Commodity Professionals

The People Behind the Trade

By
Jonathan Kingsman

Copyright ©2024 Jonathan Kingsman
All Rights Reserved

Commodity Professionals – The People Behind the Trade

Preface 1

Five Questions for the Author 4

1. Leadership and Strategy 11
    Serge Varsano – *Directoire* President 13
    Nicolas Tamari – CEO 20
    Mike Whitney – Coach 27

2. Silo to Ship 31
    James Heneghan – US Logistics and Elevation 32
    Carlos Murilo Barros de Melo – Brazilian Logistics 38
    Guilherme Cauduro – Commodity Inspection 42
    Luis Carlos dos Santos – Vessel Agent 48

3. Bulk Shipping 52
    Jan Dieleman – Owner & Charterer 54
    Anders Valentin Vogt and Mads Frank Markussen – Charterers .. 58
    Alberto Perez – Ship Certification 62
    Alexandra Hagerty – Ship's Captain 66

4. Container Shipping 71
    Estefania Gallo Prot Swarovski – Container Logistics 75
    Laia Bosch – Merchant 79
    Jack Marion – Importer 82

5. Operations 86
    Jeremy Reynolds – Forwarder 88

    Petya Sechanova – Platform Operator 95

    Saurabh Goyal – IT & AI 99

    Simon Francis – IT 103

6. Finance **108**

    Jerome Daven – CFO 110

    James Scott Wong – Commodity Finance 116

    Gijs Vos – Banker 123

7. Non-Price Risk Management **127**

    Deven Chitaliya – Risk Manager 129

    Mike Halbach – Compliance 133

    Vishwanath – Insurance 139

8. Price Risk Management **146**

    Ralph Potter – Coach & Mentortion 148

    Charles Funnell – Risk Consultant 151

    Joe Brooker – Innovation 155

9. Brokers **158**

    Kiran Wadhwana – Origin 160

    Indrek Aigro – Intertrade 167

    Peggy Olde Bijvank – Derivatives 174

10. Market Analysis and Data **180**

    The Grain Analyst 181

    Robin Shaw – ex-trader 184

    Sacha Prost – data management 190

    John Stansfield – analyst 194

11. Procurement **197**

    The Coffee Buyer 199

    Miguel Costa – Oilseeds 201

Sherif Abdeen – Sugar 206

Michael Duspiwa – Animal Feed 210

12. When Things Go Wrong 217

Swithun Still – Grain Arbitrator 218

Alex Gedrinsky – Cocoa Arbitrator 224

Brian Perrot – Lawyer 228

13. Sustainability 233

Tessa Meulensteen – Coffee 235

Nicko Debenham – Cocoa 240

Melanie Williams – Certification 245

Anita Neville – Palm Oil 249

14. Talent management 256

Julian Stow – Headhunter 259

Romina Morandini – HR 265

Bea Pupo – Team Leader 270

Kona Haque – Team Leadertion 276

15. Promoting the Sector 279

Nicole Marlor – PR & Crisis Management 282

Maryana Yarmolenko Stober – Women's Advocate 288

Florence Schurch – Lobbyist 293

Paul Chapman – Podcaster 297

16. Education 302

Eliane Palivoda Herren – UNIGE 303

Wouter Jacobs – Erasmus 306

Scott Irwin – University of Illinois 310

Ivo Sarjanovic – Professor 315

Five More Questions for the Author 320

PREFACE

At the end of 2021, I fractured my neck while on a skiing holiday in France. To my horror, I found myself paralysed from the neck down.

The first responder on the slopes probably saved my life by immediately placing me in a neck brace. A helicopter flew me to a local hospital, where I spent a week in intensive care. An ambulance then transported me back to Switzerland, where a duo of surgeons pinned my neck back together again. It took nearly one year of physiotherapy for me to recover fully. Still, thanks to the professionalism of everyone along the supply chain – from ski slope to recovery – I made a complete recovery.

One night, lying in bed in a Swiss hospital, unable to sleep, I counted the number of professionals who contributed to my recovery. There was Gilles, the first responder, the helicopter pilot, the surgeons, nurses, administrators, cleaners, cooks, managers, and accountants. I counted more than thirty professions in total. They had all played an important role. (Later, I would add Eric, my physiotherapist.)

I told a friend my happy (in the end) story over lunch. He commented that there were probably more professions in the agricultural supply chain – bringing food from the field to our homes – than were involved in my journey from paralysis to recovery.

We began to count them; within a few minutes, I had reached more than thirty – excluding all those involved in growing and harvesting the crop in the first place. We were both amazed that there were so many.

People talk about the role traders play, but few think about the professionals who move cargo to a port, inspect its quality, elevate it onto a vessel, charter a ship, organise port logistics, insure and finance the cargo, ensure its documents are fit for payment, manage the price risk, unload and process the cargo at destination, manage, account and audit the whole chain.

To that, we added the market analysts, the sustainability experts, the HR and PR departments, the lawyers and arbitrators, the NGOs, and the procurement specialists. Not all those professions are unique to the food supply chain, but they all play a vital role. The system would grind to a halt without them.

"You should write their stories," my friend told me.

I thought it over and realised I had three challenges.

I was a trader, broker, and analyst during my career. I understood markets, but I knew nothing about, for example, shipping or insurance. Still, they say writing about something is the best way to learn about it.

I knew brokers, traders, risk managers, and analysts and met the occasional sea captain and food processor. Still, I didn't know anyone from HR, PR, IT, law, accounting, etc. I had to learn what these people did and who they were.

My third challenge was that ag commodities have varied supply chains. Cocoa differs from wheat, palm oil from coffee, sugar from cotton, and corn from rice. I realised that these differences would mean the book would be, at the same time, general and specific.

"You should write it anyway," my friend argued. "People have little idea of how food ends up on their plates and of the people who make it happen. And when they do have some idea, they are often critical."

His comments reminded me of a conversation I once had with a friend's wife – a retired nurse – over dinner. She accused me of "getting between the farmer and the consumer – driving down prices for the farmer and driving up prices for the consumer."

At no stage would anyone claim that the more than thirty professions in my medical recovery had pushed up the price of my treatment or pushed down the revenue of the doctors – or that they were getting between the doctor and the patient.

I wondered why people are critical of the supply chain that brings food to their table but rarely critical of the supply chain that brings people from sickness to health. People love doctors and nurses but criticise agriculture commodity merchants; both are essential in feeding and keeping us healthy.

Perhaps it is because most of us now live in cities but still want to feel connected to the countryside. Perhaps we begrudge anyone who weakens that connection. Maybe it is because people do not understand how the food supply chain works.

During the COVID-19 pandemic, city dwellers recognised nurses' critical role in the health supply chain, applauding them from their balconies. Nurses and all the other health professionals have since faded, forgotten into the background.

This is the reason why I wanted to write this book. I wanted to recognise the thirty-plus professions that move agricultural commodities from the farm to the home. Most people don't know these professions exist, and I didn't even realise that some exist! So, if you are one of those professionals, please consider this book as me applauding you from my balcony. And thank you!

Farming is the most challenging part of the agricultural supply chain. However, despite growing up on a farm (a smallholding), I do not feel qualified to write about agriculture. I will, therefore, start my journey after the harvest.

I hope you enjoy reading it as much as I enjoyed writing it.

FIVE QUESTIONS FOR THE AUTHOR

What role do tradehouses play in the ag supply chain?

Agricultural commodity merchandising companies, usually called trade houses, transport, store, and process our food and natural fibre clothes.

They transport food from areas where it grows well (and cheaply) to places where it grows less well – or not at all – and from areas where it is not needed to areas where it is required. They move commodities from surplus to deficit areas.

Greg Page, at that time Executive Chairman of Cargill, explained it well in my first book, *The Sugar Casino*,

"*Trading across national boundaries is a necessity, not a luxury, if the world wants to serve the needs of its citizens better. And as we face a global population reaching 9 billion by mid-century, an even greater proportion of the world's food will need to move across oceans to feed the people. National self-sufficiency in food will not suffice. So, trading has always been important and will continue to be so.*"

Trade houses transport commodities across the oceans, but they also store them during periods when they are not needed and distribute them when they are. A trade house may buy wheat from a farmer after the harvest and sell and distribute it to flour mills during the year.

They process commodities from a form in which they are not wanted to a form in which they are wanted. The flour miller processes wheat into flour before selling it to a baker. The oilseed crusher processes soybeans into meal and oil. The feed manufacturer processes wheat, corn, and soymeal into animal feed.

Trade houses transform commodities in time, space, and form. They move commodities along the supply chain from producer to consumer. The key to physical commodity merchandising is sustainable and efficient supply chain management.

How do ag tradehouses make money?

They try to earn a margin at every stage of the process, but the market is efficient, and those margins are thin to non-existent. As Robert Kuok, the legendary commodity trader and founder of the Shangri La hotel chain, told me once in Hong Kong,

"The early 1960s were excellent for me in the market. I was hunting in a lake, just teeming with salmon trout. There were only three or five predators; these sharks could eat their fill. I would swim past them, and they weren't interested in me. Today, you go to the same lake: there are giant crocodiles and sharks. There is not enough fish to feed these massive predators. You must think twice before swimming in the lake.

"In the modern world, there is no back-to-back trading where you can make a simple margin on a physical transaction. Those days are long gone. Those opportunities are like golfing holes in one. I have been playing golf since 1947 and have never scored a hole-in-one. So, where there is no back-to-back trading, you must lift a leg: you must sell before you buy or buy before you sell. You must take a risk. But you can still make good money trading."

The democratisation of information has made it more challenging to make a margin. You can discover the price of anything anywhere at the click of a button. As Greg Page wrote back in 2016,

"There is a belief that the trading houses are secretive, totally opaque, manipulating markets and fixing prices. There is a belief that there is no transparency.

"That could not be further from the truth. Back in 1974, when I started, things arguably were opaque. There was no Internet, cellular phones, instant communication, flash commentary or opinion – and no email. (Sometimes I yearn for those days). The information was available on the ground, and

competitive advantage came from how quickly you could gather it and do something with it."

Trade houses can still take advantage when a commodity, calendar spread, or industrial process is mispriced. They may find that the market misprices Australian wheat versus French or Canadian wheat, and they can supply their Chinese importer more cheaply from France or Canada than from Australia. Or that the market is pricing corn for nearby shipment too cheaply compared to corn for shipment in a few months, and they can make money by storing it. Or they may find that soymeal is mispriced compared to beans and that they can make money by running an extra shift at their crushing plant.

What are the advantages of an integrated supply chain?

Having a presence at every stage in the supply chain, along with a global footprint, means that you are often the first to know when there is a supply problem – a port or transport strike, a weather issue, a change in government policy, or whatever. Prices become volatile when supply is disrupted, and mispricing becomes more frequent.

Dave Behrends, the head of trading at Sucafina, summed it up nicely:

"We are embracing a move into recurring, value-added business and away from transactional one-off differential buying and selling. But the reality is that supply and demand rarely match. We live in a world where extreme weather events will drive greater price volatility. Taking a view and trading positions (buy first, sell later or vice-versa) will always be relevant and a part of our business."

Dave Whitcomb, ex-Cargill and now CEO of Peak Trading and Research, told me:

"Commercial trading companies have a massive advantage (over hedge funds) in ag markets because of their involvement in the supply chain. They can access different price arbitrages from storage, transport, crushing, and basis. Adding all those little arbitrages across space, time, and form makes a trading house successful. They may only make a cent a bushel, but they do that thousands of times at multiple stages along the chain."

Chris Mahoney, then CEO of Viterra and now Chairman of ED&F Man, told me that 85 per cent of Viterra's profits come from distribution and logistics and only 15 per cent from trading.

ADM is possibly the agricultural sector's most integrated supply chain operator. Here is what Greg Morris, President of ADM's Agricultural Services and Oilseeds Business Unit, told me:

"Many companies operating in this space feel their job is to trade. Our philosophy at ADM is different. We trade with a purpose. We don't trade just to trade; that is yesterday's model.

"We trade to support higher utilisation rates in our assets. We trade to help provide products for our customers. So, I wouldn't say ADM is necessarily a trading company. We trade as a critical function of managing our portion of the supply chain to serve our global customer base."

Olam is another example of an integrated supply chain operator. Devashish Chaubey, who heads Olam's rice division, described how it works:

"Olam operates a large rice farm in Nigeria and is a prominent player in the domestic market. In geographies such as Vietnam, we operate mills but buy rice from millers and then upgrade it to our customers' specifications. We have facilities in Thailand and India that upgrade rice. We sell to importers in various geographies, and in some, we import ourselves and distribute the rice through the general trade and modern retailers.

"Traders often say they feed on volatility, but our business is more about making a margin at every leg of the supply chain. We don't need to feed on volatility to make margins every year. The fact that the rice price is not very volatile suits us."

The trade houses' presence at multiple points along the supply chain makes it easier to track and trace the commodities they source and ensure they are produced sustainably. Sucafina has been a leader in traceability and was the driving force behind the Farmer Connect platform. However, as Nicolas Tamari, the CEO of Sucafina, told me,

"Regarding sustainability, everybody in the supply chain must make money. We're not shy to say that you can't have social and environmental sustainability if you don't have economic sustainability."

Do ag tradehouses need both scale and physical assets?

When I asked Chris Mahoney that question, he told me:

"In our view, there is no asset-less trading model today and maybe not even any asset-light trading model of any scale that is sustainable or viable.

"There is also some advantage in being multi-commodity in that diversity helps smooth earnings. Operating across multiple regions reduces political risk. A network of offices and people representing a company's diverse interests provides some cost savings. Scale can be an advantage. When looking critically at their lending portfolios, banks prefer to lend to larger, more diverse customers where they rightly perceive the risk profile to be lower. All of this then favours large companies. A regional player can succeed, but it is not the same game."

Raul Padilla, at that time head of Bunge's oilseed crushing operations, agreed,

"You need physical assets to receive, store, and process agricultural commodities. You can't be in the business without physical assets. Processing is critical in soybeans as you can either sell beans or process them into oil and meal. And you can move down the supply chain. You can market the oil in retail bottles or, for example, biodiesel. We have 35 per cent of the packaged oil market in Brazil – a vast number of bottles!"

Brian Zachman, at that time head of risk at Bunge, summed up the challenge:

"The investment in permanent assets is expensive, the outcome of those investments is not easy to forecast, and the assets themselves act to make supply chains more efficient, which results in higher prices for farmers and lower prices for consumers. In a way, our asset base is a call option on volatility in the supply chain."

Wilmar is one company that recognises the importance of assets and successfully integrates them into the supply chain. Khoon Hong Kuok, the company's CEO and co-founder, gave me an example,

"All the animal feed mills in Malaysia were inland, and they had to buy all their raw materials in bags. I decided to build feed mills next to our flour mills so that we could use our silos to bring in corn in bulk—and use our flour mills' by-products in bulk. The savings were considerable, and in seven or eight years, we became the biggest animal feed manufacturer in Malaysia."

What about the stakeholders and the people behind the trade?

Isara Vongkusolkit, the chairman of Mitr Pohl, a leading Thai sugar producer, explained his priorities to me in 2015:

"When we do business, we involve five stakeholders: farmers, customers, employees, regulators and government, and shareholders.

"The farmer is the most important stakeholder. We were farmers ourselves. The sugar business is really about farming; it is not an industry. That's where I think people sometimes make a mistake.

"Our customer is our second most important stakeholder. We must have a reasonable price, excellent quality, and good service.

"Our employees are number three on the list. In 1997, during the Asian economic crisis, we increased our staff training to make them competitive. During the crisis, our company executives all agreed to cut their salaries. We overcame the crisis without laying off a single employee or cutting workers' wages.

"Our industry is still regulated, so our fourth stakeholder is the regulator, the government. We always support government initiatives for economic development in communities, and we recognise our responsibility to be an excellent corporate role model in all areas of governance, especially in being good taxpayers.

"Shareholders are our fifth stakeholders. We now have about eighty family members as shareholders, including nephews, nieces, and grandchildren.

"Our company is based on four important rules: we believe in the importance of leadership, the value of human dignity, standing firm in fairness and being accountable to society."

The big trade houses have a physical presence and a global footprint at every stage along the supply chain. But they readily admit that it is not enough to succeed. Greg Heckman, the CEO of Bunge, told me,

"This is a business and industry where people make a bigger difference than in any other. People have a bigger impact on delighting customers, managing risks, and ultimately creating returns. That makes it challenging and fun to join the journey."

Chris Mahoney agrees. He explained:

"An asset base is essential today. However, in addition to asset portfolios, what distinguishes companies is their people, their culture, how management and employees interact and treat each other, and their respect for each other. What kind of a company do you want? Ultimately, any company can hire bright people, but the steps to build a motivated, hard-working, entrepreneurial, fast-acting team are important for success. People spend most of their lives at work; they do not do it only for the money."

This book is about those people – the professionals behind the trade. Without them, your breakfast would not make it to your breakfast table. Your children would not have wheat for their toast, sugar for cereal, or vegetable oil for their chocolate spread. They wouldn't even have a tablecloth; the raw cotton would still be in some warehouse, waiting for a trader to transform it into cotton thread.

1. LEADERSHIP

In 1990, I set up my own company as a physical broker and market analyst, first in France and then Switzerland. We were initially a tiny team, but as the business developed, I struggled to manage the growing number of employees. The problem was that I never thought of myself as a boss. I was a broker and market analyst. I focused on our clients and left the team to manage itself.

I contacted a friend, the CEO of a small trading company, for help and advice. He explained that he never did anything in his business if it didn't increase shareholder value.

"It's my North Star," he said. "But maximising shareholder value is the end of the journey, not the start. Success comes through strategy, organisation, capital allocation, culture, and team building."

"I struggle in all those areas," I replied. "Where am I going wrong?"

"Your mistake is concentrating on your clients and ignoring your employees," he replied. "It's an old debate about whether you should prioritise your customers or your teams. I have also acted on the basis that you must prioritise your teams as they look after your customers. Happy employees mean happy customers.

"The first step, therefore, is team building," he told me. "You must build staff loyalty and motivation by developing an environment of entrepreneurship, responsibility, reward, fairness, honesty, and social awareness.

"Only once you have done that should you focus on your customers. The second step, therefore, is to maintain customer loyalty by protecting your brand and your social license to operate.

"At the same time, you must protect your business from fraud, IT, health, and safety risks.

"Only then can you grow the business by diversifying into new sectors or increasing your presence in existing ones."

"You make it sound easy," I said.

"If it were easy," he replied, "everyone would do it."

Even so, I only fully understood the importance of leadership when I retired from the markets and wrote *The New Merchants of Grain*. CEOs and senior managers often get bad press, but they play an essential role in setting a company's culture and strategy. After writing *The New Merchants of Grain*, I never again said that a CEO was overpaid!

Serge Varsano

If you make a mistake in trading, you cut the position and start again the next day. The market will always give you another chance.

I met Serge Varsano in his office in Paris on a cold and rainy Monday afternoon. I explained I wanted to interview him for the CEO section of my book, but he immediately told me that he was not the CEO of Sucden; he was the President of the company's *Directoire*.

The concept of a *Directoire* dates to the French Revolution, and the nearest translation is 'Management Board'. It is an unusual arrangement that less than 5 per cent of French companies follow – and probably unique in trading companies.

In Sucden's case, the *Directoire* consists of five people, with each member having a right of veto. Decisions must be unanimous. Every board member must agree before the company undertakes a strategy on the markets or invests in a sector or a person. If, for example, the financial director does not agree, they do not do it.

A supervisory board oversees – and determines the limits of – this management board. Serge explained that although he is the company's majority shareholder, he operates within certain limits: first, with the management board on day-to-day trading decisions and, second, with the supervisory board on more strategic decisions. He needs authorisation to exceed these limits. They ensure that the group is never in danger.

Serge introduced the dual system to protect shareholders and the group after the company nearly went bankrupt in 1990. He told me that when Sucden bought Cocoa Barry in 1982, the company's best financial and risk controllers moved from the trading side of the business to the industrial side. It left a gap in the trading operation when the company expanded into different commodities such as rice, cotton, and energy.

"Everything exploded at the same time," he admitted. "We had to sell Cacao Barry and Sogéviandes, owner of the *Charal* brand, dramatically reduce headcount and concentrate on sugar, our core product.

"Max Benamo, the former president who took over after my father died in 1990, came back to help," Serge told me. "We made a lot of money with a whole series of operations worldwide, especially in Russia, Cuba and Brazil. We had an outstanding team, a very tight team."

"In the 1990s, we began our agro-industrial activities in Russia," he said. "We bought four beet processing factories and the land with them. In 2010/12, we returned to cocoa and then coffee. Later, we added rice and sea freight by purchasing ships. We are also a market-maker in the London metals market. It is an activity that is doing well, but it experienced difficult times with the nickel crisis two years ago.

"Brokerage accounts for around 15-20 per cent of our revenue," he continued. "Our agro-industrial activities account for 30-40 per cent and trading for the rest. However, there is a large distribution percentage in the figure for Russia. I include shipping in the trading."

Although Sucden bought beet factories and land in Russia, the company did not invest in sugar cane in Brazil. Other trading companies lost a lot of money purchasing Brazilian factories. I asked Serge how he had avoided the trap.

"It's not that we were brilliant," he admitted. "It was just that we didn't have the money to do it. It was luck.

"The cane mills were expensive," he continued. "We never understood why all these people dived in. We didn't believe in the ethanol stories, and the sugar market was around 11-14 c/lb, which was insufficient to justify the prices. It was hundreds of millions of dollars plus debt.

"We got involved in logistics operations in Brazil with port terminals but did not enter production."

"But you do production in Russia," I said. "Do trading and production make a good mix?"

"We do not trade in Russia," he corrected me. "We sell our sugar locally, especially to major brands like Coca-Cola, Nestlé, etc. We export a little to Kazakhstan and Kyrgyzstan. It is not trading; it's production and distribution."

Cocoa trading was responsible for a significant portion of the 1990 losses. I reread the book *La Guerre de Cacao* to prepare for this interview, but I admit I didn't understand everything. I asked Serge if he could explain what happened.

"We were expecting a big harvest and shorted the differentials between the physical and futures market at levels of £20-30 per tonne. It was a significant operation but nothing extraordinary.

"President Houphouët-Boigny of the Ivory Coast banned exports – he thought the world price was too low – and the differentials rose to $300-400 per tonne. We had a huge potential loss on our books. Other traders went to the Ivory Coast to convince the President to reallow exports. He said he preferred to destroy his cocoa rather than export it at such a low price.

"We went to him with a different idea: accept his price and buy 400,000 tonnes, store 200,000 tonnes in Europe for one or two years and sell 200,000 to our customers. He accepted. For that, we needed FF400 million. The French government had a structural fund that they weren't entirely using, and they wrote a check for FF 400 million to the Ivory Coast.

"With the storage cost and the 200,000 tonnes we sold, we emerged from the operation almost unscathed.

"We had asked the President for exclusivity on the deal for a certain time and not to sell to others. However, he sold 400,000 tonnes to Phibros, and the market collapsed. It was a disaster for us. It was also a disaster for Phibros who were long in the market. They exited cocoa soon afterwards."

"Of the commodities you trade," I asked, "Which is the most difficult and which is the most fun?"

"Sugar is in our blood and our genes," he replied. "Sugar is complex because it is a FOB contract, unlike coffee or cocoa. You need a robust physical department to trade in sugar. You also need to have a good physicals department for cocoa, but the cocoa is already in Europe when you take delivery.

"You need a robust global network to trade sugar: Brazil, the Middle East, Thailand, China, etc. Cocoa is mainly produced in Ivory Coast and Ghana and exported to Europe and a little to the United States. Overhead costs are less expensive.

"Coffee is between the two. We are relatively small in coffee, with 7 million bags per year, compared to the big companies, which trade 12 million bags. We are among the leaders in sugar, with around 10 million tonnes per year. We are among the first in cocoa, trading around 100,000 tonnes of beans each year and the equivalent in products."

Serge Varsano has a reputation for being a speculator. Still, talking with people who know him well, I understood that he built the company on personal relationships and trust, for example, with Cuba and Russia, rather than by taking significant speculative positions on the market.

"I am more of a deal maker than a speculator," he told me. "My goal has always been to gain the trust of our customers and find solutions for them. Everyone has problems to resolve, whether financial, logistical, or pricing. That is what interests me."

"Speculation doesn't interest you?" I asked.

"Not really," he answered, "Especially on the flat price. We are not very good at the flat price, and we do very little for the size of the group, including cocoa and coffee. We prefer relative value to flat price."

"Is this Sucden's secret to success?" I asked.

"No, he replied. "The secret to success in this business is to have great teams and excellent people.

"As I explained earlier, if one of our traders wants to carry out an operation, he must have the management board's agreement. And if the board agrees, we support the trader 100 per cent. Our decisions are collective.

We make mistakes – it happens – but we don't fire a trader if he loses money on a transaction that we all approved.

"We have a strong team spirit, and our traders have stayed with us for a long time. It is our secret to success. It is our way of trading, our way of managing teams."

"Each company has its way of working," I said. "Can partnerships work in trading?

"We have few structural partnerships," he replied. "We do joint accounts, but for one-off operations. Interests can change in life and business, and getting married structurally is risky. Marrying a producer is challenging because we don't have the same interests. Traders want to buy as low as possible, and producers want to sell as high as possible. It's hard always to agree."

"I imagine it wasn't easy to take over the company from your father," I said.

"Contrary to what you might think," he replied, "it was easy. In 1975, when my father found out he had cancer, he asked me to come back from the United States. I was 20 years old. The market was dropping dramatically from 66 c/lb, and I wondered, 'What is this thing – what is happening?'

"I quickly integrated myself into the company and started doing small businesses. I had contacts in Venezuela, and we made some significant deals with them when the country became an importer in the late 1970s. I worked with my father and Elie Coriat, my father's right-hand man. My father died in 1980."

"How are you preparing your two sons to succeed you?" I asked.

"My desk is in the trading room with the traders. My two sons work three metres away, one to my left on sugar and the other to my right on cocoa. It's nice.

"They participate in the management board meetings. They are not management board members but will officially join when I retire in 3-4 years."

"What are the biggest challenges they will face?" I asked.

"Grain is our biggest challenge today," Serge replied. "We have just begun grain trading. We are small, with 2 million tonnes this year. We do not have any ambition to compete with the big trading companies, but we will find niches in complicated countries on less common products. We initially aim to distribute in Eastern and Mediterranean countries. Can we stay small? We'll see, but we might have to move to a higher level one day.

"Russia is another challenge. It is impossible today to predict what will happen. Will it normalise?

"Cocoa is always a challenge. We cannot increase our bean volumes. Exporters have built factories and export products. However, we can expand cocoa products, such as butter and cake. There will be quite a few things to do.

"There is a lot to do in coffee. It's a complex market. We had a bad year two years ago, but we slowly began to understand and anticipate the situation and had an honourable result in 2023. This year, 2024, is off to a good start for Arabica.

"Do you need more capital?" I asked.

"We have capital of around $1.5 billion, and our debt is less than our equity. We would need more capital to buy factories or grain elevators. Still, we are happy to remain in trading, brokerage in London and production and distribution in Russia. We live well and obtain excellent results relative to our funds."

"You enjoy doing big deals in sugar, cocoa, etc.," I said, "But do you get bored when there are no big deals?"

"Not at all!" he replied. "It's always interesting to follow the teams. The markets move constantly; there is rarely a year when nothing happens between sugar, coffee, and cocoa.

"I rarely get bored," he added. "But I have another great passion, which is show jumping."

Serge is a keen rider and competes in show jumping at an international level.

"I started at 10-11 years old in Neuilly," he told me. "I didn't do badly and was part of the French Junior team. However, I left for the US at 17 to study, and I never got back on a horse until I was 50."

"Was it easy to restart?" I asked.

"No, it was challenging," he replied. "It was easy at first – like golf, the first shot is easy – but it's hard to do well. Now I'm happy with what I do. I'm having a lot of fun."

"Do you ride every day?" I asked.

"No! I'm still working," he replied with a smile. "I ride every Wednesday morning and at the weekends. Competitions usually last four days, Thursday, Friday, Saturday and Sunday, so I sometimes have to take Thursday and Friday off to participate."

"Are there any similarities between trading and show jumping?" I asked. "You can be an experienced trader or rider and have a good plan, but there is always an element of luck."

"The two are similar," he replied. "The stress is about the same between show jumping and trading.

"There is always something you can't control. You can have a faultless course if you calculate and respect all your horse's strides.

"Unfortunately, there is always something which happens. The horse can swerve, add or remove a stride and, voilà, a bar falls.

"It's the same in trading! You can calculate everything perfectly, but something unexpected can happen. It might rain too much or not enough, or a delivery might have more sugar than expected. You can make a bad decision; things can go wrong, unexpected things.

"If you make a mistake in trading, you cut the position and start again the next day. The market will always give you another chance. It's the same with show jumping. There is always another competition – another opportunity.

"So, it's pretty similar. We never master everything in trading or show jumping. But that is what makes it interesting and fun."

Nicolas Tamari

Family businesses think and operate long-term. Commodity trading companies should have the management and the family as shareholders.

I interviewed Nicolas, the CEO of Sucafina, one of the world's leading coffee trading and roasting companies, for my book on coffee. The interview focused on the coffee business, but we didn't discuss leadership. I contacted Nicolas for this book, and he agreed to contribute. We met at his offices in Geneva, where the building was under renovation, and I ended up on the wrong floor. We eventually found each other and chatted in the company's kitchen. I asked him how he defined leadership.

"I define leadership as being able to do three things simultaneously," he answered.

"The first is to inspire people. The second is to manage people. The third is to contribute to the bottom line of the company. Vision is also crucial. A leader must define a clear vision and ensure everybody sticks to it.

"Culture, values, and vision make a company, but I would also add purpose. Our purpose at Sucafina is to create opportunities to improve lives. We deal with hundreds of thousands of growers worldwide; we can help improve their lives. It is what links everyone."

Whilst interviewing people for this book, I often tripped over the expression, 'Culture eats strategy for breakfast.' I was confused by what it meant and sceptical about whether it was true.

"Culture must be in people's DNA," Nicolas told me. "At Sucafina, we hire for values and train for skills. If you hire people who share the same values as you and buy into your culture, you can train them to be the best risk manager, IT person, HR person, or whatever. It's difficult if you don't have a commonality in the DNA of the culture and the values."

Sucafina employs 42 nationalities in 49 locations in 36 countries. I was impressed that a CEO could impose, develop, or nourish a common culture across diverse cultures.

"To make a good cup of coffee," he explained, "You need a blend of different origins, often from various continents. We are lucky at Sucafina to have this diversity; it is one of our strengths.

"We give everyone the freedom to speak to everyone. By sharing best practices, we learn from one another and improve. That's one crucial thing. Second, we try to adapt to the local communities, mindset, and culture. We are a global company that acts locally. We try to empower local teams while maintaining a common message at the corporate level."

"How would you define Sucafina's culture?" I asked.

"In one sentence?" he replied. "I would say it's what you see is what you get."

Nicolas took over the responsibility for the company from his brother, who took it over from their father. He told me that his brother and father had a similar leadership style and had been more hands-on. He prefers a more delegating type of leadership, but what they do have in common is that they all walk the talk and lead by example.

I was interested in discussing the advantages a family firm might have in the trading world, but I was keen to talk further about leadership. Sucafina has the Sparks program to teach leadership, and I wanted to ask how successful it is. At school, I remember some kids were natural leaders, whether in sports or arts, and others were followers. Before meeting Nicolas, I discussed the issue with a friend, the retired CEO of a pharma company. He firmly believed that leaders are born, not made. What did Nicolas think?

"Some people are born leaders," he told me. "Others are groomed to become leaders. However, to become a leader, you must have the ingredients of your personality, upbringing, and self-confidence.

"Sucafina's Sparks program teaches leadership," he explained. "It is a three-year course. Each year, we have between one and ten participants. So, on average, let's call it six. As we have three years going on simultaneously, it's 18 people. Up to now, I guess over 50 people have graduated.

"It is expensive but well worth the investment. In our industry, grooming people from inside the company rather than headhunting them from the outside is essential. By doing so, they truly live the company's vision, purpose, and culture."

Sucafina's website highlights some women who have recently completed the Sparks programme. I was curious to learn what Sucafina was doing to promote gender equality.

"Historically," Nicolas told me, "There have always been more men than women working in our industry, especially on trading desks. I have not yet been able to understand why. On the other hand, there are often more women than men in execution and operations and different departments such as HR or Communications.

"We want a mix of men and women," he continued. "But we're a meritocracy-based company. I do not want quotas for men or women. I want the most apt person to get the job. But yes, we want to promote women because we believe there are a lot of amazingly talented ladies out there who can grow and take on more responsibilities.

"For example, in East Africa, if we want something to happen on the ground with local communities, we empower women, and it's often a big success. When we empower men, I cannot say the same thing. So, we want to empower more women."

"Are there specific leadership challenges in trading companies compared to service, manufacturing, or industrial companies?" I asked.

"Humility as a leader of a commodity trading company is crucial," he answered. "That's one key difference. The second one is that in a commodity trading company, you start afresh each financial year and have your overheads to cover. Trading companies don't have recurrent built-in revenue to cover expenses, which you often find in a service industry like banking."

Some trading companies have bought industrial assets to even out volatile earnings. I asked Nicolas if he had done the same.

"To reply to your question," he replied, "I'll go to our company vision, which is to be the world's leading sustainable farm-to-roaster coffee company. We want to start at the farm, but we're not farmers. We're happy to be roasters but not brand owners.

"About ten years ago, we acquired Beyers Coffee, the largest roaster in Belgium. We also have an instant coffee business. Bayers and our instant coffee business are strategic as we can vertically integrate the supply chain. We will not be brand owners; otherwise, we will have conflicts of interest.

"These industrial assets also give us more predictability in our revenue. They indirectly help us by levelling our revenue and having a recurrent built-in margin."

"Which is better, growth through acquisitions or internal growth?" I asked.

"Initially, I would say organic growth, but sometimes opportunities arise when you don't expect them, and that's where you need to acquire. Culture is critical when you acquire. You need to make sure the company you acquire fits the culture. It's culture more than anything else."

I quickly became overwhelmed when running our little analytical company and had to impose a structure to limit the number of people who reported to me directly. I wondered how many of Sucafina's 1,400 employees reported directly to Nicolas.

"Eight," he replied. "We use the acronym FIRST. F stands for finance, I stands for information systems technology, R stands for risk, S stands for staff and human resources, and T stands for trading and execution. So those five heads report to me, plus I have three further direct reports.

"Some of our managers only have four direct reports, but it's about eight on average. It varies between five and ten, depending on the interaction between the manager and the employee, the level, and his responsibility."

"How involved are you in the day-to-day operations and trading?" I asked.

"I'm involved in the company's day-to-day operations, but it can operate quasi-normally without me. I'm aware of the trading positions we hold and the big-picture decisions."

"If you decided to go and sail around the world for a year, would the company still work as well?" I asked.

"I would say for a couple of months," he answered. "But not a year."

I now wanted to return to ownership and whether family companies have an advantage over publicly quoted companies in trading.

"Whether you are family-owned, management-owned, or even private equity-owned," he said, "I believe commodity trading companies should not be publicly quoted. Why? Because of the unpredictability of the financial results. Share price volatility is not good.

"I'm not in favour of publicly listed trading companies unless you are an industrialist and have trading as your procurement arm, which enhances or not your profitability. Family businesses think and operate long-term. Commodity trading companies should have the management and the family as shareholders."

Serge Varsano instituted a company structure that limits his decision-making power. I wondered whether Nicolas had something similar.

"I have a board of directors, the majority of which are independent," he said. "They empower me but impose certain limits in VAR, drawdown, counterparty, forex, etc. I navigate within these limits. I believe we're well structured in terms of corporate governance for a company of our size.

"I'm here to make money but also to have fun. I don't need to give a return to my shareholders of 30-50 per cent a year. They're comfortable allowing me to use the profits to grow the business."

Serge Varsano also mentioned the importance of having fun in business. It made me wonder if I had had fun running my little company. I enjoyed the challenge, but was it fun? I am not sure.

"How do you inspire innovation as the company grows?" I asked.

"Innovation must be bottom-up as well as top-down," he replied. When people have ideas, we must listen to them. We must assess whether they are feasible or not. And we must not be afraid of trying and failing fast. If you fail fast in innovation, you can fall back on your feet and re-innovate. If you don't learn from your failure – and if you don't fail fast – innovation can be a problem."

I had to think about his answer for a while. It had never occurred to me that innovation could be a problem, but then I thought about the times when companies had introduced new IT systems only to see them fail.

"How involved do you get in recruitment?" I asked.

"I don't see all candidates," he replied, "But I often participate in the last round of interviews with key people or departments needing my involvement. I enjoy interviewing people because, as I said before, we hire for values and train for skills. So, through these interviews, I can understand whether a candidate shares our values.

"I always ask a candidate to share with me one experience that happened in their life from the age of five to 20 years old that contributed to the person they are today. I want something profound and sincere, not their exam results. It allows me to understand the person behind the CV.

"Sometimes, candidates reciprocate the question to me. I answer that at the age of seven, my parents put me in a boarding school in Switzerland without me knowing that I would go to a boarding school. I do not remember my parents telling me I was going. I suppose they did, but they didn't explain the meaning of boarding school. You can imagine the trauma.

"It taught me how to survive in very unusual circumstances. On the other hand, it did not teach me to ask for help. It did not teach me to communicate. So, I often do things by myself. I've learned in the last decades how to work more with teams.

"The fantastic thing is that the kids I met at that school – I'm now 54 – are like brothers to me today. I can see them on the other side of the planet, and we can sit and have a meal, and it's as if we haven't seen each other for 20 minutes."

"Last question," I said. "What advice would you give someone taking up a leadership position for the first time?

"One: Listen and listen. Two: Lead by example. You cannot expect your people to do something you are unwilling to do. Three: Don't be an asshole. We have an official "no-asshole" rule at Sucafina. It is independent of how much you contribute to the P&L or how great you are."

Michael Whitney

Leaders have a life cycle and a sell-by date. Things change around them, but they may not adapt.

A friend recently sent me a McKinsey report on the role of a CEO. It argued that the fundamental core of the CEO role consists of six things:

- Set the direction.
- Align your organisation in that direction.
- Mobilise your leaders to deliver in that direction.
- Work with your board.
- Connect with a group of stakeholders.
- Manage your personal effectiveness.

I contacted Michael Whitney, a leadership coach and recruitment consultant with Kincannon Reed, to ask him if he agreed with McKinsey.

"How you behave as a leader will characterise how others in the organisation behave," he told me. "Your behaviour as a leader is essential. Take just one example: if you stifle discussion and jump all over somebody, they will think twice about stepping up in the future. You may miss something vital if you don't allow people to contribute.

"A CEO must trust the employees, and the employees must trust their CEO. It is particularly relevant in a trading company where the bets are big, and decisions are taken quickly. A trading environment requires an awful lot of trust. As a leader, you must look people in the eye and ask them: Can I trust you to deliver this?"

"But doesn't the McKinsey article concentrate on strategy rather than culture," I insisted.

"Culture is embedded in all of those things," Michael replied. "You can have the best strategy in the world, but if you cannot forge a good relationship with your board chair or board, you will not be around for long. Your capacity to manage up will determine the success of your strategy. The board must trust you.

I asked Michael how easy it was to tell the difference between a manager and a leader.

"Sometimes you meet somebody, male or female, and just say, wow, they have an aura. They exude a level of self-confidence which is not brash or in your face. They can listen, engage with you, and make you feel you're the most important person in the room. You feel drawn and connected to them. Many people are leaders, but great leaders have that aura, that natural presence.

"A leader can move seamlessly between two things," he continued. "They're confident and happy doing strategy, thinking at a high level, and setting a direction of travel. But they are equally as good at making it happen and executing against it. It sounds easy, but it is challenging.

"Looking at leaders through history, it's also about the moment. A specific set of circumstances will dictate having one type of leader versus another. It goes back to that war versus peacetime scenario. Look at what a great leader Churchill was during the war, but he was soon voted out of office once the war ended. Leaders have a life cycle and a sell-by date. Things change around them, but they may not adapt.

"The manager is functionally strong. There isn't much you can't tell a manager about how to run a trading desk or a crushing plant. They master their market and the S&Ds that drive it. But ask that manager how they will double the company's revenue over the next five years. They can't extend to that."

Michael spent 13 years in the British Army, and I asked him to list three things he learned there that helped him in his later career.

"First, the armed forces prepare you to lead from a young age," he answered. "Leadership training is a constant throughout your career. The army teaches you to think logically when making assessments and judgment calls and how to write and communicate succinctly.

"Second, the armed forces teach you cadence. There are periods of intense activity and periods which are less intense. You go off on operations, and the intensity can be extreme, but you can't sustain that level of commitment and effort. There are periods when you must reduce the cadence to focus on other things and rebuild the capability to operate again at an intense level.

"Business can learn from that," he continued. "In business, you have what I call the Duracell bunny syndrome. People think their ticket to success is continually moving at a hundred miles an hour. I am not sure it's the right thing to do in business. People get tired. They burn out. Pausing and thinking gives you the springboard to get back in and reposition.

"The third thing I learned was the value of constant self-reflection. The armed forces expose you to people with more experience than you – strong personalities who will firmly state their case. You must be mature and humble enough to reflect on what they say.

"I'm unsure of the extent to which many business leaders are open to that reflection, to ask why their personality is conditioning them to behave in a certain way. The armed forces continually expose you to your peers. You don't have a choice but to pause, reflect and think.

"Leaders must understand themselves. They must be able to say, "This is where I stack up and where I don't." They must understand their weaknesses and where they need to improve.

Finally, I asked Michael what advice he would give to someone taking a leadership position for the first time.

"First, you must understand yourself," he answered. "You must have emotional intelligence and deep levels of self-understanding and self-awareness. You must understand your weaknesses.

"Second, you must understand that there will be times when you will have to draw upon the support of others. You must nurture people with complementary skills and personalities, even if these people tell you what you do not want to hear."

2. SILO TO SHIP

During my career, I frequently visited Brazil to meet clients, talk with sugar millers, and discuss crop progress. I was always impressed at how efficient and professional the agricultural sector was but surprised by how it struggled to move its production to the ports for export. The roads often disintegrated into a mud bath, and trucks backed up for kilometres on the highway to Santos. Ships could wait months to load if the weather was unfavourable.

The sector has invested heavily in rail freight, and the situation has improved somewhat, but the roads still clog up during harvest season.

I also frequently travelled to the US but never got much further than New York City and their annual Sugar Dinner. Admittedly, I worked for Cargill for two years in Minneapolis at the beginning of my career, but that was a long time ago. At the start of this book project, I knew little about the US agricultural export flow from field to port.

Nor did I know much about the supervision companies that inspect the goods at each stage of the supply chain. As a broker, I often negotiated the shipping documents and inspection certificates the seller should provide. Still, I rarely enquired about the process of producing and obtaining them. Nor did I ask who was responsible for the vessel at the load port. Who ensures that a ship is refuelled, and the crew changed?

I am almost embarrassed to say it, but this chapter has been a steep learning curve for me. As such, it is one of my favourites. Enjoy!

Jim Heneghan

The US is moving more towards a Brazilian model of corporate farming driven by demographics and the search for economies of scale.

When Jim joined Louis Dreyfus in 1999, his first job was to buy and sell CIF (Cost Insurance Freight) barges from the interior of the US along the US River systems, primarily the Mississippi River System and, to a lesser extent, the Ohio, and Illinois, and Missouri Rivers, flowing to New Orleans for export.

"US agriculture is blessed to have the Mississippi River System," Jim told me. "It has 20,000 km of navigable waterways reaching the heart of the country's grain belt.

"Moving crops to export ports by barge gives the US a tremendous cost advantage over our competitors in Brazil and Argentina," he explained. "The cost of moving grains to the ports in those countries is huge. US farmers don't have to rely on the road system, like in Brazil, where they must truck their exports across some tough kilometres. It is a natural cost advantage. It can ebb and flow with currency, and a weak *Real* can offset some of that advantage. Still, our natural advantage is not going anywhere. It's there."

Jim left Louis Dreyfus in 2013 to become the global ag business manager for BTG, where he was involved in setting up agricultural commodity trading from scratch. He now sits on the board of Greenfield Holdings, a company building the first new grain export elevator in Louisiana since 1979. The elevator will have an annual capacity of 11 million mt with an upside of 22 million mt. It will receive grains and soybeans, predominately via barge, and load them onto oceangoing vessels for export.

"We are working on the final permits with the Army Corps of Engineers," he told me. "While building out that ship-loading facility, we have a barge-loading feeder facility in Lake Providence, Louisiana. I don't trade or merchandise that facility, but I see the positions and am on the risk committee."

The CIF barge market to New Orleans is the largest US cash market for corn and soybeans. It's also the primary delivery mechanism for the CME corn and soybean futures contracts. I asked Jim what the main drivers of the CIF barge market were.

"The supply and demand for exports out of New Orleans," he replied. "You're looking at the interior supply of crops that can lead to an exportable surplus into the river system for exports. Then there's a big operational component, everything it takes to load, insure, ship, and manage a barge. We must also watch out for quality and phytosanitary aspects, and then the risk management."

"When people talk about exports from New Orleans," I asked, "does that include all of Louisiana?"

"There's a mile marker system," Jim explained. "When ocean vessels come into the river system, they pass the South West Pass (SWP), where the captain hands over his ship to a pilot who takes it up the river system.

"Regarding commodity loading within the river system, nothing exists for the first 50 miles because of the delta. The main loading corridor is from mile marker 60 up to about 210 miles north of the sea, above the SWP. A bridge in Baton Rouge has an air draft that doesn't permit large vessels like Capsize or Panamax to go further north. The main commodity corridor is from Baton Rouge to the south of New Orleans. Call it a 100-mile corridor.

"It's tidal, but the river levels depend more on the water flowing from the Mississippi River system. At Baton Rouge, you can have a low of 5 feet on the river gage to a high of 40 feet. It is tidal but is more dependent on the upstream variability.

"We heard a lot about low water levels restricting barge activity. Is it something that will happen regularly?" I asked.

"I sure hope not," he replied. "Low water levels made loading and shipping barges at the proper draft and ideal economics difficult. The whole system backed up due to the historic droughts in the Southwest and Western Corn Belt. That's recovered somewhat, and we're returning to a more normalised flow.

"The river system is also prone to flooding. If you have too much water in the system, you can get flooding on the lower Mississippi River around Cairo, Illinois. That's a big area with a lot of flow coming in. It can flood in Missouri, along the Mississippi, Arkansas, Memphis, and Tennessee. As the water rolls down to New Orleans, the authorities can open spillways to relieve the flow. But yeah, there can be severe flooding episodes.

"Floods will affect the downbound transportation and grain supply to New Orleans. It can be hazardous to take a tow downbound. The river authorities will restrict the number of barges you can transit. Rail freight can somewhat mitigate it, but the system is set up to be barge-served. Typically, 90 per cent of the supply arrives via barge and 10 per cent by rail.

"The upbound also becomes difficult as it's a throughput and a backhaul system. If barges can't get downbound, they can't get upbound. But even if they can get upbound, going against the current requires a lot of power.

"Then, at some point, if the river levels are high enough, it's hazardous to have anything in transit as you're putting projectiles on the water that can eliminate docks and bridges. There have been episodes of tows or vessels breaking away.

"I always imagined," I told Jim, "barges would be empty going back up."

"You'll get some empty barges upbound, but the barge companies try to do a backhaul if they can – often fertilisers and metals. The downbound is usually grain and coal.

"Does agriculture compete with coal on the Mississippi for barge capacity?" I asked.

"The barges are different. Grain barges are covered, whereas coal ones aren't. You have a different barge capacity and fleet for different products, but you still have throughput and need tows and schedules to go up and down. It can be complementary, but it might be competitive at other times. It's hard for the ag space to move the energy space. It's the other way around."

"Could you talk me through the CIF barge market?" I asked him. "How does it work?"

"If you have a farm close to the river system, the best market for your grain is probably for export. You would sell it to a silo operator who would put it on a barge. These river facilities typically don't have a lot of storage. They're throughput facilities, like New Orleans, but on a smaller scale.

"If you're running a river terminal, you would look at the export bid FOB New Orleans and back that up to the interior, including all the transport and surveying costs and an elevation margin for the grain facility on the river system. The grain barge loading facilities will try to buy enough grain to load up barges and build a program. The barge quantities, roughly, are 55,000 to 60,000 bushels, call it 1,500 mt.

"If you are in the heart of the Midwest, you may get competitive bids from oilseed crushers, food processors and biofuel producers. Farmers will ask, 'What's my best market today, spot or forward, export or domestic?'

"At Louis Dreyfus, we owned some loading facilities, and we bought grain directly from the farmers or cooperatives and loaded it on barges. We didn't buy FOB the river; we covered the whole supply chain."

"How much weight is typically lost during transport to the export terminal?" I asked.

"Some people argue there's a weight pickup as grain is shipped downstream, but I don't know if it's a mass or volume pickup because the grain was cold, is shipped downstream, gets humid in Louisiana and expands. I've seen some weight pickups, but typically, you have a loss of around one-quarter of one per cent.

I had read somewhere that as farms get bigger, they are taking over the inland storage role from the trade houses and cooperatives. I asked Jim if it was true.

"Yes," he replied. "On-farm storage has increased due to good farmer profitability over an extended period. Farmers have become more corporate over time and are now handling assets previously held by the big co-ops or the multinational players. The multinationals have gotten out of that business; regional co-ops and farmers have replaced them.

"The big co-ops like CHS have international operations and do everything from agronomy to services, fuel, distribution, handling, owning assets, merchandising, etc., all the way through to financial services. Then, you have regional versions with big co-ops in Iowa. Some own processing facilities and crush plants to serve renewable diesel demand.

"The old romantic co-op model where the farmer drives down to a small co-op elevator in the middle of town is dated. The US is moving more towards a Brazilian model of corporate farming driven by demographics and the search for economies of scale."

Around 40 per cent of the annual US corn harvest goes to produce ethanol and Dried Distillers Grains with Solubles (DDGS). With the country developing its Renewable Diesel Programme, I wondered whether its agricultural exports would decline. And would it result in export overcapacity on the Mississippi?

"It ebbs and flows," Jim told me. "It's never been structurally oversupplied, and elevation margins are usually positive. The problem is more in the other direction. Elevation margins surge when export demand picks up. It's not easy to build a new export terminal. You've had natural expansion from the existing players, but little new capacity has come online.

"We've mandated more demand for biofuels, and maybe we will have fewer soybeans and corn to export, but we could increase meal and DDG (Dried Distillers Grains – a by-product of ethanol production) exports. Chinese crushers have a duty advantage in importing soybeans and crushing them domestically rather than importing meal," Jim told me. "But if that ever changed, we could see meal shipping to China rather than soybeans.

"It's been part of our thought process at Greenfield regarding our new facility. The river system is so expansive there are ways of shipping meal rather than beans. The US system can adapt quite well. If that's an opportunity to adjust, it can do it."

"What are the biggest changes you've seen in your career in the US domestic market?" I asked Jim. "Is it biofuels, corporate consolidation, or something else?

"The two episodes of biofuels expansion in the US. The first was ethanol with the 2005 RFS, Renewable Fuel Standard. It significantly altered the economics of domestic processing versus export demand. The second is happening now with renewable diesel. It is increasing the domestic consumption of soybeans.

"The other ones would be on the transportation side with competing flows for rail and barge. The US has gone from a significant coal exporter to nothing. It changes the economics of how you rail your ag products and how you compete for barges."

"Can you tell me three things about the CIF barge market," I asked, "that everybody should know but nobody thinks of?"

"The first goes back to the delivery system. It is one of the most transparent, liquid, visible agricultural physical markets. It is standardised and well thought out regarding rules, regulations, and trading and has a heterogeneous trading base. It ties directly into the futures instrument and is an excellent mechanism for connecting physicals to futures. How the Chicago corn and soybean futures markets converge with physicals at expiry depends on the CIF barge market.

"The second is that the US flat price depends on the US balance sheet, distilled down to supply and demand, stocks or stocks to use, which you can quantify, but the variability is with exports.

"The third is that the corn and soy futures listed on the CME are for US corn and soybeans. The CME sets a benchmark for world prices, but it's a US corn and soybean contract. You cannot deliver Brazilian corn. Corn in Brazil is fungible with corn in the US, but it's not deliverable."

Carlos Murilo Barros de Mello

Moving commodities by rail increases our economic costs but not necessarily our environmental costs. Our rivers are not easily navigable, but they provide green energy.

Murilo is an old friend from my many years in the sugar market. He has worked all along the supply chain for a trade house (Louis Dreyfus), a bank (Macquarie), a producer (Raizen), and a food company (Tharawat in Saudi Arabia). He is now Hedgepoint's head of sugar and ethanol for the Americas.

With over ten years of experience in price-risk management for agricultural and energy commodity chains, Hedgepoint became an independent company in 2021 following a spin-off from EDF Man Capital.

"I've been on both the sell and buy sides," Murilo told me. "It allows me to put myself in my client's shoes. When you do so, you know where it hurts. You know where the hurdles are. You know where the opportunities are. You know how they think. It makes it easier to shape a product.

"It helps with the language you use and how you communicate. It also helps in terms of my network. Ours is a small community, and I've been in the business for so long that I have ended up knowing everybody. Sugar is a big family."

I asked Murilo about the production and logistics challenges that Brazilian agriculture faces.

"Agribusiness is undoubtedly the most efficient industry in Brazil," Murilo told me. "We are second to none globally in terms of productivity and efficiency. People tend to think of agriculture as an old craft with small farms. It's not that at all. It is at the cutting edge of technology, not only for the seeds but also for best management and industrial practices.

"Our first challenge is growing the sector to meet expanding global demand through higher yields and more efficiency without damaging the environment. People often paint Brazil in a bad light in agriculture because of deforestation in the Cerrado and Amazon, but nobody mentions that Brazil's energy matrix is 90 per cent renewable.

"Infrastructure is our second challenge. Agricultural production has been increasing so quickly that it is hard for the country's logistical infrastructure to keep up. Brazilian interest rates are among the highest in the world, making it complicated to get a return on infrastructure investment, whether rails, roads or ports.

"The country's politics can be challenging. Policies and priorities change when the government changes, making investing riskier. It doesn't help build confidence for long-term investors. That said, there are many things that the government has done right. During the eighties and nineties, the government privatised the railways and the ports, reducing government interference and increasing efficiency. It allowed the sector to tap international capital markets.

"The rail system has expanded significantly, making rail transport cheaper, safer, and more reliable.

"Some new roads are also being built privately, especially in the far north. The privatisation of logistic infrastructure has allowed agricultural production to flourish."

"Are poor logistics holding Brazil back?" I asked.

"Logistics struggle to keep pace," he replied. "However, things are improving fast, allowing expanded grain production in the frontier lands in the north. Previously, if you wanted to bring grains from North Mato Grosso to Santos, you would have to ship them 3,000 kilometres over poor roads. The new ports and roads in the north have cut these distances to 500 kilometres. The northern ports have also reduced ocean freight transport distances to Europe and the Panama Canal."

From my days as an analyst, I remembered how Brazil's high cost of inland transport influenced which crops farmers grow. When I started in the sector, Brazil's sugar distillers provided all the ethanol in the country. However, corn ethanol production is taking market share in regions far from the ports. It makes more sense for these regions to use their corn for ethanol to supply the local fuel markets than transport it to the ports. The cost savings are further improved as the fuel distributors no longer transport gasoline to these remote regions.

People often complain that moving soybeans to Santos Port costs more than moving beans from Santos to China. I asked Murilo if that was true.

"It's true," he replied. "It's partly because ocean freight is much more efficient and cheaper than road and rail freight. There is also less weight loss with ocean freight than with road and rail – particularly road. You lose a small but significant percentage of weight when you move grains by trucks over poor roads. However, rail is taking an increasing share of the transport from farm to port; weight loss is becoming less of a factor."

Jim Heneghan mentioned that US farmers are blessed with the Mississippi River Basin. River transportation is more environmentally and economically efficient than road and rail transport, giving US farmers a significant advantage over their Brazilian colleagues. I asked Murilo if he agreed.

"You are right," he told me. "Brazil's rivers are less workable than those in the US. We may increase barge transportation a little, but rail is the future for Brazilian crop exports.

"Moving commodities by rail increases our economic costs but not necessarily our environmental costs. Hydroelectricity accounts for about 60 per cent of Brazil's energy matrix. Our rivers are not easily navigable, but they provide green energy."

"Let's move now to port elevation – the receiving and loading of grain onto oceangoing vessels," I suggested. "How much does it cost to load a vessel at Santos?"

"This information is private," he replied. Still, it should be about $11 per mt. Elevation used to cost as much as $36 per mt before privatisation.

It initially fell to $18 per mt and stayed there for a few years, but it has been on a downward trend for the last twenty years.

"The ports have invested in faster, more efficient ship loaders. Thirty years ago, daily load rates were 2,000 to 3,000 mt/day. A terminal in Santos can now load as much as 40,000 mt/day.

"They have also invested in bigger and better warehouses, making segregating different qualities of commodities easier and speeding up reception.

"What's the secret to a good elevation operation?" I asked.

"Efficiency is the secret to elevation," he replied. "You must keep the costs down. It is a capital-intensive business. Maintaining high throughput shrinks your fixed costs per tonne. Every penny counts.

"It can sometimes lead to a fight between the producers, trading companies, ports, and logistic operators. Traders and producers like to concentrate shipments and sales when prices are highest. Logistic operators like to ship a similar quantity every month and don't want the port and rail systems to stand idle.

"However, this is less of a problem now because Brazilian agricultural production has increased significantly. The ports and rail systems run at 85-95 per cent capacity all year.

"There is a difference in how the sugar sector has developed compared to grains and oilseeds," he concluded. "The country's sugar producers have become the biggest traders and exporters of sugar and have bought and built rail and port infrastructure. They have constructed an integrated value chain. The trading companies play that role in grains and oilseeds. Traders, not producers, own the grain and oilseed logistics infrastructure."

Guilherme Cauduro

Testing, inspection, and certification are all about trust. We must maintain an excellent relationship with our clients. They must trust us because we protect the quality and quantity of their goods.

Bureau Veritas is a French company specialising in testing, inspection, and certification. Founded in Belgium in 1828, it moved five years later to Paris, where it is now publicly quoted on the Euronext exchange. The company has 82,000 employees in 140 countries with a network of over 1,600 offices and laboratories. It operates in various sectors, including building and infrastructure, agriculture, food and commodities, marine and offshore, industry, certification, and consumer products.

Veritas' role in the agricultural supply chain is to inspect commodities to ensure that they meet the description of the goods in the agreement signed between buyers and sellers and to meet international commodity regulations and rules.

Guilherme Cauduro has a master's degree in agronomy from the Federal University of Rio Grande do Sul, where his father is a professor. Although Guilherme grew up in the city, his father spent much of his time on the family's soybean farm, and he accompanied him when he could.

"I didn't enjoy the noise of the big city," he told me. "I preferred the quiet of a farm."

On leaving university, Guilherme began his career with an agricultural research firm, where he stayed for two years before realising it was not for him. He had a friend working for Schutter Group, a Dutch inspection company headquartered in Rotterdam. The work sounded interesting, and he applied for a job there. He started as an inspection and certification manager at Rio Grande Port.

"I learned on the job when I started in the business in 2007," he told me. "I stayed in the port for 10-12 hours daily to understand how it all worked – the trucks, the terminals, and the conveyor belt loaders. I also learned how to do a draft survey.

"Most of the issues occur at night and weekends. I initially spent many nights and weekends at the port. I would often get home at three or four in the morning. It was tough on my wife, but she supported me."

In March 2007, Bureau Veritas acquired Schutter, and Guilherme stayed with them. He has effectively worked for the same company for 16 years. He is the Executive Director of the company's AFC Division in Brazil. AFC stands for Agriculture, Food and Commodities and is one of the company's five divisions in Brazil.

"We have a massive operation inland," he told me. "In the harvest season, we have around 3,000 – 3,200 inspectors working in our division in Brazil. In the mid-season, we have 1,500-1,800 people.

"When the trading houses originate soybeans or corn from farmers, they send the trucks to the farms to load and transport the commodities to the ports or the crushing plant. They hire our services to inspect the trucks when they load to ensure the quality is according to the contract between the farmer and the trading house.

"Bureau Veritas is involved in farm transhipment," he continued. "When the trading houses tranship cargoes from trucks to rail cars or trucks to barges, we are in the transhipment points collecting samples from trucks, from the barge, and from the rail cars to see if the quality is OK.

"Another business we do upstream is credit monitoring," he said. "The trading houses, banks, and chemical companies prefinance the farmers and cooperatives who need money to plant and harvest. We are on the farms to check how the crops are growing and to see if the harvest will be good enough to pay back the money to the financier."

"We also work for seed companies, protecting their royalties from GM crops. In Brazil, seed companies can charge royalties against GM crops for ten years, and we have teams that inspect the crops to ensure farmers pay royalties.

"Nowadays, our upstream accounts for around 60 per cent of our income – that's for the agriculture division."

"What is it like being a surveyor?" I asked him.

"We have a saying in the business that 'we must kill a lion each day.' Every day is a new story, and every crop season is different. We never have a crop season that's the same as another. As an inspector, you can expect something different every day.

"We have a lot of responsibilities and pressure from the clients. The costs can quickly mount if we fail to do our job correctly, whether quality inspection or crop surveying. It can be a considerable amount of money for a trading house. If we make a mistake in our analysis, we have problems with the farmers because they have guaranteed a certain quality.

"Testing, inspection, and certification are all about trust. We must maintain an excellent relationship with our clients. They must trust us because we protect the quality and quantity of their goods.

"We operate 24/7. In our business, we are always available to perform operations or to attend to a client; readiness is one of the critical factors of Bureau Veritas' success in the agri market in Brazil."

"What are your biggest challenges?" I asked.

"Our business is people," he replied. "We train our people and help them develop their skills. We are present in fifteen ports in Brazil, and our clients expect – and need – the same standard of service in each port. So, our biggest challenge is to ensure our inspectors and local managers provide the same high standard of service to the client regardless of where they are based. Our business assets are not computers or cell phones; they are people.

"We must guard against corruption. People often try to corrupt our people by asking them to issue fake certificates – to lie about the quality of the goods. Ethics is one of the absolutes of Bureau Veritas. We invest a lot in training our people about the fundamentals of our core business, principles, the relevance of our role, code of conduct and the absolute values of the company, among others.

"We must also keep our teams motivated. Working 24/7 means working weekends. People usually want to relax on weekends with their families. My job is to keep our teams motivated to supply the same standard of service to all our clients, to guard against corruption and to maintain integrity throughout our business. Integrity is the big thing.

"Do you travel much in your present position, internationally and domestically?" I asked.

"I started to make overseas business trips when the company promoted me to commercial director. It was an opportunity to meet people, get to know different cultures, and make friends in the business. Before the pandemic, I made seven or eight overseas business trips yearly as Commercial Director.

"You may have an excellent relationship with your clients in Brazil," he explained, "but you must also develop relationships with end buyers – the final receivers of the cargo.

"When a trade house sells cargo to China, Vietnam, or wherever, it is often the final receiver who chooses the inspection company at load. Remember, weight and quality are final at load. A trading house may prefer a different inspection company but will not say 'no' to a client. My job as commercial director was to persuade the end-buyers to choose us rather than our competition.

"In December 2021, I started in this new position as Executive Director. I still travel overseas but take a maximum of two trips a year. There is much to do here in Brazil, and I cannot stay away too long. That will change over time. I'm training my colleagues and passing all my client relationships on to them."

"Is it usual for a buyer to appoint a surveying company and a seller to nominate a different company?" I asked. "And what happens if they disagree?"

"Yes, it is widespread," he told me. "The buyer and the seller may want to appoint their own supervisory company. If there is a discrepancy or a disagreement, the seller, the buyer, and the inspection companies talk together to come to an agreement. They may agree to remove, for example, part of the cargo that may be off-spec – or the seller may compensate the buyer financially."

"You mentioned earlier that issues often occur at night or the weekends," I said. "Why is that?"

"First, people sometimes try to load off-specification quality goods at night or on the weekend when they think our inspectors are less focused. If a seller has a quality issue with a portion of the cargo, they may try to load it at night or on the weekend.

"Second, more accidents occur at night, especially in winter in southern Brazil. Temperatures sometimes fall below zero degrees, and surfaces can become dangerous.

I had read that there have been issues with traffickers smuggling cocaine in commodity shipments, particularly in containers.

"It is a big problem," Guilherme told me. "The traffickers have a lot of money and a lot of power. It is not only in containers. Nowadays, the traffickers have divers in the load ports, attaching boxes with cocaine onto a vessel's hull, and then divers removing these boxes from the ships at the destination. Rotterdam Port Authority employs divers to randomly check arriving vessels to see if they can find these boxes. It is a problem for the entire Brazilian agricultural sector."

"How has technology changed the business over the past few years?" I asked. "And how do you imagine it changing in the future?"

"It's incredible how technology has changed our business," he replied, "especially in digitalisation. Only five or six years ago, our inspectors in the ports would note their weight and quality observations on paper and send them to our local office, where a guy would manually enter the information onto an Excel sheet and then send it by email to the client. Our port inspectors now enter the information directly into their tablets or smartphones, and the system sends it automatically to our clients. It's not 100 per cent digitalised, but I would say it's 85 per cent digitalised in Brazil.

"We now have a machine that measures the moisture content of a commodity underload and sends the results through our system, which goes directly to the client. We don't need people typing in the moisture anymore. It is a significant change.

"The conveyor belts in Brazil load about 3,000 tonnes per hour. It's fast, and you don't have time to waste. Continual automated quality screening will be more efficient and accurate.

"We already have some grading machines in Brazil that screen for damaged, mouldy green beans, foreign matter, and impurities. We must calibrate these machines correctly and manually double-check they provide accurate results for the sample. This technology will help our inspectors to work faster and more efficiently."

"What do you like and dislike about your job?" I asked.

"I like the job dynamic," he replied. "I like meeting people, connecting with them, getting to know their cultures, and doing business in their countries. I like the speed of the sector – the adrenaline. I like that every day is different. You don't sit in front of your computer doing the same thing daily.

"I don't like my job when people try to bribe our inspectors to issue fraudulent certificates. Corruption is a big problem in Brazil, as it is throughout South America."

"Is there anything you'd like to add?" I asked.

"Only that a surveyor's role is essential to the agri-commodity supply chain. We, as surveyors, are responsible for checking the weight and quality of the goods traded between seller and buyer, and we are pleased to see that the clients understand how valuable our job is."

Luis-Carlos dos Santos

Never stop dreaming.

Luis is a vessel agent in Santos, Brazil, representing the Unimar Shipping Agency.

Before a vessel arrives in a port to load or discharge cargo, its owner or operator must nominate an agent to take care of all the formalities while the ship is in port. The agency is usually a full agency where the agent looks after the interests of both the vessel owner and the charterer. Occasionally, the ship owner will not be comfortable using the charterer's agent and will appoint a protective agent to look after his interests.

Vessel agents are responsible for handling all the vessel's necessary documentation for the health authorities, the federal police, and customs. The port or local authorities have no direct contact with the vessel owner or operator. Everything must go through the agent.

Vessel agents also look after the embarkation and disembarkation of the crew. Everything related to the vessel comes under the agent's umbrella. The agent is legally responsible for the ship in the port or on the roads. If, for example, it leaks oil into the port, the agent is legally responsible for the damage. The vessel agent is an essential part of the chain. A ship in port makes no money, and there must be no delays.

I asked Luiz why a client might choose him rather than a competitor.

"Information is one differentiator," he replied. "We provide statistics and market-relevant information, such as vessel line-ups. Traders and analysts use them to track import and export flows.

"Service quality is another differentiator. We try to provide our clients with the best service possible – consider it the difference between flying Ryan Air and Swiss. Remember, time is money, and efficiency is everything.

"We build personal relationships with our clients over the years. These relationships are based on trust – trust that we will do an excellent job for our clients.

"There is a standard cost, but some vessel agents might offer discounts or rebates to loyal clients or tempt prospective clients to try their service. We don't do that as we prefer to differentiate ourselves on quality rather than price. You usually get what you pay for in life."

"You mentioned vessel line-ups," I commented. "How do you put those together?"

"A vessel line-up is a list of the vessels nominated to load or already loading in the port. It includes the commodity, the shipper's name, and the declared destination. We don't have any information as to the sales price of the shipment. Analysts find line-ups helpful in tracking the quantity of a commodity that the exporting country ships – and hence, how much is left to ship from the harvest – and the amount a country imports.

"Of course, the vessel may not end up in the declared destination and might be resold or traded to another destination once it has left the load port, but traders can track the vessel using various tracking services.

"We put the line-ups together from both public and private information. The information is in the public domain whenever a vessel is nominated to a port. The Santos vessel agents meet regularly to coordinate the vessels they manage, and we often share information about where our ships are going. Not everyone wants to share. In addition to our weekly meetings, we also share information electronically.

"What is it like being a vessel agent?" I asked.

"Hard work! Except for 1st January each year, ports never stop. Ports work 24/7, and so do we. Our senior controllers work regular office hours from eight to six, but we also have a night shift when junior staff man the phones and emails.

"We usually handle more than one vessel at a time, which can sometimes be stressful. Technology has made our lives easier. Everything is linked electronically to the Brazilian health, police, port, and customs systems. In the past, we physically had to go to the various authority buildings with the paper documents, but now we file everything electronically. There are heavy fines if we do not complete the information correctly or on time.

When I first met Luiz, he had just completed an endurance event in the Amazon jungle. I asked him about it.

"Yes, I participated in endurance events for three years before I injured myself. The longest I did was 300km – a mixture of cycling, running, hiking, and canoeing – often over 48 hours. We competed in a team of either two or four people. We had to be self-supporting. Things began to get serious when our team won a 220km event. We also did 260km in 36 hours, which was fast.

"It was my way to boost adrenaline as you must push yourself. I love being in nature. Competing in these events was an excellent way to be outside. I found it relaxing."

"When I first met you, you also worked with the local schools," I said.

"I still do," he replied. "I started a social project in Santos in 2008, teaching English to underprivileged children. I also teach classes on the environment and biodiversity.

"In 2012, I purchased six cameras on a trip to Japan and began teaching photography to 15–18-year-olds on Saturday mornings. It is a great programme – a big success. Some of the kids I taught now work as photographers.

"In 2016, a contact at National Geographic asked me to extend the programme to Mozambique. I went there with my six cameras and two of my former students. We taught 24 kids over two weeks, with twelve kids and one camera for two kids each week. A Geneva company sponsored the cost.

"One of my former students in Mozambique recently messaged me to tell me he now works as a photographer and is training to be a tracker for

National Geographic. He sent me some of his photographs. It made me cry with happiness."

"Last question," I said. "What message would you give a young person thinking about a career in our industry?"

"I have four messages?" he answered.

"Never stop dreaming.

"Whatever you do, do it with passion.

"Constantly reinvent yourself and adapt as the world changes.

"Always look for ways to grow personally and professionally."

3. BULK SHIPPING

God must have been a shipowner. He placed the raw materials far from where they were needed and covered two-thirds of the earth with water.

I suspect maritime transport is the link in the agricultural supply chain that has changed the most over my career. A typical bulk carrier would carry 12,000 mt of sugar when I started in the business in 1979. Sometimes, if we were lucky, we could find a vessel that could hold 14,000 mt. The current record is 108,900 mt for a bulk sugar shipment and 108,500 mt for soybeans.

Traders now move bulk sugar in Handymax vessels, capable of carrying between 40,000 and 65,000 mt. They ship white sugar in breakbulk (in bags, stowed in the hold) in the smaller Handysize ships that take between 10,000 and 40,000 mt.

Traders typically ship grains and oilseeds in Panamax vessels, small enough to transit the Panama Canal. They carry between 65,000 and 100,000 mt. Grains and oilseeds account for around 10 per cent of the total dry bulk trade. Iron ore accounts for about 30 per cent, and coal accounts for about 25 per cent.

Shipping transports 90 per cent of the goods in the world and burns 7 per cent of global oil consumption. It contributes 3 per cent of the GHG emissions in the world.

A critical change over my career has been the development of the market in Forward Freight Agreements, FFAs. These now trade daily in thousands of lots, allowing operators to hedge their freight needs. The FFA market has traditionally been an OTC market, where counterparties enter into direct agreements. It is still an OTC market, but since the crash of 2009, all FFAs have been cleared either in London or Singapore.

(When the freight market collapsed in 2009, Panamax time charter rates fell from $70,000 per day to $7,000 per day. Daily Capesize rates dropped from $200,000 to $5,000 in less than one month. People hadn't realised how volatile freight rates could be, and several shipping and FFA-trading companies went bankrupt.)

FFAs are closely correlated to the physical shipping business. The physical shipping market determines the FFA prices, not vice versa. Many ships are now time-chartered on floating rates, at plus or minus the Baltic indices.

Another significant change over the past forty years has been how the trading companies have developed their freight activities. When I started at Cargill in London, the company had one freight guy chartering vessels on a voyage basis.

Cargill and the other big traders now have separate freight departments with P&Ls that can reach tens of millions of dollars. Forty years ago, they might have sold a cargo to China and then looked for a ship to transport it. Now, they can be short or long on tonnage and take positions. It's become a trading market.

There is another thing that has changed significantly over the past forty years. When I started in the business, the average lifespan of a cargo vessel was 25-30 years. Today, it is more like 15 years. Some 25-year-old ships are well-maintained and safe for carrying grain. Others are less well maintained and are a problem at 12 years old. At the end of their lives, ships usually sail to Turkey, Bangladesh, and India for scrapping.

Shipping faces the same challenges as those faced by commodities. Technology has made communication fast and seamless in both chartering and trading. It has led to thinner margins. As a result, traders seek economies of scale, and shipping is evolving with bigger and bigger ships.

Jan Dieleman

Shipping is under-recognised and under-appreciated. People often think of shipping as a service or logistics operation, but it's much more than that. It is a market – and a volatile one.

Jan joined Cargill in the Netherlands as a trainee. After three years in grain, he worked in shipping for eight years before moving to the energy markets for six years. He returned to shipping in 2016 and is currently president of Cargill's Ocean Transportation business. Cargill charters around seven hundred ships yearly: 25 per cent for Cargill and 75 per cent for external customers, operating mainly in dry bulk.

I was trying to imagine the challenge of managing seven hundred ships.

"We have developed AI-assisted analysis to predict where ships will go once loaded," Jan told me. "And we have some systematic trading where our models look at the data to produce a trade recommendation. We use these tools on the operational side. We can see each ship's daily fuel consumption and advise the master of the best speed to sail. There's a lot to be done to optimise this. There are still instances where we speed up a ship only to find it stuck in a port lineup."

When I started in commodities, shipping was an old-fashioned male-dominated sector with alcohol-fuelled lunches. I wondered how it had changed.

"When I started," Jan said, "The business was, to some extent, as you describe it. When you walked into the room, everybody looked similar. Things have changed for the better. If you step on our trading floor here, you'll see we have a diverse group of people in terms of gender, nationality, and skillset. It's much more a reflection of what society is today."

Jan outlined three reasons for this change.

"First, shipping has become more dynamic. In the early 2000s, when Cargill began growing its freight presence, many commodity markets were being deregulated, notably coal and iron ore. Previously, those markets traded on ten-year contracts. Then, in 2008-9, we had a massive spike in freight rates, spotlighting shipping as a significant input cost. It attracted new talent to the industry.

"Second, there has been a drive for more sustainable shipping, an essential topic for the younger generation. It has helped us attract bright and diverse people into the industry.

"Third, there has been greater use of digital tools. In the old days, you had to use a particular broker because he was the only one who knew where ships were. It meant you had to have a good relationship with the broker. Now, you look at a screen and count the vessels yourself. It has made the industry more professional.

"I like shipping," he continued. "It touches on the underlying commodities and the energy landscape. Energy accounts for around 40 per cent of the cost of moving goods from A to B. I like the challenge of decarbonisation. Transiting to new fuels will have a massive impact on the sector.

"We won't achieve our GHG goals by doing things more efficiently. To achieve our goals, we must shift to zero-carbon fuels. We'll run into a wall if we only work on fuel efficiency."

"What about wind – cargo carriers with sails?" I asked.

"Wind power will not get us to zero carbon," he replied. "But it is a step towards zero. Sails could reduce emissions by up to 20 to 30 per cent. They could also reduce fuel consumption by 20 to 30 per cent, giving us an immediate return on investment. Wind will make the hydrogen, ammonia, or methanol problem 20 to 30 per cent smaller.

"Energy-saving devices, biofuels, and supply chain optimisation are solutions. We, as Cargill, are doubling down on all three of those."

"The cost of decarbonisation in shipping will be huge, but in the container sector, it might mean only an extra half dollar on a pair of shoes. If you can pass the costs down to the end user, you can start scaling this and lower the cost of these new technologies. You can then roll them out to the broader industry.

"What are the other sustainability issues in shipping?" I asked.

"When people talk about sustainability in shipping, they only speak about decarbonisation. Sustainability is a much broader issue. It's about human rights and labour conditions at sea. It's about the recycling of ships. Look at the SDGs. They are a lot broader than just GHG emissions."

"I read you once walked out of a conference panel because it consisted entirely of men," I said.

"The conference was in Norway," Jan replied. "The organisers changed what they had promised a little bit. I decided to say that that was not what we agreed, and I didn't show up on the panel. It was a small thing, but it's gone a long way, and we have gotten a lot of credit for it.

"Many event organisers now put gender parity as a minimum requirement. It is becoming an industry practice. It is great to see."

"Are you seeing any move to gender diversity among crews?" I asked.

"The latest number I've seen is that females make up only 2-3 per cent of the workforce on ships. That's far from gender parity, but it's a complex issue. Ships' facilities can be basic, and crews can be away from home for extended periods, which makes things more challenging."

When people think about shipping, they think of flags of convenience, tax avoidance, pollution, safety, and poor crew treatment. I asked Jan whether he felt that image was justified – and if it is, what the sector is doing to improve things.

"You're right that the sector has a track record of not being the most transparent and maybe not being the most proactive," he replied. "You have good and bad spots in any industry, but we must be careful not to paint a whole industry with one brush.

"Things are changing rapidly, especially in transparency. When you get transparency, you gain clarity as to what needs improvement. An excellent example is taxation and beneficial ownership – who owns the ships? From a compliance point of view, we are in a completely different world than fifteen years ago.

"Finally," I said, "What advice would you give somebody starting in shipping or thinking about going into shipping?"

"Shipping is under-recognised and under-appreciated. People often think of shipping as a service or logistics operation, but it's much more than that. It is a market – and a volatile one. The Capesize market is possibly the second most volatile market after Natgas. There is much more going on in freight than people realise.

"If you're interested in the decarbonisation drive, there's a lot you can do in shipping, even though the sector is viewed as hard to change. There are a lot of opportunities. Our recent hires are excited about the green side of shipping and the contribution they can make.

"For people already in freight or just starting, I would say, 'Be curious. Don't zoom in too quickly on one market or one commodity. Keep your eyes open, see how the interactions work and identify the risks and the opportunities.'

"I would tell them not to pursue a career where they don't have a passion. You can be okay, but you will never excel. Go where your passion is and be curious."

Anders Valentin Vogt and Mads Frank Markussen

We are already seeing consolidation among major players in the freight trading sector, driven by the desire to achieve economies of scale, improve operational efficiency, and enhance their ability to weather market volatility.

Anders and Frank work within the Copenhagen Merchants Group – CM Group, a second-generation family-owned company involved in commodity brokerage and trading, shipping, logistics, terminals, production, and market intelligence. Anders heads the newly established entity CM Navigator, and Frank works as a freight trader in Navi Merchants.

Anders has been with the group for over eight years, working initially in the Agri and Biomass (wood pellets) markets. His roots in agriculture run far back, having grown up on a farm.

Frank was a freight trader for ten years, most notably in Denmark with DS NORDEN but also with Louis Dreyfus in Switzerland, where, incidentally, he read the Sugar Trading Manual (now, unfortunately, out of print).

CM Navigator is a subscription platform with S&D analysis, trade flows, physical prices (nominal and actual bids & offers), and dry bulk freight rates. Its freight calculator runs 360,000 freight rates, updated daily (approximately 30.000 voyages 12 months forward). Navi Merchants is a shipowner and charterer who trades freight, taking market positions, mostly on European trades and primarily in European short sea routes.

I asked Frank to explain how the FFA market works.

"The FFA markets work the same way as other derivative markets," he told me. "FFAs are swaps cleared via exchanges with brokers acting as go-betweens. Freight sellers can lay off their flat price risk via FFAs; in that sense, it is like basis trading in many other markets. The main difference between FFAs and wheat futures is that the MATIF or CBOT settles through physical delivery, while FFAs are financially settled based on an index of global routes.

"It makes FFAs more volatile than other futures because you cannot take delivery of ships against an FFA, forcing physical and derivatives to converge. If I am not mistaken, the FFA market is one of the world's most volatile derivatives in percentage swings.

"I would love for you to interview some hedge funds that have entered FFA markets in recent years," Frank continued. "My feeling is they put too much money into a relatively illiquid market. The ensuing volatility means shipowners and freight traders must constantly revise their bids and offers as customers buy an all-inclusive price, not a premium to a financial product. It is, of course, an opportunity for the smart traders!"

"Can you charter a vessel on a basis against an FFA?" I asked.

"Yes," he replied. "You can charter a ship on index-linked pricing, the same index that FFAs settle on. It is a popular way for traders who want to add physical presence without incurring huge flat price risks. It has other risks, though. There is no free lunch."

"Do you use AI in your programming, and how do you see it changing your freight world? I asked Anders.

"I will leave the freight trading part to Frank, he replied. "But in a CM Navigator context, we rely on old-fashioned fundamental analysis. We see the potential for AI to increase the accuracy of lineups and S&D forecasts using satellite imagery.

"However, AI could significantly impact market dynamics regarding the speed with which the markets react to disruptive events and capture opportunities. It may give the bigger trade houses an advantage or introduce new players into the industry, shaking things up a little, as in other industries."

"I am part of a network at the Danish Technical University," Frank told me. "We try to combine business knowledge with students and academics, funded primarily by Maersk Foundation".

"Ships operate under the constraints of physics," he continued, "making them suitable for modelling and optimisation. Whether it's engine performance, hull design, or port logistics, AI-driven solutions are on the horizon.

"Some shipowners are exploring AI-driven trading models, and companies like Cargill use systematic trading models to generate trade recommendations. While these models exist, their effectiveness can vary widely. However, AI's current limitations in price prediction shouldn't overshadow the fact that humans also have limitations. While top traders excel, not everyone in the shipping industry consistently makes profits. The future likely involves a combination of human expertise and AI."

"What does the future look like for the freight trading sector?" I asked.

"I think the next step is consolidation – amongst shipowners, freight traders and data providers," Frank replied. "We are already seeing consolidation among major players in the freight trading sector, driven by the desire to achieve economies of scale, improve operational efficiency, and enhance their ability to weather market volatility. You need serious IT, data subscriptions and human resources to compete with the best."

I couldn't interview two Millennium-generation Danes without asking them about diversity and sustainability.

"Diversity is on our agenda," Anders told me. "Diversity of ethnicity and nationality comes naturally in a global industry. However, when it comes to gender, it is not so easy, especially within these traditionally male-dominated industries like tech, commodity trading, and shipping. For example, last time we advertised for a software developer, 1 of 20 were female. In CM Navigator, we are a team of five nationalities based in three offices with around 40 per cent women."

"Sustainability is essential," he continued. "Customers must have it, and they ask for it to be free. We calculate carbon costs and emissions on the freight along with every freight rate. We aim to combine our data into a full carbon data solution."

Do Danes have shipping in their blood," I asked. "Are you modern Vikings?

"There's certainly a unique connection between Denmark and the shipping industry, Frank replied. "What struck me in Switzerland was that very few locals seemed interested in pursuing careers in shipping or commodities. In Denmark, it's a different story altogether. Shipping, especially through companies like Maersk, is a matter of national pride."

"You could say maritime traditions run deep in our veins," he added. "My family has ties to the industry – my parents were part of the Maersk family when they met."

"You mention Switzerland," I retorted, "But a Swiss company, MSC, is currently the world's largest shipping company, just ahead of Maersk."

"That's true," he replied. "But MSC has a Danish CEO!"

Alberto Perez — Lloyd's Register

By 2050, most of the world's fleet will be using alternative fuels, a combination of pure synthetic hydrogen-based fuels like green ammonia and methanol, LNG, and biofuels.

One of the great things about writing this book is that I discovered professions I didn't know existed – or that I kind of knew existed but never really thought about them. While looking for someone to talk to about marine insurance, a friend suggested I speak to Alberto Perez from Lloyd's. I only found out later that he knew no more about insurance than I did.

Alberto is Spanish and has a master's degree in electrical engineering from the Polytechnique University of Madrid. When he finished his studies, he took a position with ABB, a Swiss engineering company, as a commissioning and technical engineer in their marine division gave him. He spent long periods in the Republic of Korea.

In 2013, he completed an MBA at the IE Business School in Madrid and transitioned from engineering to a more commercial career within ABB. He stayed with ABB in Spain, developing the local business and working on decarbonisation. In 2014, ABB transferred him to Geneva, giving him responsibility for their energy efficiency business, a position that involved extensive travel.

In 2022, he completed the University of Geneva's Advanced Diploma in Commodity Trading. He joined Lloyd's Register, establishing and leading an entity in Geneva to cover commercial maritime markets for non-ship-owning entities, predominantly charterers, financiers, and insurance companies.

Lloyd's Register, commonly called LR, was founded in 1760 at Edward Lloyd's Coffee House in London, a meeting place for merchants, ship owners and insurers.

The underwriters, owners, and merchants had no standards or criteria to help them evaluate the risk of insuring a ship. They began to employ technical experts to inspect vessels and rate them against specific criteria. As a next step, they started to develop shipbuilding rules. They published a book, the Lloyd's Register of Ships, which listed and rated the ships they inspected.

Lloyd's Register of Shipping evolved into a technical society known as Lloyd's Register and expanded into non-maritime areas. The company has recently transformed and now acts as a professional services company with predominantly two lines of work. The first is the ship inspection and rating business, mainly on behalf of governments, representing several flag states and doing inspections on their behalf. The second work is advisory, which is anything not exclusively related to ship certification.

"So that's what we've been doing for the past 261 years," Alberto told me, "Trying to make the maritime trade and the sea safer for all working there."

I asked Alberto to tell me more about ship inspections.

"There are different types of inspections," he told me. "There are annual surveys for the class and the flag state. The same inspector typically does both at the same time. Then, there is usually a significant survey every five years, often occurring while the ship is dry-docked for maintenance. In addition, an insurance company will typically require a class survey after an incident or accident."

One of the criticisms levied against shipping is that ships typically sail under flags of convenience. I asked Alberto if the criticism was justified.

"There was a debate some 30 years ago as some flags had looser standards than the traditional flags," he said. "Many countries agreed to inspect vessels when they entered their ports. Port State Control (PSC) has become an essential element of marine regulation. Inspectors have the authority to detain ships if necessary.

"All the information is public. If inspectors find that ships from a particular flag start to present problems, they might grey- or deny-list that flag. It's the last thing a flag wants because any ship under their flag will be inspected whenever they visit specific ports. Generally, inspectors always find something wrong, which helps maintain standards across all flags. Shipowners will choose a flag state for tax reasons rather than to get away with lower technical standards."

There has been a lot of media criticism of the merchant shipping sector for its GHG emissions. However, ships carry 90 to 95 per cent of the world's transported goods but are responsible for less than 3 per cent of all GHG emissions. It's an economically and environmentally efficient means of transport. Even so, the IMO has set a goal to achieve net zero by 2050. I asked Alberto if it was achievable.

"It will not be easy," he replied. "Alternative fuels do not yet exist in meaningful amounts. The policy will concentrate on increasing fuel efficiency for the next few years. It alone will not solve the problem, but it could reduce it by 20 to 30 per cent.

"The goal is to get to a point where most of the ships in the world use alternative fuels. Some of the fuels are carbon-negative; using them will remove atmospheric emissions. By 2050, most of the world's fleet will be using alternative fuels, a combination of pure synthetic hydrogen-based fuels like green ammonia and methanol, LNG, and biofuels.

"Will adding sails to cargo ships help?" I asked.

"Absolutely," he replied. By the beginning of 2024, we should have 50 ships on the water equipped with sails, commonly called Wind Assisted Propulsion Systems (WAPS). And there is an order book of 200 more. The technology is heading for massive adoption in the next five to ten years. You can significantly reduce the use of your main engine by using sails. We're talking about high single-digit to low double-digit per cent savings in power.

"There's a shipping regulatory framework starting next year in Europe called Fit for 55, where regardless of the flag and the ship's ownership, any ship entering or leaving a European port will be subject to EU legislation on shipping emissions. The penalties will be significant. Part of this regulation, FuelEU, will provide incentives for using WAPS. As a result, if you operate a five-year-old tanker regularly visiting European ports, retrofitting it with sails is more than likely economically worthwhile."

I asked Alberto about the life expectancy of a ship.

"It depends on the ship type," he said. "It is often more of a commercial consideration than a technical one. For ships that trade internationally, it is roughly 20 years for a bulk carrier ship and 15 years for an oil tanker. There are some 30- or 40-year-old cruise liners still operating."

Dismantling ships is dangerous for workers and the environment. Injuries, fatalities, and work-related illnesses often occur because of the hazardous materials onboard the vessels. I frequently saw reports of workers taking terrible risks breaking up old vessels.

"Is it controlled in any way?" I asked.

"In 2009, policymakers and regulators came together to address the issue and introduced the Hong Kong Convention for Safe and Environmentally Sound Recycling of Ships (HKC), which came into force in June 2023. As part of the convention, ships must have an Inventory of Hazardous Materials onboard, which must be prepared, verified, and kept up to date, in line with the IMO's guidelines.

"Whilst ship recycling remains hazardous due to the above points, we are certainly seeing a shift towards safer and sustainable practices for vessels that have reached the end of their lifecycles."

Captain Alexandra Hagerty

You come back ashore and realise that you have changed so much; your perspective has changed as you have navigated around the globe.

Around one-third of people who work in the agriculture commodity supply chain are women, but few are seafarers. A 2021 survey by the IMO (International Maritime Organization) found that the percentage of women in the shipping industry is 29 per cent worldwide, but nearly all are on land.

In the US, in 2020, there were 15,465 females in a total shipborne workforce of 210,000 merchant mariners – just above 7 per cent of the total. Unfortunately, very few held leadership positions. Among those 15,465 female merchant mariners, 4,729 had a credential endorsed as "Master", and only 149 held a certification endorsed as "Master Unlimited Any gross tons", effectively certified to command ships of any size globally.

In 2020, only 149 US female captains could command a ship globally out of a US merchant marine workforce of 210,000.

I managed to track down one of them: Captain Alexandra Hagerty, who has spent the last 13 years as a mariner. In a 2021 interview on her website, Captain Hagerty explained why she took to the seas.

"I fell in love with sailing when I worked as a sailing instructor for physically disabled children when I was nineteen. It was a fantastic experience getting them on the water, some of them for the first time. I realised how exciting it was to be on the water, with its inherent sense of adventure and a means to travel the globe. I wanted to experience more.

"Some of the most significant challenges in this career are your sacrifices. You miss special engagements, ceremonies, conferences, and occasions with family and friends. Sometimes, you are forgotten and lose touch with the communities and networks you once had on shore because you are gone for months. You come back ashore and realise that you have changed so much; your perspective has changed as you have navigated around the globe. It takes time to re-enter yourself into a community that has been continuing without you.

"Loneliness is a huge challenge, and this industry is not for everyone. You must have grit and integrity to wake up daily, work 12–15-hour days for months, and realise you will reap the rewards upon signing off. This lifestyle is premised upon delayed gratification. If you can't play the long game shipping out for months, this isn't for you!

"I have been challenged in the past as a woman. However, being physically active and motivated helps break some of these stigmas. I also am not afraid to speak up and over someone if they are trying to cut me off in a conversation or confront someone if there is an issue.

"Sometimes the greatest reward, strangely enough, is having the regular comforts you expect to have daily on land taken away from you for an extended period, and when you come back from sea, you appreciate them so much more.

"On some ships, you are constantly moving and working. However, the hard work pays you back in vacation time. What 21-year-old graduating with a four-year degree can make six figures in six months of work and have six months of vacation a year while obtaining excellent medical and retirement benefits? An American Merchant Marine Officer!

"I will never forget seeing the Northern Lights (Aurora Borealis) coming out in Iceland. It felt like it was engulfing our vessel in a greenish spiritual light. It was stunning, and the pictures from that evening of the Arctic Circle will never do justice to watching its movement across the sky.

"I also remember watching flying fish fly the length of a swimming pool off the coast of the Northern Marianas Islands and blue-footed boobies landing on the vessel while transiting through the Panama Canal. It was terrific talking to a Panama Canal Pilot and fellow graduate from our school who brought local coffee and Panama Canal Pilot hats to my crew as we transited the canal, talking with him about local customs.

"Meeting a 75-year-old Japanese pilot in the Naikai Sea (Inland Sea) who told me that age is just a number. He started his career as a pilot at 55 after working 20 years as a Ship Captain. He was so inspirational and kind."

Captain Hagerty has sailed and commanded many vessels, including MV Africa Mercy with Mercy ships. I asked her what had prompted her to volunteer and what she learned.

"I realised there was an opportunity for people in seagoing professions to give back – pro bono work. I had heard of doctors and lawyers doing pro bono work, but I didn't know I could volunteer as a captain and give back to the world. It was like, wow, there's an opportunity to take my skill sets to a different level and give back.

"I was also attracted by the challenge of getting a ship underway that hadn't moved in two years due to COVID.

"The ship had to leave Africa in 2019 due to the COVID pandemic, and thousands of Africans held on to their ID cards, hoping and praying every day that the ship would return. It was a fantastic experience to be the captain of a ship that brought 14 pallets of medical supplies and 450 crew from around the world to Africa.

"The weather was perfect; we didn't encounter any storms. It was strange. It was as if the seas were ready for us, and everything was meant to be. I was so happy to be asked to be the first female captain of this hospital ship. It was the only job where I wasn't paid, but it was the best job I have ever had."

It was during this voyage that Captain Hagerty had the idea of *Captains Without Borders,* and she started thinking about how she could help seafarers while at the same time alleviating their shortage. She realised that with women making up less than one per cent of ship's officers, the sector was not tapping into 50 per cent of the world population.

"If you look back 100 years," she told me, "People never imagined that women could become professional lawyers and doctors, but 50 per cent of doctors and lawyers are now women. My idea was to break down barriers and give young people from disadvantaged backgrounds – women or people from different castes, societies, or countries where seafaring is not a typical job or career – the opportunity to attend school and join the maritime industry.

"We're now seeing a huge change where doors are finally opening for a new plethora of people to enter the sector. I see more young women getting into it than ever before.

"I also thought about the war in Ukraine. I was a Vice President of the American Council of Master Mariners and IFSMA, the International Federation of Shipmasters Associations. With ISMA, we worked with the Ukrainian Seafarers Union to help seafarers stranded worldwide. Some of them ended up being on my ship.

"We also gave seven scholarships to young cadets at the Ukrainian Maritime Academy to finish their studies. They started crying when we told them; they were so happy and excited to have a scholarship. Half of them were women."

Finally, in the 2021 interview, the interviewer asked Captain Hagerty the same question I always ask interviewees: what advice would she give to a young person contemplating a career in the maritime industry, especially a girl?

"This career is not for the faint of heart," she replied. "Nor for someone who wants to stay home or local. This career is for someone who is flexible, ready to be delayed on the other side of the world because of international relations or a pandemic and can handle the consequences.

"High school girls interested in this career must be okay with being physically active 10-12 hours daily. This will never be the 9-5 job unless you want something shoreside. Most graduates work on average for 3-5 years at sea and then move shoreside. However, I encourage those who want to move up the ladder because there is a big difference in responsibility from Second Mate to Chief Mate and from Chief Mate to Captain.

"Responsibilities change and gain complexity, and your day-to-day problem-solving skills must grow and adapt as you advance in rank and position."

4. CONTAINER SHIPPING

Growing up in the UK during the 1960s and 1970s, my mother often sent me out to search the local shops for sugar and cooking oil. My father, at the same time, would drive around the local petrol stations in search of fuel. The dockworkers were going on strike again!

I can remember a joke at the time. A dockworker turns around and stamps on a snail.

"Why did you do that?" asked his co-worker.

"Damn thing has been following me around all day," he replied.

Containerization did not just mean that I no longer had to scour the shops in search of sugar. It revolutionized world trade and was both the catalyst and the driver for globalization. In the process, it transformed port cities, turning dockland warehouses into shopping malls, lofts, and coffee shops.

Before containerization, workers would handle goods manually and load them onto a truck, train, or barge, transporting them to a port warehouse where they would offload and store them until a ship turned up. When it did, stevedores would move the cargo to the vessel's side and either carry it on their backs up a gangplank or use a crane to lift it into the ship's holds. Once at its destination, other workers would unload the goods and transfer them to a warehouse to await collection. The process was costly, time-consuming, unreliable, and open to theft.

The concept of container shipping dates to the early 20th century, but it was not until the mid-1950s that it gained traction. In 1956, the American trucking entrepreneur Malcolm McLean launched the first container ship, the SS Ideal X, which transported 58 containers from Newark to Houston.

The Japanese shipping company NYK built the first container ship, the Hakone Maru, in 1968. It could carry 752 of the new standard-size containers. Modern container ships can hold more than 24,000 containers.

Container capacity is usually expressed in Twenty-foot Equivalent Units (TEUs), equal to one standard 20 ft × 8 ft container. It is an approximate measure because containers vary in height, while 20 ft containers are a few inches short of 20 ft, which allows two to be fixed together and stacked on top and below 40 ft containers. One forty-foot container is equivalent to two TEUs.

There are no exact numbers, but 40 ft containers account for at least 70 per cent of the world's container fleet, mainly because they fit easily onto a truck or railcar. However, container ships carry containers of various sizes. About 90 per cent are dry containers; the rest are refrigerated (reefers) or flex tanks for moving liquid products.

Shipping lines prefer 40-ft containers and usually only charge 30 per cent more to move them than 20-ft boxes. Shippers prefer to move heavier cargo, like sugar, in 20-ft units, placing them at the bottom of the hold to help stabilize the ships. As a result, they sometimes offer discounted rates for agricultural commodities.

Carriers will now stack as many as 25 containers on top of each other inside the holds and on the decks. As heavy agricultural goods usually go towards the bottom of the stack and inside the vessel hold, few are lost overboard during a storm.

As I mentioned earlier, containerization has driven a massive expansion in world trade. In 2021, ocean-going ships transported about 1.95 billion mt of cargo globally, up from some 0.1 billion mt in 1980. Over the same period, the[202F?]deadweight tonnage of container ships[202F?]grew from about 11 million mt to roughly 293 million mt.

Nine of the world's ten busiest container ports are in Asia. In 2022, Shanghai was the most active, with about 47 million TEUs, followed by

Singapore at 37 million, Ningbo-Zhoushan at 33 million and Shenzhen at 30 million. Los Angeles was the ninth busiest at just under 10 million TEUs. The Port of Rotterdam topped the ranking as the largest container port in Europe, handling over 8 million TEUs. Santos in Brazil is the busiest container port in South America, running 5 million TEUs.

Remember, though, that as most containers now are 40 ft, the actual number of containers shipped could be around 60 per cent of the total TEUs.

Container shipping companies have built increasingly large vessels to exploit economies of scale. In 2023, the Swiss-based MSC (Mediterranean Shipping Company) launched a staggering fifteen ULCSs (Ultra Large Container Ships) – 400-metre-long monsters that can carry more than 24,000 TEUs. OOCL (Orient Overseas Container Line) – a subsidiary of COSCO (China Ocean Shipping Company) – built five vessels of similar size in the same year.

In the same year, MSC overtook Danish-based AP Moller-Maersk as the world's largest container shipping company, a position Maersk had held since 1996. MSC added almost 100 ships to its fleet in 2023 and now manages over 740 container ships with a carrying capacity of around 4.9 million TEU. Today, MSC operates a vast network covering over 200 trade routes and calling at more than 500 ports around the globe.

Maersk runs a fleet of around 700 container ships with approximately 4.2 million TEU capacity. France's CMA-CGM is the third largest company, with over 623 vessels and a carrying capacity of about 3.4 million TEU. COSCO is the fourth largest, with approximately 480 container ships and a capacity of 2.9 million TEU. The German-based Hapag-Lloyd is fifth, with about 250 ships and 1.8 million TEUs in carrying capacity.

The four biggest container ship operators account for over half of the world's container fleet capacity, while three alliances account for nearly 75 per cent. In 2015, Maersk and MSC launched the 2M Alliance, a vessel-sharing agreement on the Asia-Europe, trans-Pacific, and trans-Atlantic trades that covers nearly 30 per cent of the global shipping market. The two shipping lines announced in 2023 that they would terminate the alliance in January 2025.

The Ocean Alliance is the second largest, consisting of COSCO, OOCL, Evergreen and CMA. THE Alliance, between Hapag-Lloyd, ONE, HMM, and YML, is the third largest.

These alliances were scrutinized during COVID-19 when container shipping rates shot higher. The cost to ship a container of coffee from Vietnam to Europe rose from $1,000 to $13,000. Some blamed the shipping companies for price-gouging, but there simply wasn't the capacity to meet demand. When demand exceeds supply, prices move higher to ration demand and increase supply. The higher rates rationed demand, and the container shipping companies made record profits. Since then, they have invested much of those profits in new capacity.

Estefania Gallo Prot Swarovski

I have no regrets. MSC, Cargill and Fracht proved to be better than any university.

On 10th January 1992, a container ship, the Evergreen Ever Laurel, ran into a severe storm in the North Pacific Ocean, and some shipping containers washed off the deck. One container split open in the waves, and its cargo of 28,800 children's bath toys – red beavers, green frogs, blue turtles, and yellow ducks – made a bid for freedom. Oceanographers have been tracking their progress ever since, using them to help map ocean currents.

The toys began to wash up along the Alaskan coast within a year. Others spent years trapped in Arctic ice before gradually drifting to Japan and Europe. Beachcombers still look out for the toys; they have become collector's items, selling for as much as $1,000 per duck.

Containers rarely fall from ships; when they do, they usually sink quickly. They float low in the water when they don't, making them a shipping hazard.

Our Brazilian office used to specialize in brokering white sugar shipped in containers from Santos. I think we brokered perhaps the largest-ever shipment of sugar in containers to India. (The country was an importer that year.)

Even so, when I began this project, I knew little about containers – nor anyone involved in the business. A mutual friend introduced me to Estefania – Steffi. They had known each other at Cargill, where Steffi oversaw the company's sugar container shipments. Before working with Cargill, she had worked at MSC.

"I started on the cruise side with MSC," she told me, "I spent two years there before moving onto the cargo side for three years. I have a connection with the MSC family through my godmother, and I married one of MSC's trade managers when I was only nineteen."

Steffi joined Cargill in 2011 and then moved to Alvean, Cargill's sugar-trading joint venture with Copersucar. In 2018, she joined Fracht, a Swiss freight forwarding company that handles more than 70,000 containers annually.

"Although my job is based in Miami," she told me over a Zoom call, "I am currently in Buenos Aires. My daughter was born in Geneva, but we moved to Argentina when I divorced. She was 13. She fell in love with Argentina, and I cannot persuade her to move. She's 19 now and studying at the university here. Fracht kindly allows me to split my time between BA and Miami."

I wanted to bring the conversation back to shipping and asked her if any of her containers had ever washed overboard.

"It has never happened to me," she told me. "But it occurs when there are big storms. You will understand why if you have seen a video of a vessel going through a storm. So, you had better hope that your container is not the one at the top."

"Have you ever lost track of a container?" I asked her, "Like a suitcase at an airport?"

"Rarely," she replied, "Although we have had two containers in India for a year and a half. They were supposed to go to Minnesota, but the shipping company sent them as empties to India. I have lost containers only three times in my 19-year career."

I remember that our Brazilian office regularly complained when a ship left containers behind at the port, even when they had been booked on the vessel. I asked Steffi if it happened often.

"It happened a lot during the Pandemic," she replied. "There are various reasons why a vessel might leave a container behind.

"One would be if the vessel arrives late to a port. Vessels have certain hours agreed with each port, and they must leave by a specific time to reach the next port and maintain a reliable schedule. So, let's say a vessel was supposed to have 10 hours in port, but because of bad weather or whatever reason, it arrived late and only had 3 hours. The ship must cut and run to the next port, even if it leaves cargo behind.

"The second reason will be when carriers are overbooked. Sometimes, they are 30, 40 per cent overbooked. It's not happening now, but it used to occur during the Pandemic. The world went wild. Everybody was moving cargo, and there was not enough capacity.

"The third reason could be a last-minute change of schedule, or maybe your cargo is too heavy, and the vessel is too low in the water. If it is, the ship will leave heavy cargo behind. As sugar is heavy, it is often the first cargo left behind."

Fracht is a private Swiss company founded in 1955 and still owned by the founding family. Cargill is also family-owned. I asked Steffi if the two companies were similar.

"Not really," she told me. "There are more similarities between Fracht and MSC, where I started my career. Cargill is family-owned, but it is a big machine, and you never get to see the family. At Fracht, I talk regularly with the owner and update him on the business. It would never happen in Cargill.

"But there are other advantages to working at Cargill," she continued. "It is like a university in ag trading. I learned a tremendous amount while I was there. I started in my mid-20s and took every course that Cargill offered. I'm very grateful for that experience because it changed how I think."

I asked Steffi whether she had been to university.

"Yes," she replied, "But, as I said, I married young and never finished my degree. I regretted it for many years. I had always been top of my class at school, and my teachers had big expectations for my university and academic career. But life, as they say, had other plans for me. Now,

I have no regrets. MSC, Cargill and Fracht proved to be better than any university.

"When I joined Fracht, they told me that many top managers in the company didn't have a university degree, so welcome to our family. They trusted me so much that I just flew.

"I was hung up for a long time that I hadn't finished my university degree and lacked self-confidence. I needed approval to think that I was good, that I was smart, that I was capable. It would have been better if I had worked on that earlier to understand my capabilities better."

"What advice would you give to your 19-year-old self?" I asked her.

"To trust herself and be more self-confident," she replied. "I would tell her not to run. I spend my life running, but life slips through your fingers when you run. Take life one step at a time. Slow down. Don't be in such a hurry.

"I would tell her that what matters the most is not how life treats you but your attitude towards how life treats you.

"Finally, I would tell her that the people she builds connections with will become her biggest asset."

"Do you think she would have listened?" I asked.

"Probably not!" she replied.

Laia Bosch

I like my job because I see its sense, need, and purpose.
It's a job full of stories.

I have known Laia for many years. She joined Kingsman in 2008 as a Biofuels Analyst before moving to Nestlé, working first as an analyst and then as a vegoil procurement manager. She took up her current role with ADM in January 2022. She is one of the few people I know who have had three professions in a short time: analyst, procurement manager, and trader. That was enough reason to chat, but she is also a container expert.

Lea lives and works in Switzerland, where she manages her teams in the Netherlands and Singapore, moving crude and refined vegoil from ADM or third-party plants to customers across the globe.

I asked her if it was challenging to ship food-grade refined vegoil.

"The challenge in shipping refined oil is freshness," she told me. "For example, we ship to New Zealand, which is almost two months of transit time. Some parameters, for example, peroxide values, increase over time. It's still edible, but the quality deteriorates.

"We have hundreds of containers moving worldwide daily," she continued. "Anything can go wrong in a shipment. A container may miss a ship or have the wrong documents. It may have quality issues. Sometimes, we must export containers from a war zone. Every container is a potential source of problems, but we work with excellent partners, freight forwarders and shipping lines. They know where our containers are. They track them. We do not have many scares."

Laia explained that they can access the shipping line's digital platform to track the location of each container at any time. I asked her if she considered herself a trader or a supply chain manager.

"I call myself a trader," she told me, "But a significant portion of my role is managing a supply chain. We supply customers in the middle of Africa or the Pacific Islands who have been buying from us in containers for years. We have been strong in exporting oil in containers from Ukraine during the war. We have a robust global footprint and a network of ADM people working with customers at destinations.

"What do you like most about your current role?" I asked her.

"I like my job because I see its sense, need, and purpose. It's a job full of stories. It could be a Caribbean mayonnaise manufacturer or a Pacific fish canner without a refinery in the country or a neighbouring country. They need to import a container of oil to their facility.

"Another example could be a food manufacturer in a market with only one supplier that wants to import oil to lower their ownership price. Or a small crusher in Ukraine that wants to export its oil but doesn't have enough capacity to fill a big vessel. They all rely on us.

"I find it very satisfying. It is what I most like about my job, that I see the purpose of it."

I was curious whether her friends approved of her job as an agricultural commodity trader.

"Do they see you as a wicked speculator," I asked, "Or do they say you're helping feed the world?"

"They usually ask a lot of questions," She replied. "I do have friends who are critical, but I think I have more supporters than critics."

I wanted to know whether she preferred being an analyst, procurement manager or trader.

"Procurement is about price risk management, negotiating, and cost savings," she told me. "It's not an income-generating activity by itself. If you manage cost savings and price risk management well, and the brand is selling well, then you see the returns of your job. What I like about trading is that you see your P&L daily; it's a business by itself.

"They all have their charm," she continued. "There is an excellent link between them. I'm happy to have gone through the three.

"None of the steps I have taken in my career have been a piece of cake. But I think it should be like this, right? If you move, you move to stretch yourself. I was lucky enough to have people that believed in me and trusted and supported me. I would be lying if I said it was not challenging, but that's what I like as well."

I asked her how she managed her work-life balance.

"I have an intense job in terms of watching the market, my position, and my shipments. But I'm a mom of two children. I don't know if it's because of them, but I know when to stop before being overworked.

"I also make sure I do things outside work and family. So that's how it works for me. We work a lot and are always alert, but I still want to keep time for myself."

I asked her what advice she would give to a young woman seeking a career in ag trading.

"I would suggest you find a woman who inspires you," she told me. "Ask her to mentor you – and then to give it back to the industry, your company, and women in general. Be a mentor to another woman."

Jack Marrian

People need to understand the sheer volume of drugs that get smuggled around the world in shipping containers. We traders need to understand the risks.

One Friday night in July 2016, 32-year-old Jack Marrian was woken from his bed in his suburban Nairobi home, handcuffed and taken to the city's central police station. It was the beginning of a three-year nightmare that saw him spending weeks in a crowded Kenyan jail, deprived of his passport for two years, charged with drug smuggling, and faced with the prospect of spending 30 years in prison.

The previous evening, Kenyan Customs officers—accompanied by the local media—had opened one of four shipping containers that had arrived in Mombasa port. They found that two of the 50kg bags of white sugar in one of the containers had been replaced with 100kg of cocaine, with an estimated value of US$6 million.

The sugar was part of a total consignment of 22 containers shipped from Brazil to Kenya, with transhipment in Valencia, Spain. Mshale Commodities (Uganda) Ltd, the East African arm of British sugar-trading company EDF Man, was the importer of the sugar, and the company's name was on the documents. Jack is a director of the company.

Unknown to Jack at the time, the US Drugs Enforcement Agency, the DEA, had been tracking the drugs from the moment the smugglers had placed them in the container while it was waiting at the port of Santos in Brazil. The DEA had warned their counterparts in Spain that the drugs were on their way and suggested that they wait to see who came to pick them up. Somehow, the warning leaked out, and no one turned up to collect them. Before the Spanish police could get a mandate to open the container, it was whisked off on the next boat to Mombasa. The DEA then informed the Kenyan authorities that the cocaine was on its way.

Smuggling drugs in legitimate containers is known as Gancho Ciego or Rip-on/Rip-off. UNODC, The UN Office on Drugs and Crime, describes it as:

A concealment methodology whereby a legitimate shipment, usually containerized, is exploited to smuggle contraband (particularly cocaine) from the country of origin or the transhipment port to the country of destination. Neither the shipper nor the consignee knows their shipment is being used to smuggle illicit cargo. For this method to succeed, there will always be a local conspiracy in the country of origin or the transhipment port and the destination country.

The European Monitoring Centre for Drugs and Drug Addiction adds,

The drugs are usually loaded in the dock area, so the 'rip-on' team must be able to get the drugs into the container terminal and locate the container, which must be in an accessible position. In most cases, the security seal must be replaced with a duplicate to avoid obvious signs of tampering. At the port of arrival, the drugs must be retrieved, which can be achieved in various ways. The drugs can be removed from the container by corrupt port workers or by external teams who gain access to the terminal. After the 'rip-off', the container is left open or resealed with another false /duplicate seal.

In Jack's case, the smugglers cut the locking bars of the container to gain access to it and insert the drugs without disturbing the original seal. The Kenyan authorities found a spare MSC seal in the container.

When the Kenyan police arrested Jack, they showed him a photograph taken at passport control in Nairobi airport of three Caucasian men; they asked him if he knew them. He did not, but they were subsequently identified as suspected members of the 'Ndanghreta crime syndicate, which controls up to 60 per cent of the cocaine traffic between South America and Europe and operates in ports all along the Iberian Peninsula, as well as in Italy.

They had arrived at Nairobi airport a few days before the four containers arrived in Mombasa. No one is sure, but the plan was probably for the smugglers to bribe their way into the port, recover the drugs, and rescue an operation that had gone wrong. Unfortunately for them—and Jack—the Kenyan police got to the drugs first.

The DEA wrote a letter to the Kenyan prosecutors saying, "The DEA would like to stress that there was no indication the cocaine was to be received in Kenya." They added, "The company owning the consignment had no knowledge that the cocaine was secreted inside their shipment of sugar."

Unfortunately, the Kenya authorities continually denied ever receiving such a letter, and the case against Jack and his co-defendant Roy Mwanthi, a Kenyan clearing agent at the port, dragged on. Only in March 2019, nearly three years after his arrest, did the authorities finally dismiss the case.

"I don't want this to happen to anybody in our business ever again," Jack told me.

"Surely the solution lies in the hands of the shipping and trading companies," I asked him. "It must come rather from the port authorities increasing security at the ports."

"The challenge," Jack admitted, "is that you are up against a large-scale, well-funded organization, especially from Brazil."

The UNODC states that less than two per cent of the more than 500 million containers shipped yearly are inspected. Drug gangs often target sugar containers because sugar does not show up on scanning equipment. As such, the containers must be searched by hand – a monumental task. It makes the rip-on / rip-off method relatively cheap. Even if a container is seized, there is only a relatively small quantity of cocaine in each container, reducing the cost to the gang.

Jack is the nephew of the Earl of Cawdor, whose family seat is Cawdor Castle in the Scottish Highlands. His case received considerable coverage in the UK media. I wondered to what extent his aristocratic background might have explained the Kenyan authorities' reluctance to drop the case, even considering the DEA evidence.

I asked Jack if he felt he had been singled out and made a scapegoat. He replied that he didn't think so, although he "believed it was politically expedient for the Kenyan authorities to accuse and prosecute me publicly."

"In a way, I was fortunate to have had all that support from the media," he continued. "I think it helped."

"Has the experience put you off trading?" I asked him.

"It has made me cautious about trading anything out of Brazil," he replied. "Brazil is extremely high risk. People need to understand the sheer volume of drugs that get smuggled around the world in shipping containers. We traders need to understand the risks. And we need to take the issue seriously."

5. OPERATIONS

Contrary to what you might imagine, traders don't trade commodities; they trade documents. A trader who sells Brazilian soybeans to China doesn't get paid once the beans are loaded onto a vessel in a Brazilian port, when they are unloaded in China, crushed, or even eaten. The trader gets paid when he presents his buyer with documentary proof that he has shipped the soybeans according to the contract terms.

The initial document in any transaction is the contract. It doesn't matter what the buyer and the seller may have agreed verbally; what matters is what they wrote in the contract. Unfortunately, no matter how much they discuss a deal before concluding it, the buyer and seller may sometimes interpret a contract clause differently. If that is the case, and they cannot resolve the disagreement amicably, one or either party may go to arbitration. (See the *When Things Go Wrong* section later in this book.)

If a seller knows his buyer well and trusts him to pay without problems, he may ask him to pay for the soybeans Cash Against Documents (CAD). In other words, the buyer pays for the soybeans once the seller presents all the previously agreed shipping documents. (They usually do this through a bank.)

If the seller doesn't know his buyer well or doesn't trust him to pay for the commodity without any problems, he would ask his buyer to open a Letter of Credit (L/C). It is a letter from a bank guaranteeing that the buyer will pay the seller on time and for the correct amount. The L/C will stipulate which documents the seller must present to the bank to effectuate payment. Once he presents these documents in good order, the bank must make the payment. The L/C is, therefore, the pivotal document in the transaction process, and the trader must make sure that the terms of the L/C match the terms of the contract he has with his buyer.

What other documents are typically needed to prove that the seller has shipped the commodity in good order and per the contract terms?

A commercial invoice is the first one. After all, no one (usually) pays for anything without first receiving an invoice. The Bill of Lading (B/L) is the second document. A completed B/L shows that the carrier has accepted the cargo as described and that he is obligated to deliver it to the consignee in good condition. In the case of a shipment by sea, the ship's captain or his accredited agent will sign the B/L once the cargo is loaded. It becomes a receipt with a detailed list of the transported cargo.

But apart from a commercial invoice and a bill of lading, what other documents might our soybean seller need to supply to get paid?

Traditionally, they may include an inspection certificate issued by an independent supervision company at load, an export license issued by the exporting country, a certificate of origin, and a phytosanitary certificate.

If documents are more important than the commodities, you could argue that the trade execution professionals who look after those documents, making sure they are all in order and presented on time so that payment is made on time – are as important, if not more important than the traders who buy and sell the commodities.

However, operators do much more than ensure sellers get paid for their goods. They also ensure that the supply chain operates efficiently and smoothly. It's another reason why good operators are worth their weight in gold.

Jeremy Reynolds

There are three broad buckets of functions within a trading organisation

Jeremy is from Richmond, North Yorkshire, in the UK. He studied business at Nottingham University and took a job with Cargill.

He started in grains and oilseeds – supply chain, plant logistics of farm collections, raw materials, and planning for the UK crush plants. He worked on the transportation, distribution, and management of NGFI (Non-Grain Feed Ingredients).

In 1997, Cargill asked him to move to Geneva for three months to work with the sugar team. The company sent him to Moscow for a three-month assignment the following year. He stayed there for nearly four years, working on the supply chain, trade, execution, operation sites, warehousing, and distribution.

From Moscow, he moved to the Philippines for eighteen months to help build the company's sugar business there. He then returned to Geneva to head up the global sugar operations.

In 2010, he took over responsibility for regional trade execution for Cargill International, which included grains and oilseeds, sugar, coal, metals, and energy, for five years. He then spent four years with Alvean, Cargill's joint venture with Copersucar, before joining Tereos in 2019. In 2023, he launched Crest Trade Services, a company offering consultancy and managed services in trading and shipping.

I asked him if he would call himself a forwarder, logistics manager, or trade execution specialist.

"We used to call it forwarding," he answered. "The term dates to the eighteenth century in the UK when innkeepers forwarded goods to the next inn. Most companies now call the role trade execution coordinator, but as that is a bit long, we tend to use the term operator.

"It is difficult to categorise as it covers so much," he continued. "The role coordinates all the actors in the supply chain: buyers, sellers, freight suppliers, brokers, agents, document services, and supervision. It is an open system in which the trade execution coordinator manages and coordinates all those different parties to ensure that actions are taken correctly to execute the contract.

"The job differs from supply chain management, where you manage supply to meet expected demand. Supply chain management is not the same as contract management."

I was surprised that Jeremy had travelled so extensively in his role as a trade execution coordinator. I asked him if it was usual.

"I wouldn't say so," he admitted. "Still, the tradehouses often view relocation as a talent development opportunity. It can involve working on new infrastructure projects or covering short-term assignments. These opportunities help an individual understand the activities from origination to destination.

"The trading houses have a pipeline to fill future leadership needs, and travel and overseas assignments are part of that process. My moves to Geneva and then Moscow were pivotal. They allowed my career to progress much faster than if I had remained in the UK. I don't think there's anything stopping anyone from moving. You just need to have the aptitude, and you need to ask.

"When I moved to Moscow in 1998, few people spoke English. My Russian wasn't good enough to hold business conversations, but I soon learned enough to get around and live in the city. And then you turn these obstacles into opportunities. It's fun. There is something to learn from every culture.

"The Philippines was challenging from a cultural and business aspect, but Switzerland was the hardest, possibly because I expected it to be the same as the UK. But now my wife and children are Swiss, so you adapt. You need to approach everything with an open mind and treat relocation as an opportunity."

"Where does trade execution sit within a trading organisation?" I asked.

"There are three broad buckets of functions within a trading organisation," he explained.

"The first is value creation, which is the role of traders. The second is value measurement – a financial and risk process. The third is value capture. Our role in trade execution is to capture the value traders believe they have realised on paper.

"If the mark-to-market is $10 per mt, good contract execution can ensure the company captures $10 per mt. We guarantee that every party, including ourselves, meets the contract's obligations. We can sometimes add incremental value through good execution. However, our primary role is to capture the existing value rather than add additional value.

"Could you talk me through the various functions?" I asked.

"Before a trader makes a trade," he said, "We discuss document requirements and payment instruments. We also discuss any optionality in the contract, including origin, quantity, quality, packing, load, or destination port. We discuss deadlines for when we must declare those options.

"As a trade execution coordinator in a smaller organisation, you may need to book the freight and negotiate the charter party. In organisations of all sizes, you must understand the vessel's location and when it will arrive. You must appoint surveyors to ensure that the ship is in the proper condition to load with the holds clean and the hatches watertight. You also must know what to do if they aren't.

"You must give the correct nominations to your suppliers at the right time so that they can get the goods in the right quality and quantity to meet the vessel.

"If you are the vessel charterer, you must coordinate with local vessel agents and the port elevation operators, ensuring that everything is in place for the vessel to arrive and load and that all parties know their obligations.

"Once the vessel is loaded, you must manage the documentation. Buyers pay against documents, usually without seeing the goods, so those documents must be accurate and per the contract. You must ensure the documents are in order and you can get paid. It sounds simple, but it's not!

"There is an old rule that 80 per cent of trades go smoothly – and take 20 per cent of your time – while 20 per cent of your transactions require more attention and take 80 per cent of your time. The quality may be off; the vessel may be late; the vessel master may want to clause the Bill of Lading, etc. – all great opportunities for learning the business!

"You then present the documents through the agreed channels and coordinate payment. After the buyer pays, you must finalise matters such as laytime or demurrage."

"What happens when things don't go well?" I asked.

"As a trade execution coordinator, you are part of a team that includes a controller, legal and compliance. Together, you work on a solution. I always tell my teams that we seek a pragmatic, not a perfect, solution to any problem.

"Everybody wants to achieve the same goals. The seller wants to be paid, and the receiver wants to be happy with the goods they receive. We can spend days trying to find a perfect solution, but it may cost you hundreds of thousands of dollars in demurrage. Instead, we look for a pragmatic solution where parties say, "Well, that's not ideal, but let's mitigate the costs and get things moving." No one wants to let a ten-thousand-dollar problem become a hundred-thousand-dollar problem.

"What makes a good operator?" I asked.

"You must have a good knowledge of UK law in contracts and taxation to understand the function of a Bill of Lading or a Letter of Credit, for example. However, the application of that knowledge is a fundamental skill. You take decisions contextually. Applying your knowledge to the business in different contexts makes you a great operator.

"How you approach a problem may depend on your contract price and whether it is lower or higher than the market.

"It may also depend on whether the customer is strategic to your business or only buys on price. You may treat each differently. This ambiguity may annoy you and be challenging to accept, but it's not personal. You must be good at dealing with ambiguity. The ideal solution may not be best for the business long term.

"Remember, one of the critical roles of a trade execution specialist is to anticipate where issues might arise so they don't happen."

"Could you give an example of that?" I asked.

"Suppose you sold a vessel for March arrival, and you realise it will arrive in April. The earlier you start working with your buyer, the better. You don't wait until the vessel arrives at the discharge port before talking to your buyer.

"The same applies to quality issues, particularly around the condition of the cargo. The vessel master may sometimes clause a B/L (to note that the goods are damaged). The earlier all parties get together and resolve the issue, the better. It may make sense to pause the load and clean the cargo load belts or offload the portion in question. Again, it is a question of pragmatism, moving things along to protect your company's interest and reduce its risk."

"How important is trade execution to a trade?" I asked.

"A customer may not buy from you because of your company's trade execution, but they will certainly not if your trade execution is terrible. There is a base level of expectations. You won't get plaudits if you exceed them, but your customer will think twice about trading with you if your execution is terrible."

"What's the most challenging thing about being a trade execution specialist?"

"The sheer quantity of information can be challenging. I have seen organisations where people get 20,000 emails a month. You can't control what people send you, but you can control what you choose to read. You must distinguish between what is and is not essential and act accordingly.

"It's not abnormal in our industry to have 120 people on copy of an email asking about a vessel's arrival date. You can't act with speed and agility when 120 people think they have a voice. The best organisations will have procedures as to who is involved in what. The execution coordinator, the trader, the trading manager, and the controller may need to be part of a decision-making process – that's four people, not 120!

"I have been in managerial roles for the past few years and concentrated on organisational transformation – leveraging scale. When you look across an organisation, you see silos of operations which duplicate tasks three, four, five, and six times. There is a lot of productivity to be gained and value extracted. If you improve productivity, you reduce costs and improve team engagement."

Traditionally, the front office is glamorous and highly paid with large bonuses, while the back office is less glamorous, less well-paid and with fewer bonuses. I asked Jeremy if that was still the case.

"It is still the case," he replied, "But, although it pains me to say it, I think it is probably justified.

"Physical commodity merchandisers drive a trading company's profitability. They bring the clients to the table, negotiate the deals, and manage the price risk. They get paid more because they create more value. It's as simple as that. If they create value, they get well rewarded. If they don't, they get fired. It comes with the territory.

"We're not taking risks in the back office. We work with the traders to help them manage their risk.

"Trading companies do recognise and reward trade execution and have traditionally viewed it as a differentiator in terms of their business. However, I don't know whether that will continue to be the case with the major trade houses joining a consortium to digitalise their operations."

"You've managed several trade execution teams," I said. "What profiles would you look for when hiring somebody for one of your teams?"

"Good communication skills: People don't need to be extroverts, but they need to be able to communicate what is required when it's needed and be willing to share knowledge and information.

"Determination and resilience: Things don't always go your way. Executing a contract has its frustrations, and you need to be able to manage that.

"Intelligence: the ability to absorb, process and apply information in different contexts.

"Curiosity: you need to be curious to learn and ask questions.

"Adaptability: the world is changing, and you can't assume that something you knew yesterday will still apply tomorrow.

"Proactivity: the ability and willingness to grab opportunities. Don't sit back and wait for things to happen. An operator must know when to let things happen and when to make things happen."

"What is one piece of advice you would give to someone starting as a trade execution specialist?" I asked.

"People will try and put their problems onto you," he replied. "But you don't have to take them on. Their problem is not your problem."

"Last question," I said. "Would you recommend a young person to become an operator?"

"Traders will always need operators, not just for execution but also for advice. If you like problem-solving, logistics, and working in a dynamic and international industry, I would absolutely recommend you take it up as a career. It's a great place to be. I have loved my career so far and still love it!"

Petya Sechanova

We wanted to create a project that was "by the industry, for the industry.

Petya was born and raised in Sofia, Bulgaria. After earning her bachelor's degree, she completed an MBA with SDA Bocconi in Milan, focusing on international business. She then moved to Belgium, beginning her career with DHL, working in logistics.

In 2009, she joined Cargill in Belgium as a trade execution operator and relocated to Geneva, Switzerland, a year later. In 2011, Cargill acquired the Australian Wheat Board, and Petya moved to Melbourne, Australia, where she spent two years working on merging the trade execution functions for the two companies.

Petya returned to Geneva in 2013, where she worked herself up to become the global head of execution for the Cargill agricultural supply chain. I asked her to take up the story from there.

"As I moved into management positions," she told me, "I found that my biggest challenge was to attract and retain talent. People would join the team and quickly master and manage the routine work, but they got bored and moved on to more exciting parts of the business, like trading, analytics, or IT.

"I increasingly tried to digitalise the trade execution function. I became passionate about the potential for new technologies, such as Blockchain or Artificial Intelligence, to take over the routine parts of trade execution. I knew we had to modernise the sector and make it more attractive to the younger generation.

"I also knew we couldn't just do it on our own. Digitalisation had to be a cross-industry initiative, pulling together like-minded professionals from other trading organisations.

"All trading companies are spending a lot of effort and investments in innovation and IT – but we knew we couldn't do the job alone. The industry is interconnected. It is a complex ecosystem that includes banks, supervision companies, agents, vessel owners, governmental organisations, and chambers of commerce. These participants work together to ensure the supply chain operates smoothly and efficiently.

"We wanted to create a project that was "by the industry, for the industry." So, in 2018, we joined forces with ADM, Bunge, and Louis Dreyfus Company to start working on the project. COFCO and Viterra (then Glencore Agri) joined shortly afterwards, and Marubeni joined in 2022.

"Our initial challenge was deciding on which sections of the value chain to focus on. Should we start with farming and move to retail or narrow the scope? Should we concentrate on grains and oilseeds or broaden the range of commodities? Should we focus on origination – and if so, in what geographies?

"As you can imagine, setting up an organisation that at that time brought together six of the world's largest agricultural trading companies, we had to ensure that we would be 100 per cent compliant with international anti-trust legislation.

"We worked this all out, and, in 2020 – in the middle of Covid – we set up Covantis SA as a legal entity in Geneva, co-owned by its six founding members. It was effectively a technology start-up.

"As I mentioned, I was part of the project team from day one and one of the initiators of the idea. I applied for the position of CEO, and I was selected."

"Could you give me your Covantis elevator pitch?" I asked. "How would you explain what you do in a few sentences?"

"Covantis aims to accelerate global trade transformation by solving technology-related industry challenges. Our vision is to create a fair, trusted platform that brings better efficiency, transparency, and information exchange for everyone working to feed the world."

"Can Covantis add value in terms of traceability?" I asked.

"We can add value by making the document flow more transparent. It helps visibility regarding environmental and social sustainability certificates.

"However, most end-buyers want to trace their agricultural inputs back to the farm while our system starts at the loading port. One possible solution might be to partner with someone who covers the flow from farm to port.

"Does Covantis have a role in finance and payments?" I asked. "Does its transparency facilitate commodity trade finance?"

"Absolutely, yes – and that role will grow!" she answered. Most of the international trade in agricultural commodities is conducted under UK law. In October 2022, the UK officially introduced into parliament "The Electronic Trade Documents Bill", which enshrines the idea that electronic trade documents such as bills of lading, warehouse receipts, and promissory notes can be "possessed" and exchanged. The bill provides the legal basis to transition to a digital trade document environment and will provoke other jurisdictions to follow suit. We are considering allowing our clients to present electronic documents to the banks for payment and discharge the cargo."

"How does Covantis generate revenue?" I asked. "And how do you measure the return on investment for your shareholders?"

"We charge all participants – including our shareholders – a fee for using our platform depending on their role, the volumes they transact and the value they can extract.

"We have been modest in our pricing to encourage adoption. We want to make Covantis the industry standard, but that will take time.

"The investment to date has been significant, and our revenues are not yet providing a return on that investment. Building the infrastructure and the network is a front-end load investment that will pay off over the next few years. We believe that our shareholders will see a good return on their investments in terms of money and cost reduction (from using the platform).

I know competition between big trading companies is fierce, even if this is not the public's belief. I asked Petya how she managed the optics of having seven trade houses "controlling" the food supply chain through Covantis.

"Controlling is not the right word," she replied. "We use "equal ownership" instead. Covantis is independent of its shareholders, with its own governance, organisation, and decision-making structure. Covantis is based on a type of governance known as a "shifting alliance model", where no shareholder can veto strategic business decisions. Our mission is to build a fair and trusted platform.

"Covantis was never intended for the exclusive benefit of the large commodity trading houses. It is for all the actors in the value chain, no matter their size or geographic location.

"One of the main reasons why the competition and anti-trust authorities gave us approval was that no one has access to data other than their own. There is no sharing of information stored on Covantis, nor can Covantis JV be used as a forum for the prohibited information exchange between shareholders.

"We do not favour – or privilege – shareholders above other users, including in our pricing approach."

Saurabh Goyal

Open AI is a game-changer in traditional applications because it does the job 100 times better, but there are 100 other use cases that were not even possible earlier.

Saurabh studied at the Indian Institute of Technology and began his career as a programmer with Tata Consulting Services before doing an MBA in marketing and finance. He then worked as a program manager for the New York Mellon Bank, Accenture Capital Markets and Prudential Asset Management.

Olam International hired him in 2009 as their head of CTRM – Commodities Trading and Risk Management Systems – where he developed trading systems for physical commodities. He was with Olam for eight years, working in almost all aspects of commodity trading operations, including supply chain and risk management, hedging and trade finance. In 2016, he left Olam to start his own company.

"As Olam grew," he told me, "The company replaced their in-house systems with SAP. I was initially involved in SAP implementation, but I quickly realised that SAP was more complicated, expensive, and challenging to implement than our in-house systems. That realisation gave me confidence that there was a market for small and medium-sized commodity traders – like Olam 20 years ago – who could not afford to implement SAP or develop an in-house solution.

"Some companies provide front-office applications for order and risk management. Still, few give end-to-end solutions, including the front office and hedging, operations, accounting, middle and back-office activities, trade, and finance.

"We do almost everything from order management to sustainability. Our latest project is to help companies manage the traceability required under the new EU deforestation rules."

"Do you work with Blockchain?" I asked.

"We were initially optimistic about Blockchain," he replied. "But after one year of working on it, we realised it was not a solution and stopped. Blockchain was designed specifically for Bitcoin; it is the technology behind it. Our biggest mistake was to think we could separate Blockchain from cryptocurrency. Taking the technology that drives cryptocurrency and using it for something else does not work. It is like trying to fit a square peg in a round hole."

"Do you use AI?" I asked.

"We began using AI three or four years ago," he told me. "We used it to scan documents like bills of lading, invoices, packing lists, and origin certificates and then auto-fill forms in the system. It saved someone manually filling them. We used AI technology, but it was not 100% reliable. It made mistakes in reading the data and importing it into the system. As a result, we were cautious about including traditional AI in our applications.

"Chat GPT and Open AI have made things 100 times better. We now feed all our documents to Chat GPT through the back-end APIs (Application Programming Interfaces). It has so far provided 100% reliability and accuracy in reading the data from the documents and importing it into our application.

"It exemplifies how generative AI has completely changed the landscape. You previously had to put a lot of investment and effort into integrating traditional AI into your systems, but with Chat GPT, all that hard work is gone. You apply basic software engineering to integrate Chat GPT and ensure the process flow works fine. Chat GPT provides the intelligence to read, interpret, and structure the data, leaving us free to focus on the engineering part.

"Some might say that our enthusiasm for AI is like what we initially had for Blockchain, but it isn't. With Chat GPT, we are already reaping the benefits."

"Will Chat GPT be transformative for our business?" I asked.

"I believe so," he told me". We are now looking at many different use cases where we can start using Open AI and similar models.

"User support is one obvious application. No matter how excellent your system is, you must provide client support, especially regarding ERP (Enterprise Resource Planning). Our scalability as an organisation was dependent on being able to hire resource people to give that service to our customers. Chat GPT can automate most client support functions, leaving human interaction only for critical use cases.

"Open AI is a game-changer in traditional applications because it does the job 100 times better, but there are 100 other use cases that were not even possible earlier. For example, we have a customs module where an international trader can make a customs declaration without using a customs broker, an agent, or a freight forwarder."

"How will AI transform the agricultural commodity trading business?" I asked.

"It is a difficult question to answer," he replied. "As software developers, we see that it is transformative in developing and providing our systems to our users. GPT is excellent with the English language, but it is ten times better with software programming languages.

"Chat GPT will transform the way users consume software. Users currently consume software in a form-like interface, entering and saving the information. It's a data-driven approach. In a few years, we will see conversation-driven user interfaces. You will tell the system what you want to do. For example, you will tell it that you have received a new contract to supply a commodity to a customer. It is lying in my email. Can you please check and store it in your system?" And the system would be able to do that."

"Will AI make some professions redundant?" I asked.

"The politically correct answer is, "No, it won't. It will help professionals do their jobs better, remove the mundane tasks and empower workers to focus on higher-level thinking."

"The correct answer is, "Yes, AI will make some professions redundant. We're already seeing it. The biggest tuition-assistant company in the US (Chegg.com) – once worth $3 billion – lost more than 50% of its business within six months of Chat GPT launching. The company connected kids to different teachers, helping them with their homework. Chat GPT destroyed their business model and, in many cases, does a better job than most teachers."

"Should we be afraid of AI?" I asked.

"I don't think so," he replied. "AI doesn't have an agency; it will not suddenly wake up at night and start thinking for itself. It is a programme residing on a system that is waiting for you to ask it a question. When you ask a question, it looks back into all its learning and provides an answer. It is not fundamentally designed to think for itself. The doomsday scenarios are not applicable here."

"Could AI learn to trade on the futures markets for speculating or hedging?" I asked.

"Electronic and high-frequency trading, identifying micro patterns and then acting on those patterns, have existed for many years," he told me. "Companies have made fortunes using the technology. However, their success has depended not only on their mathematics and algorithms but also on their better connectivity to exchanges and some information-based edge.

"Chat GPT will not revolutionise short-term trading because short-term traders analyse real-time tick-by-tick data; it is not Chat GPT's model. Short-term trading will continue to rely on statistical probabilistic models already out there. It's a mature industry. Chat GPT may be better suited to longer-term trading, looking at supply-demand imbalances – crop and weather reports and the like – and then taking a direction-based strategy. I think it can work."

Simon Francis

Platforms facilitate the information held within the organisation. The collaboration of the information after that is still a work in progress.

Simon has spent his career in dry cargo with intermittent ventures into the digital world. During his career, he worked with all ship sizes in the dry cargo sector, from coasters to capes. Within this sector, he has worked for owners and charterers in their operations and chartering departments.

"What's the most significant change you've seen in freight in the 30 years you have been in the sector?" I asked.

"The way we do our work," he replied. "Thirty years ago, we would handwrite a telex on a piece of paper, which we would pass to a secretary, who would type it up and send it via the only telex machine in the office. The process moved to a mix of fax and email in the mid to late 90s, but a lot of it was still paper-based – printing off, giving copies to colleagues, filing, all that sort of thing. Email helped because you could do it digitally, but you still had to go through many emails. Now, you're in a world where the email is read for you, automatically filed, and tagged.

"There have been other changes. In my early days, we would do voyage calculations on the back of a cigarette packet and measure distances on the map with compass points. It is now all done electronically.

"So, from a chartering point of view, the process of putting together a piece of business now can be done much quicker and more accurately than in the past.

"Is the current trend to move from emails to platforms?" I asked.

"It is," he replied. "But email is still the backbone of it all. Counterparties still communicate via email. A freight broker sends everything via email to his principals. Principals send everything to the ships via email, and so it goes on.

"Platforms facilitate the information held within the organisation. The collaboration of the information after that is still a work in progress.

"You have recently launched a new company, SHINC," I said. "What does the name stand for?"

"It's an abbreviation the shipping world uses for laytime working days in Charter Parties. It stands for *Sundays and Holidays Included*. I could have called it SHEX, which would have been *Sundays and Holidays Excluded*."

"Many of my readers are young people learning about the business," I said. "Demurrage, despatch, and laytime may be unfamiliar to them. Could you just briefly explain them?"

"When a charterer contracts a ship to carry cargo, they stipulate in the contract how long it will take to load or discharge the cargo. It is known as *'laytime allowed.'*

"If your cargo is 100,000 mt and you agree to load at 25,000 mt a day, that's four days' laytime allowed. It won't take exactly four days to load in practice. Suppose the laytime used to load the cargo exceeds the laytime permitted. In that case, a penalty payment is payable to the ship owner by the charterer for keeping the vessel in port longer than the contracted period. That payment is called the *demurrage payment*.

"If the vessel is loaded quicker than the laytime allowed under the contract, the shipowner pays a payment called despatch to the port at (usually) half the demurrage rate. It is like a bonus to the port for loading the ship quicker than the contracted period.

"So, is laytime the time the vessel spends in the port?" I asked.

"Yes," he replied. "The time spent in port is subject to the contractual laytime clauses. So, you have laytime allowed, and then there will be events stipulated in the contract where the laytime clock stops.

"You can't load sugar or grain cargo when it rains, so laytime will not count during rain periods. Laytime will not count when shifting from anchorage to berth. Laytime may not count if the vessel loader breaks down. Clauses like that stop the laytime clock as the port call continues. It is where the interpretation of the contractual clauses can cause disputes, negotiations and time wasted processing the demurrage claim."

"In the contractual clauses," I said, "Sundays and holidays are sometimes included in the laytime and are sometimes excluded – which is why you've chosen that name. I have got it now."

"Exactly. The standard terms are SHINC and SHEX, and then there are variations."

"What problem is your new company, SHINC, looking to solve?" I asked.

"The laytime process is still manual, from entering port events from the Statement of Facts into the laytime calculator to collaborating and agreeing demurrage claims via email with multiple PDF documents attached.

"Users have long email chains of communications and spend time comparing one laytime calculation against another produced on different systems. They monitor and manage their laytime claims, often on an Excel sheet. It is still a manual process open to errors and sits at the bottom of the logistics chain. One error in calculating the laytime can cost users thousands of dollars. The data is so opaque that both users and management often never know the mistakes being made and the money they are risking!

"The agreement of a demurrage claim can also be a cumbersome process as users often interpret the clauses in the contract differently, leading to protracted negotiations.

"We hope to enable and encourage people to be more precise in their contract clauses, which will help to have fewer negotiations and quicker processing.

"SHINC solves these inefficiencies by enabling information to flow live, both pre-arrival and whilst a ship is in port. It will allow parties to make commercial decisions proactively rather than reactively.

"SHINC will then use a combination of AI and digitalisation to enable demurrage claims to be agreed upon and settled more as a process than a negotiation.

"Finally, once the demurrage claim is settled, SHINC provides data to help chartering departments make better commercial decisions in the future.

"When you say that it enables commercial decisions during the voyage and the port," I asked, "what type of commercial decisions would those be?"

"A good example would be whether to work overtime or not in a port. One would probably have to sit down with a pen and paper to manually calculate how much lay time is left on the port call to ascertain if the shipowner should pay for overtime or the port. SHINC aims to enable users to track laytime remaining during a port call on a live basis, allowing them to make more informed decisions like, 'Do we pay for overtime or not?'

"What sorts of disputes occur over laytime?" I asked.

"The classic example is when the contract says that shifting from anchorage to berth does not count as laytime. We all agree, but the question then is which event counts as moving from anchorage to berth? Some say it is from 'pilot is on board' to 'first line ashore'. Others say it is from 'anchor up' to 'all fast'.

"If the contract isn't clear, you can waste time disputing that one point. Some more modern contracts explicitly say shifting from anchorage to berth means' *anchor up* to *'all fast'*. It's explicit and clear. But so many of the contracts are historical. They've been used year after year, and they're not explicit in the terms. So, people then interpret it in different ways."

"How much money are we discussing here regarding demurrage and despatch?" I asked. "Is it significant?"

"Absolutely," he replied. "I don't think anyone knows the global annual demurrage bill for tankers, dry cargo, and barges. Educated estimates are several billion dollars a year."

"How much might it be on an average grain cargo in Santos?" I asked.

"The most significant claims are at the beginning of the grain season when you have 60 vessels outside the port for 40-45 days. If it's a $20,000 per day demurrage rate in the contract, you're talking of a claim of $800,000 to $1,000,000."

I had read that SHINC was working to become a B Corp. I asked Simon why.

"We're here to generate a profit for SHINC," he told me. "But we also want to look at the bigger sustainability picture. From helping ports reduce the time ships spend in port and thus reduce emissions to reducing the amount of paper used in the laytime process by going digital. Every little bit helps towards the greater goal."

6. FINANCE

In his excellent book, *The King of Oil*, journalist Daniel Ammann writes that Marc Rich left Phibros in 1974 to set up his eponymous trading company in Zug, Switzerland. Although he stayed in the US, he chose Switzerland as his company's HQ because of the low tax rates and because it was a neutral country; it was not even a member of the United Nations. As Marc Rich himself said, "The only bad thing about Zug is the fog."

In 1983, US authorities charged Marc Rich with evading taxes and trading with Iran during the 1979/81 hostage crisis. Rich fled to Switzerland and lived there as a fugitive for 17 years. Switzerland did not have an extradition treaty with the US then.

Marc Rich admits to buying oil from Iran during the embargo, as well as to supplying oil to apartheid South Africa and bribing officials in countries such as Nigeria. Bribing foreign officials was legal in the United States until the passing of the Foreign and Corrupt Practices Act of 1977. In Switzerland, it remained legal – and tax-deductible – until 2000. As a non-US company based in Switzerland, Marc Rich & Co was legally (if perhaps not morally) exempt from the embargoes on Iran and apartheid South Africa.

Switzerland's political neutrality and stable government still provide a secure business environment. The country offers competitive corporate tax rates and various tax incentives, particularly for trading companies. The regulatory environment for trading companies is relatively light compared to other financial centres, reducing compliance costs and operational burdens. It also has a multilingual, well-educated workforce.

It is called a cluster effect, a self-reinforcing phenomenon where the more trading houses there are, the more come.

However, there was another, perhaps more significant, reason why Marc Rich chose Switzerland: access to finance. Switzerland was where the banks (and the money) were. They still are. Finance is critical to the agricultural supply chain. Nothing would move without it.

Jerome Daven

It can be challenging to separate the great ideas from the good ones – to decide where to allocate our resources and ensure that we have covered all the risks and business implications, such as tax.

Jerome is Swiss and grew up in a little village in the Swiss Alps. By his own admission, he spent more time on the ski slopes or the hockey pitch than in the classroom. However, he was good with numbers and decided to go into accountancy, joining KPMG and then moving to PWC, where he passed his accountancy qualifications.

One of his audit clients at PWC was an oil trading company, and he spent a lot of time in their offices. He quickly became interested in supply chains and trading, finding it fascinating to put together the global news that he was reading in the newspapers with his day job. Geopolitics has always interested him.

A friend on his accountancy course suggested he apply for a position with Cargill. He went through the interview process, and Cargill gave him a job, not in Geneva as he had expected, but in an animal feed nutrition mill that Cargill had recently bought in Switzerland.

"It was a family business," Jerome told me. "It had to be integrated – financially, system-wise, and culturally – into a big multinational. It was a fabulous experience. I learned agribusiness there, stocks, shrink, and cash flow – all pragmatic and tangible activities."

After two years at the feed mill, Jerome moved to Geneva to become the controller for their energy business. Cargill then sent him to Minneapolis for four years to work as a financial controller in their North American energy business.

I had spent two years in Minneapolis with Cargill, and I asked Jerome how he had enjoyed his time there.

"You cry twice when your company transfers you to Minneapolis," he replied. "Once when you arrive and once when you leave. It was a fantastic time for the whole family – and we visited 28 states in our four years in the US!"

When Cargill sold its energy business to Macquarie Bank, Jerome took a position as a financial controller for ADM's grains business in Hamburg, Germany. After three years in Germany, he moved back to Switzerland with ADM to be the divisional CFO (Chief Financial Officer) of global trade – the company's international distribution and marketing arm. In 2023, ADM also made him CFO of its international corn milling business – starch and sweeteners.

"Could you tell me about the CFO role in an organisation like ADM?" I asked him.

"I see my principal role as the glue between trading, execution, and the other functions within the company," he replied. "I act as a chief of staff, supporting the BU (Business Unit) presidents in their roles and providing the financial information they need to make the best possible decisions. I work with them to develop and implement the strategy.

"I coordinate with corporate headquarters and the group CFO, ensuring we align with corporate strategy.

"I am in charge of the contract execution function overall and have a role in seeking efficiencies and increasing productivity. Trading is a high-volume, low-margin business, so productivity gains are always welcome.

"Lastly, I have a fiduciary responsibility to ensure our financial accounts and reporting are timely. ADM is a publicly listed company."

"What is the difference between a CFO and a Financial Controller?" I asked. "I see you were both during your career."

"The role of a financial controller is to ensure that accounting and reporting align with US GAP (General Accounting Principles)," he explained.

"Besides a fiduciary role, financial controllers ensure that internal controls are respected and follow up on internal audits. Financial controllers report to the CFO. They ensure that the company respects internal and external financial controls.

"Each BU has a yearly plan, and we have a monthly meeting to ensure everything is on track. Part of my job is forecasting capital requirements and updating those forecasts in line with any market changes or events.

"I work with the BU president to ensure that the BU's plans respect the company's capital limits. I also look at the expected returns of new investments."

"Is it fair to say that a financial controller would focus more on the past while a CFO would look more to the future?" I asked.

"I think that is a fair way to put it," he told me. "One of the biggest challenges a CFO faces in a major trade house is managing the intracompany information flow.

"We have a fantastic bunch of people here at ADM, and they constantly come up with ideas for new businesses or how to develop our existing businesses. It can be challenging to separate the great ideas from the good ones – to decide where to allocate our resources and ensure that we have covered all the risks and business implications, such as tax.

"It can sometimes be frustrating for team members when their ideas are turned down or shelved for later, but we all understand that we must prioritise the best ideas.

"I don't work on my own. We have a finance team, a controller team, a financial analysis team, and a business development team. Together, we ensure that we continue to invest and that our existing businesses operate profitably.

"I also work closely with the company's risk managers."

I asked Jerome what the main risks were.

"Credit and counterparty risk– the risk of a client or supplier defaulting on a contract – is one. However, operating along the supply chain and sourcing commodities from local ADM companies reduces counterparty risk.

"People in the energy markets often trade ten years forward. We don't deal that far ahead in agriculture, and that reduces our performance risk. We trade this crop year and the next one, so the mark-to-market risk is less than in the energy markets.

"Operational risk – a boat stuck somewhere that could lead to a vessel arriving late and being out of contract – so default risk.

"There is also weather risk, for example, a hurricane in the US or a drought in Argentina. We have an advantage because we are a global company with a geographically diverse portfolio. It reduces our market risk compared to local players. If there is a drought in Argentina, we can source soybean meal from Brazil or the US.

"There is also a risk of having a rogue trade somewhere. I experienced it earlier in my career, and it's not nice. One of the worst nightmares for a financial controller is to have "bottom draw contracts," transactions that traders don't put into the system.

"I am fortunate to work with great leaders who set the environment – the tone – from the top. They acknowledge that traders can make mistakes and that errors happen. If the trader declares it immediately, they know they will be treated fairly. However, they will be harshly treated if they try and hide it."

"Do you have trouble sleeping?" I asked him.

"I have two teenage daughters," he replied. "They can sometimes be more challenging than a ship running late."

"Let's move back to the finance function," I suggested. "What is the difference between transactional – or cargo-by-cargo finance – and overall finance?"

"Big companies can issue bonds and syndicate bank loans," he replied. "We don't have to worry too much about financing our treasury operations. Smaller companies are in a less fortunate position and often struggle to obtain the financing they need. Banks will usually only finance them on a cargo-by-cargo basis.

"CFOs in small companies will spend more time obtaining financing than allocating it internally. I spend most of my time not raising funds but ensuring we allocate them efficiently.

"We compete internally for capital. Most big companies set thresholds below which a BU president can make investment decisions. Above those thresholds, they would have to take the plan to HQ and compete for internal funds.

"But before doing that, we must ask, "Is the projected investment a good strategic fit?" For example, we would not invest today in a banana plantation, even if the expected returns were good.

"Second, we must evaluate expected returns. We have a weighted average cost of capital and need to beat that by a certain percentage.

"Compared to our processing businesses, we don't have significant CAPEX requirements in our trading business. The capital we employ is mainly working capital. If we get a decent return on our working capital, we don't have to worry too much – but we must ensure we get the returns!"

I recently read a McKinsey report that the commodity trading sector would need an extra $300- $500 billion in trade finance. "Do you agree?" I asked.

"The world trade in agricultural commodities will not grind to a halt for lack of finance," he replied. "I am a great believer in markets. If the margins are there, the finance will be available. The margins will adjust to enable the sector to finance its activities.

"Sometimes, a bank might come into commodity trade financing without understanding how trading works and how traders manage risks. It eventually leads to problems, and the banks will exit the sector. We work closely with our banking partners to ensure they understand our business and we understand theirs.

"There is sometimes a spread – a margin – between our internal cost of capital and our client's cost. Some companies may look to capture that margin, but it is not something we do. We are physical commodity traders.

We are not a financial institution. I would not use the company's balance sheet to play the role of a bank. We may offer credit line financing to a client, but only if that client is strategic to our business."

Commodity prices rose dramatically in 2022, and I wonder if some smaller companies found it challenging to finance their margin calls on futures exchanges.

"It was challenging for some smaller companies, especially those specialising in origination," Jerome replied. "They buy commodities at the origin and then hedge them by selling futures. When prices rise, they must pay variation margins on their short futures positions even though they have offsetting positions in the physicals. Even if a company is hedged, it will still have to pay variation margins on its futures positions. Of course, if futures prices fall, the exchanges credit their account with the money against variation margins.

"I didn't hear companies failing to make margin calls when futures prices rose. It shows that the system works and that the necessary finance is there. Remember that the trading companies were more profitable during this period, and I imagine that this gave the banks more confidence in supplying finance. At ADM, we had no problem financing our trading during this period.

"Final question," I said. "What advice would you give to a) a young trader and b) someone considering getting into the business?

"I would tell a young trader to spend time – at least six months – with your finance and operations teams. It will make you a better trader. It will also help you realise that you can have a great career and a lot of fun in a support function. You don't have to be a trader to enjoy a fantastic career in commodities. Other jobs within a trade house can be just as satisfying as trading.

"I would tell a young person thinking of joining the business that they must be passionate about the job. All the people here are driven. They think and breathe commodity trading all day long."

James-Scott Wong

You can't have a purpose if you don't have profit. Profit makes the world go around, but how do you effect purpose once you have profit?

James-Scott is of both British and American nationality but grew up in the US. He came into agriculture from an investment banking and trading background focused on distressed and restructuring. He joined ED&F Man in 2012 as Head of Fixed Income Credit.

"The most refreshing thing about moving from investment banking into commodities is that commodities are more about relationships," he told me. "You develop a deep relationship with your customers. You break bread with them on their farms. You need to be there in person. In 2013, while with ED&F Man, I flew to 40 countries in six months."

In 2017, James Scott founded AlmaStone.

"I left ED&F Man for two reasons," he explained. "First, I was in the investment business in a trading firm. I'm naturally long- rather than short-term. My business was about investing and making loans. Second, I outgrew the relationships. I started financing beyond ED&F Man's core commodities and geographies. So, it made sense. In 2017, I spun out with the backing of Warwick Capital, a $2.5 billion private equity fund.

"We do direct, senior-secured lending to middle-market agribusinesses," he explained. "We're a combination of three businesses in one.

"In one way, we're no different from a classic private credit shop, where it's heavy desktop analysis, looking at the borrower's creditworthiness (e.g., historical financial ratios and forecasts.) Where we differ –

because of my background in distressed and restructuring – is that we take an intrusive M&A approach every time we look at a company.

"Second, we're no different than an asset-backed lender. We always look at downside protection. We try to factor in worst-case scenarios. We structure against enforceable collateral. We might do pre-crop, starting upstream with producers and processors. If we are talking about sugar, we follow the chain from when the sugarcane goes into the ground through the factory that processes it into raw sugar or ethanol and down the supply chain to the soft drink manufacturer.

"Third, although we masquerade as financiers, we think and act like merchants. We have a combination of talents on the team. My colleague in Brazil was the former CEO of the third-largest grain trader in Brazil. My COO was the head of market risk at ED&F Man. We know how to move stuff.

"We take a partnership approach in our business. We come in as informal advisors and are proactive in helping the client. We look at the agricultural and operational aspects and assist with pricing and hedging. It gives us a comprehensive preview of the business from upstream to downstream. We see the flow of goods. It gives us a holistic perspective."

Rabobank told me a few years back that they only finance the big trade houses because of the weight of the financial and ESG due diligence. They don't fund the smaller players. I asked James Scott if he was looking to fill that gap.

"Banks and trade houses dominate the finance within the supply chain," he said. "Traders would typically secure a five-year agreement and give a prepayment. The conditions of that prepayment are often better than a bank's terms, but the traders make it back through their trading.

"Due to Basel 3, the major banks tend to gravitate towards investment-grade counterparties and concentrate their risk. They must do the same due diligence, whether it is a $5 million or $200 million loan. However, every time the cycle shifts and things improve, they come down the curve towards the middle market.

"We don't compete with the banks for the big company business because bank financing is cheaper than ours. Likewise, we don't focus on SMEs (Small and Medium Enterprises) because of their level of corporate governance and client sophistication. We focus on middle-market counterparties, where you're beginning to transition to a better governance structure and more transparency. It's just trying to find that sweet spot in the middle.

"When I first started the business, I wanted to finance the Guatemalan coffee producers, but they are smaller leasehold farmers, and the risk is significant. We now focus on processor-producers like sugar mills or soybean crushers. They act as informal banks at the start of the supply chain. They finance the farmers, take that risk, mitigate it, and then create the value conversion.

"When we do transactions to mitigate performance risk, we approach it partly like a bank with a credit agreement and contractual remedies, partly like a trader following the flow and goods, and often inserting a third-party collateral manager. Then, to mitigate payment risk, we usually take assignments over offtake agreements of friendly traders. In that way, we follow the cash payments and logistical movements. It gives us a lot of levers to pull.

"The nice thing with crops is that you can follow the cycle. The nice thing about logistics is that you can see when things get stuck. The last challenge always starts with the people and relationships. You want to finance people you know, people with a similar philosophy and alignment, and you grow with them."

"What keeps you awake at night?" I asked.

"It is easy to make a loan, but getting the money back is not always easy," he replied. "It's a delicate balance between control and influence.

I don't kid myself about the countries we're in. Most of our business is in Latin America, Africa, the Black Sea, and the Middle East. We constantly evaluate probabilities. Risk is always apparent.

"We haven't had any outright defaults, but anyone in the lending business who survived COVID who tells you they don't have any NPLs (Non-Performing Loans) would be lying. It's the nature of the business.

"We finance one of the largest agricultural producers in Ukraine. It's incredible how they are coping with the war, and they only recently have begun to have issues honouring their obligations to us. That's the nature of the business, right? It is what it is."

"Can you insure some of those credit risks?" I asked.

"Absolutely, but the question is whether the insurance pays," he replied.

"When we think of risk mitigation, there are four recovery levels.

"If you know the goods are delivered to an off-taker, given that I have an assignment, the off-taker pays me directly. That's level one.

"I focus on middle-market counterparties because they can pay me out of their liquidity if a crop is delayed or something goes wrong. That's level two.

"The third level is the "Can't pay, won't pay" scenario. If there is a $13 million pile of sugar against our $10 million loan, I will enforce against it to seek recovery. We have the mechanisms and know how to do that.

"The fourth, as you mentioned, is insurance. We're probably one of the few non-banks that carry our own dedicated cargo policy. We still actively use Lloyds's, but that capacity has waned for ags.

"Fraud has recently been in the headlines in metals warehousing," I said. "Is fraud less prevalent in the ag trade than metals – and how can you avoid it?"

"Fraud is everywhere. It's in commodities, financial markets, crypto, etc. You can't prevent it. You can build a higher wall, but someone will find a way to get around it. You can introduce more regulation, but fraud is a purposeful evasion of the rules and systems.

"There's a theoretical understanding where things look good on paper, and then there's the practical side of being on the ground and having a commercial understanding of how things work."

"Can you give me an example of a loan you've made?" I asked.

"We provide pre-export financing for sugar mills in Latin America," he replied. "In Africa, I tend to start on inventory. I finance stocks in the warehouse and get paid when they leave.

"We finance tobacco. I know it's a controversial crop from a Western standpoint, and we do have a phase-out strategy in our ESG documentation, but you look at it differently when you are on the ground and understand its social impact. For example, tobacco in Zimbabwe accounts for approximately 20 per cent of their exports, and it's the most viable cash crop for many farmers."

"How do you deal with environmental and social issues in your supply chains?" I asked.

"We do formal investigations regarding land and company registries, but we get a better feel when we're on the ground, where we hear and see what goes on. It gives us a better overview."

You do as much diligence as possible – it's part of your process – but there's a certain level of trust, right?

In crops, issues often arise when a company hires a third party to bring in and manage migrant labour. You try to mitigate it as much as you can from a top-down perspective by choosing a partner who does what they say they do. And then, you try to evaluate the situation on the ground. That's why I travel so much. You trust, but you must always verify.

"It's a rule of mine to never lend to someone without visiting them first. It's essential in any business. You can put any metric you want on risk, but there's no transaction if there's no relationship."

I saw from the company's website that they called it a purpose-driven business. I asked James-Scott to explain what that was.

"I'm Roman Catholic," he replied. "This morning, I talked with a friend about God and Mammon. The Bible teaches us that humans can't serve two masters: God and money. One is virtuous; one is materialistic. There is, however, always a balance. How do you balance people, planet, and profit?

"You can't have a purpose if you don't have profit. Profit makes the world go around, but how do you effect purpose once you have profit? We're blessed in the West because most of us don't have to worry about sustenance, but there are emerging markets where sustenance is still a factor.

"When we started the business in 2017, it was about CSR or corporate social responsibility. Since our inception, we have included ESG in our investment process but never formalised an accreditation as I believed it was not genuine and pay-to-play. It was a new metric for raising capital, but people didn't necessarily do what they said. And sure enough, at the end of 2022, you saw the tide go out with many greenwashing headlines.

"Our metric is always, "Is our intention matching our output?" We believe in ESG and continue to evolve our policies; however, it must be balanced relative to the circumstances."

"How do you measure success in a purpose-driven business? I asked.

"It's challenging," he replied. "I struggle with it constantly. There's a financial metric, and there's your heart. It's knowing we were put on Earth for a greater purpose. If I can extend the table for another person, that's fantastic. If I can enable others to put themselves in a better position, that's even better.

"We are meant to give; we're meant to serve. But you can't serve if your vessel is empty. When you do things of virtue, you only need one witness – yourself.

"Do you only work with commodities certified to be sustainable?" I asked.

"No, we prefer to do our due diligence," he replied. "Many of the companies we finance are bridges between agriculture and industry. A crop might be certified as sustainable, but you get a different viewpoint when you're on the ground and see wastewater from the factory flowing untreated into a river. "

"Final question," I said. "How do you manage your work/life balance?"

"I try to lead by example. Building this business has been a great sacrifice for my family. It's funny. I say I do all this for my family, but I'm not with my family. It is something I am trying to correct.

"I am a private person. That's always been my mentality. Opening and sharing are foreign to me. My father used to tell me that if you lay low in the weeds, people never know where to attack. That's served me well my whole life. But my friends tell me I need to tell my story."

Five questions for Gijs Vos

You've had an extensive career in commodity finance. Could you talk me through it?

After graduating from university in 1997, I enrolled on ABN AMRO's Management Training program and joined their commodity finance division after three or four years. There was something about commodities that I have always found fascinating. Commodities have a tangible element that banking per se doesn't have.

I started with inventory finance in the early 2000s with commodity repos. It was a small group initially. We did the simple stuff on LME metals, but then we dabbled around a bit in coffee, orange juice, and cocoa. It was a learning process, but it quickly grew.

The commodity world is incredible. It's the people, it's the business, it's the mindset. But for me, it was about understanding how commodities are traded. You must be curious and willing to go down a rabbit hole or two – to keep digging and trying to figure things out. There's always something to learn. It's always intriguing. There's never a dull moment.

I moved to AMN AMRO London in 2005, working more on the futures and derivatives. ABN AMRO sold the business to UBS in 2006, and I left after six months to join Standard Chartered Bank in New York. I worked in New York for nearly eighteen years with Standard Chartered and Rabobank before returning to ABN AMRO.

I met my wife in New York. She's a coffee trader. She recently took a senior position with Starbucks in Lausanne, so we moved to Switzerland.

When I interviewed Karel Valken from Rabobank for my book The New Merchants of Grain, he said that Rabobank only finances the ABCD+ traders as the due diligence workload is not worth the time for smaller companies. Is it still the case?

When I started at Rabobank, for example, you had to have a minimum equity of $10 million to be a wholesale commodity finance client. That's probably increased to over $100 million, with annual revenues of a billion. Capital is getting more expensive, so banks are looking for better returns. You put the same amount of due diligence and credit work into a $10 million or a billion-dollar deal.

Here in Switzerland, the smaller cantonal banks service the smaller and medium-sized clients, but their financing comes at a price. They're more expensive. This lack of liquidity puts the smaller and medium-sized traders at a funding disadvantage.

Banks finance the smaller commodity traders contract by contract (transactional finance), which is operationally intensive. The ABCD+s are essentially corporate borrowers with revolving credit facilities. You lend against the balance sheet and the profitability.

Banks come in and of commodity trade finance. Do they misread the risk and then blow up? Is fraud a factor?

A few banks have exited the sector in the past few years. Most notable would have been BNP and ABN AMRO. Banks have become less keen on commodity trade finance in recent years. It is primarily driven by lower returns, higher capital requirements (partly caused by fraud losses), and increased regulation such as Basel, Dodd-Frank Act or MiFID. The combination of these factors makes commodity trade finance less attractive to employ capital compared to other sectors.

There have been numerous frauds in commodity trade finance recently. Some made the news, and others disappeared. Fraud undermines the banking sector's confidence in commodity trading and changes its risk management culture. They prefer to put their money in an industry like FMCG, where they get paid good margins with little trouble.

I don't think anybody starts a trading company and says, I'm going to defraud a bank. More often, something goes wrong, and rather than confessing to it and breaching their covenants, companies might say, 'We'll lie about it and hope we trade out of it.'

Even if it starts innocently, the fallouts are severe. The knock-on effects include additional scrutiny, more audits, and less access to credit insurance. Everything becomes more expensive and more complex. The whole process takes longer.

What advice would you give a young banker to watch out for fraud?

Be aware of herd mentality. Don't go along with something just because the other banks do.

Don't always rely on the financial reporting.

It's part risk management and part plain old greed. You need to meet a budget, and this client pays more. Nobody wants to walk away from a client who pays a good margin. Still, the moment the music stops, everything falls apart.

One red flag would be if a client fully utilises their credit lines. The rule is, "If it's too good to be true, then it's not true. If your client is willing to pay double or triple the margin than other comparable clients do, then that's not right.

Meet your clients at their offices or industrial premises. It's a red flag if you always meet clients in a restaurant.

I once had a processor client, and we were financing stocks in a warehouse. I went to visit the warehouse for a due diligence check. The place was a mess. The floors were dirty, and the pallets were badly stacked and falling over. The office was filthy, covered in dust. What's the administration like if that is how they deal with their physical commodities?

A year later, multiple containers went missing. We should have pulled our financing, but we didn't. I learned to look at the surroundings when I do due diligence. Are the buildings maintained? Is everything as you would want it to be?

Is reputation risk a factor for the banks?

Reputational risk is a factor for sure. There are two elements to reputational risk.

The first is the incidental reputational risk caused by, for example, consumer sentiment or social issues. It could be related to financing oil production, intensive farming, environmental damage like deforestation, or social issues like child or slave labour, etc. As a result, the bank could be subject to environmentalists' protests and boycotts. It is a moral corporate citizen question that not only applies to commodity banking. And it also changes. Palm oil is a good example. It used to be a wonder crop and the renewable biofuel of the future. It was the best thing ever, but now it's frowned upon because of deforestation.

The second element is more severe and related to breaches of regulations such as KYC compliance, money laundering, etc., resulting in significant fines and penalties. The reputational fallout can be enormous. It's not always quantifiable beyond the fines and penalties. Are you going to lose clients over this? How much revenue is associated with the loss of these clients?

In any case, you'd rather not be in the news. There is a saying that there's no such thing as bad publicity, but I don't think that is true for banks. You want to avoid those headlines.

7. NON-PRICE RISK MANAGEMENT

Non-price risk in a commodity trading company encompasses risks that do not directly relate to markets but can significantly impact the company's operations, reputation, and long-term viability. These include operational, regulatory, compliance, environmental, social, geopolitical, and cybersecurity risks.

Operational risk is loss from failed internal processes, people, systems, or external events. In commodity trading, this can result from interruptions in the supply chain due to transportation issues, natural disasters, or supplier failures. It can also be because of inefficiencies or human error in trading, logistics, or settlement processes that lead to financial losses, legal penalties, and reputational damage.

Trading companies must manage environmental and social risks such as pollution, deforestation, and social welfare liabilities, ensuring their operations do not negatively affect local communities, fair labour practices, and respect for human rights.

Trading companies often operate in high geopolitical risk areas where changes in government, civil unrest, or international sanctions can disrupt supply chains and affect market access. Similarly, tariffs, quotas, and trade agreements can impact the flow of commodities across borders.

Cybersecurity risk is critical, whether unauthorised access to data or cyberattacks such as ransomware. Competitors or malicious actors may attempt to steal proprietary trading algorithms, strategies, or other intellectual property, undermining a company's competitive advantage.

Compliance officers play an essential role in trading companies. They ensure that their company adheres to relevant laws, regulations, and standards set by governmental and international bodies. They include international trade laws, such as export/import regulations and customs requirements, environmental laws on deforestation and pollution, and food safety standards,

They develop and implement internal policies and procedures to ensure regulatory compliance by establishing ethical employee guidelines. They set up systems to monitor compliance and enforce policies while maintaining records of regulatory filings and incident reports to document compliance breaches and actions taken to resolve them.

Compliance officers act as a bridge between the company and regulatory authorities, communicating with regulatory bodies to stay updated on new laws and regulations while ensuring that management and staff are informed about compliance issues and updates. They provide guidance on ethical issues and conflicts of interest that may arise in commodity trading, ensuring that their company conducts all trading activities ethically and transparently.

Insurance also plays a critical role in risk management. Trading companies can't insure against all risks, but they can insure some.

Today's marine cargo insurance policies offer comprehensive coverage options, addressing risks such as physical damage due to accidents, mishandling or environmental factors, theft and piracy, contamination or spoilage, and losses arising from political instability, war, or sanctions.

Five Questions for Deven Chitaliya

Deven, you are Senior Vice President & Head of Risk Management at Olam Group in Singapore, responsible for risk management across 12 agri-business platforms spread across more than 70 countries. Please tell me a little about how you manage risk at Olam.

All organisations must manage risks effectively to endure and thrive. Traditionally, most organisations assign risk management to business unit leaders within their areas of responsibility. We call this "silo" or "stovepipe" risk management. For example, the Chief Technology Officer is responsible for managing risks related to information technology operations; the Treasurer is responsible for managing risks related to financing cash flow, and so on.

However, risk does not respect organisation charts; it can be anywhere and take any form. Some risks fall between siloes, unnoticed by individual leaders. Others can affect different units differently – managers may not know that a decision taken for one silo can cause or escalate risk in another. The upshot is that risk can go unnoticed or not be effectively tackled until a catastrophic event is triggered.

Another challenge with traditional risk management is that it is often internally focused and granular – looking within the organisation's four walls, with minimal focus on risks that may emerge from outside the business.

At Olam, we have mapped 51 risks (including 19 quantifiable risks) across 11 risk categories that the Risk Office monitors, measures, and reports on regularly with each department.

What are the most important considerations when implementing a Risk Management Framework for a company?

The most important is a robust governance structure and the independence of the risk management team. You also need a "holistic risk capture'" that is both outward and inward-looking and covers the entire company, not just individual business platforms. Risk must be consolidated and assessed both at the business and corporate level.

You need to measure risk wherever you can and keep on stress testing and analysing different scenarios. You need proactive operational risk controls in credit, counterparty, stock, and quality. You also need strict 'drawdown' and 'stop loss' policies at a platform level.

But perhaps most importantly, you must assess your company's risk appetite. That may sound obvious, but many companies go into trading without assessing their risk-taking capabilities.

Could you tell me the most significant risks Olam currently faces?

The most significant risk we face is our employees' health and safety; we spend a lot of time ensuring we minimise those risks.

Cyber-security risk is our second most significant risk. The innovative ways your systems and people's information can be hacked and misused, sometimes even surprise experts. With widespread operations across product platforms and geographies, standardisation of IT controls and effective implementation of the latest security controls across the company are crucial to counter and reduce losses in actual cyber-attacks or cyber fraud.

Supply disruption is currently our third most significant risk. Labour shortages and transport/logistics bottlenecks can also be an issue. We do see some slowdown in select countries. However, most of the Agri products fall under the list of essential commodities, so the trade is still immune from a complete shutdown.

There have been some relatively short-lived food export bans from certain countries, but they have not had much impact on the food supply. Ports have remained open, and the food supply chain has shown itself robust and flexible in dealing with the current crisis.

I would put demand destruction as our fourth most significant risk. This risk is less with food products, as demand is more or less constant. People must eat. However, things can be more complex with industrial products like cotton, where end users can defer purchases for extended periods.

For example, we must ask ourselves how a drop in retail clothing demand in Europe and the US might lead to the cancellation of their orders, say, with Bangladeshi clothing manufacturing factories, which might affect cotton sales contracts.

In-depth regular risk reviews with a business team focusing on operational checks and controls and assessing high-risk areas and bottlenecks help us take proactive actions as a "One Olam" team.

What about counterparty risks?

Olam is unique among the major agricultural trade houses in that we are very involved at the origin. Our vertically integrated supply chain for our Upstream businesses means we have minimal and well-managed counterparty risk on our supply side.

Our counterparty risks tend to be downstream, where we depend on timely contract performance and payments from our customers. Market volatility plays an important role. The higher the volatility, the higher the 'mark to market' exposures, the higher the risks.

Not only do we have to assess the risks to our businesses, but we also must constantly monitor the risks to our client's businesses: are they facing supply issues; has a significant buyer defaulted on them; how is their cash flow relative to their stock levels; how is their payment performance with us, what are the inputs from our market network, etc.? These things can show us an early warning sign / red flag for timely and corrective action.

It goes a long way to ensure long-term relationship building and trust when we offer innovative solutions where possible to support their businesses. e.g. short-term cash-flow issues, bank-assisted structures to support payments, credit insurance, collaterals, deposits, parent guarantee-backed exposures, etc.

What keeps you awake at night?

That there is something out there that we don't know about. I am not worried about the things we know about any event that may occasionally occur in the usual course of business; we have robust systems in place to monitor and manage these known risks.

One unknown, of course, is technological development and innovation: will something be invented that might negatively affect one of our businesses? There is no easy way of knowing that except to remain current on the major initiatives, experiments and actions undertaken across the industry!

Mike Halbach

Compliance, for me, means managing the grey. We need to figure out the middle. It's where the problems start and where risk assessment kicks in.

Mike works with Sybius, a boutique consultancy firm offering compliance services to the commodity trading and financial sector. Before joining Sybius, Mike worked for 16 years with Cargill, most recently as compliance director for derivatives and commodities.

"My job at Cargill was in the trading compliance areas," he told me. "I specialised in the intersection between trading in physical commodities and trading in financial instruments on regulated markets.

"The intersection usually occurs when pricing the physical transaction. If you sell wheat and your customer prices it against the Chicago futures, are you acting as a futures broker or providing investment advice?

"No, neither of the two. A commodity trader like Cargill is not a financial institution but must comply with regulations when trading on regulated markets. My role was to ensure that we had internal policies and procedures to comply with these regulations. It included ensuring traders and others do not give the impression of acting as futures broker or providing investment advice."

Mike told me that he faced three main challenges in that role. The first was that he needed to understand the business. He had people in his group who were fantastic professionals from the world of finance, but they were new to the world of physical commodities. They had to quickly learn how it worked.

His second challenge was translating compliance in a way traders could understand.

His third challenge was the speed at which the regulatory landscape changed. He had been with Cargill for one year when Lehman Brothers collapsed. It was the kick-off for long-term change in the world of finance.

"It is an evolving space," he told me. "More regulation will come If we as an industry do not operate properly. There are ongoing discussions about how commodity firms should be regulated, particularly in Europe, the US, and elsewhere.

"Are there specific measures legislators are looking to introduce?" I asked.

"Regulation will come into our sector through the financial markets," he replied. "One suggestion is to introduce capital requirements. If you want to take risks in the market, you need to have the necessary capital resources.

"The US, EU and other jurisdictions already restrict risk-taking by limiting the size of traders' positions on a futures exchange. The exchanges already impose financing requirements through initial and variation margins.

"Europe is also approaching the question through the lens of market abuse and conduct, looking at how traders hedge their physical transactions. A trading book will have a portfolio of positions without a one-to-one relationship between them. It has the potential of being vulnerable to abuse from a regulatory perspective.

"Don't expect compliance to go away," Mike warned. "The more you embrace it, the easier it will be to deal with."

"Do you think physical brokers will ever be regulated?" I asked. It was a question I had often asked myself during my years as a physical broker.

"I believe they could be," Mike replied. "The regulators are looking at physical brokers in standardised contracts such as sunflower oil in Europe or the Mississippi barge market in the US. They could ask whether they are physical cargoes or standardised financial instruments."

I have often argued that the agricultural business is largely privatised and has less room for corruption than in the oil and mining industries, where governments grant licences and permits. I asked Mike if he agreed.

"The US and Europe have already imposed massive fines for bribery and corruption," Mike countered, "albeit in the oil sector and for events many years ago.

"But think about cocoa," Mike continued. "You're buying from government entities in both Ghana and Ivory Coast. If you sell soybeans to China, your buyers may be state-owned companies. Countries like Iran, Nigeria, and Algeria also buy through state companies. The magnitude is less than oil's, but you are still vulnerable in agriculture."

"Does compliance cover reputation as well?" I asked. "Would that come under your remit?"

"Everybody in a company is responsible for the reputation of that company. A single trader can destroy a hundreds-of-years-old company in a second. As such, senior management, divisional managers, all employees and even beyond, like contractors – rather than just compliance officers – need to look out for reputational risk. "

"But what about legal compliance?" I asked. "There seems to be a fuzzy frontier between compliance and legal."

"Compliance starts where legal compliance ends," Mike answered. "Legal compliance clearly defines what a company can and can't do. However, there are grey areas in the legal world, and that's where compliance starts. Compliance, for me, means managing the grey. We need to figure out the middle. It's where the problems start and where risk assessment kicks in. It defines how much risk a company may be willing to take."

"There's so much legislation, and it's changing all the time," I said. "Cargill operates in so many countries; how do they keep up with it all?"

"Large commodity traders clearly define multiple compliance areas such as sanctions, competition, anti-bribery, food safety, etc," he replied. "You must organise and structure it. And you have priorities within each function. It's a volume problem and a prioritisation problem.

"You must also do a risk assessment depending on your area of compliance. If it is competition law, you must look in every country where you operate. If it's futures trading, you look at the countries where you trade the futures and where the futures exchanges are located. You have plenty of people following the rules. However, digesting that information can be a challenge."

"Doesn't that make it harder for you, Mike, now that you are in a smaller organisation?" I asked. "How do you track all that information and ensure you're up to speed?"

"It is a good question," he replied. "I agree I don't have the resources I had at Cargill, but information today is much more available than it was twenty years ago. We are linked to a lot of trading organisations and have a network of people with whom we share information

"I'm not advising the Cargills of this world. Smaller organisations have different risk profiles. When you have a specific client, you go through the list of things they're exposed to and focus on those. It reduces your workload. Besides, I advise more on compliance strategies and structures – how you can practically deal with your risks – than on day-to-day activities.

"There is another element here. You get into a routine working for one company and can become a victim of groupthink, attached to a particular way of seeing and doing things. As a consultant, I am exposed to a variety of views. I am no longer factually and emotionally attached to one pre-determinate view. I believe it is called 'non-attachment' in advanced organisational thinking."

"Where does compliance end and risk management start?" I asked. "Is compliance a subcategory of risk management?"

"Too many people in the commodity world misunderstand risk management," he replied. "They too often think risk management is market risk management, but there are many other risk areas you need to think about. Risk management is mitigating the risks in your business activity, irrespective of where they're coming from.

"You have market, compliance, counterparty, funding, and financing risks. People in accounting have to manage risk. There is a whole range of risks in trade execution. You have cyber security and IT risks. You have fraud and payment risks. The people responsible for managing these risks are not necessarily in compliance, but compliance provides a framework and interacts at every level of risk management.

I saw on his LinkedIn profile that Mike had experience in forensic accounting.

"Forensic activities, not forensic accounting," he corrected me. "Forensic activities are part of the compliance role. I'm not examining a crime and how a person died, but there is a comparison. We try to understand what happened and see if it is still happening. We try to find patterns. It is an intense role, but it is a crucial part of compliance to prevent further damage to the company.

"It may also lead to an improvement in trading activities. Suppose you are not contravening any market regulations but still move the market when you hedge a physical transaction. In that case, our forensic activity can highlight possible ways to improve your hedge execution. It is the advantage of business-oriented compliance."

"Is this something that artificial intelligence could help with?" I asked. "It seems an obvious candidate for artificial intelligence."

"Absolutely," he replied. "It's an example of where artificial intelligence can help. Regulators already use or at least consider the use of AI extensively.

"The only issue is that AI doesn't tell you what it did, how it did it, or if it did everything. It can be challenging from a regulatory perspective.

"One downside is that AI can send out too many false positives. As a compliance officer, you must confirm and document that every false positive is false."

"What are the best and the worst things about being a compliance officer?" I asked

"The best thing is I can look into everything and learn about the business. Today, risk management is natural for me, for example, but I discovered it through the compliance journey.

"The worst thing is that traders often view you as a 'no-sayer'. I have had to learn not to say 'no' too quickly, and I am still learning. Looking back, I have often said 'no' too quickly. Traders are not doing things wrong intentionally – some do, but the vast majority don't.

"Even so, you need a lot of courage and resilience to say 'no' when everyone wants you to say 'yes'."

"Are you a policeman or a detective?" I asked.

"I am neither," Mike replied. "People often think of us as the police, but if we do our role correctly, we are more of a business enabler. We ensure the business can continue to operate and has the license to operate. In one sense, we are policemen who protect that licence to operate. In another sense, we set up the processes that facilitate business. We are an enabler.

"I like to think of myself as more of a harbour pilot," he continued. "If I were a policeman, I would keep the vessel miles from the coast without the ability to do business. A pilot must navigate the ship through the rocks and keep the company safe. If you need to slow down, you slow down but speed up when you can.

"People in the trading world should see their compliance people as partners, not policemen. They're there to help you. They are there to keep the business functioning and you out of jail."

K.S. Vishwanath

The most important thing is to spend time on insurance. Benchmark your program and spend some time on risk engineering.

When I started working on my new book on agricultural commodity supply chain professionals, I quickly realised that I had significant gaps in my knowledge. One of the biggest was my complete ignorance of the world of insurance. I had worked for many years as a physical trader and broker, but we always traded FOBS or C&F. I don't think I ever traded a CIF cargo.

As I started to delve into the matter, the first thing that struck me was the connection between marine insurance and the law.

Lord Mance, formerly Deputy President of the UK Supreme Court, said, "Insurance and the law are inextricably linked at all points. Insurance is not like making cars or widgets. It depends on agreements and wordings for its force and effect, and agreements and wordings depend on the law for their force and effect".

The second thing I learned was that insurance is so incredibly complex that someone could write a whole book about it. Therefore, I was delighted to find someone who had done just that.

K.S. Vishwanath (Vish) has nearly 40 years of experience in marine insurance in India and the Far East. Since 2008, he has been a freelance consultant based in Bangalore. He has written a highly acclaimed book, Insuring Cargoes—A Practical Guide to the Law and Practice, published in the UK. The second edition was released in March 2023.

Vish told me that although there are many scholarly works on the subject, he felt there was still space on the bookshelf for a book written by a practitioner that focused on practice rather than theory. He wanted to write a book that provided solutions to the issues a practitioner confronts daily.

"The shipping industry is in turmoil with the events in the Red and Black Seas," he told me. "Still, on a different level, the insurance sector's most significant issues are excess capacity and severe competition. In many parts of Asia and Africa, this leads to the commodification of complex risks. The European markets are less affected.

"Many risks are complex to price. Insurers, hungry for premiums and profits, may not price them correctly.

"Insurers develop volatility in their books and must make a profit to build a reserve for any significant loss. An insurer will take a pyramid approach, where most of their business comes from a low frequency of claims, but one or two of those claims will be of high severity.

"The bottom line should always be at the back of your mind as an underwriter. Still, market and broker pressure may force you to introduce excess volatility into your book. Competition is severe. If I say no to a business, the brokers will say, 'You're cherry-picking—if you want profitable business from this client, you must also do some high-risk areas.'

"As an insurer, you must ask yourself, "Is my business sustainable over a long period? Am I being fair to the clients as well as my shareholders?" These are things which I would lose sleep over."

"You mentioned that the insurance market is in turmoil because of the Red and Black Sea situations," I said. "What are the issues there?"

"The Red Sea is one of the world's most important shipping zones," Vish told me. "An underwriter with less appetite for risk may say they will not write business for voyages via the Red Sea, but most companies will do the business but increase their rates. It increases traders' costs.

"The other issue is that avoiding the Red Sea will increase transit time and adversely affect a moisture-sensitive cargo like grain. Going from the

Red Sea through another climatic zone may lead to condensation issues in bulk cargoes.

"Sweating and condensation can be a particular problem for containers but may be excluded under the insurance. Desiccants only work for a limited time; they stop working if containers take longer routes or are otherwise delayed.

"Piracy is still a risk if you go through the Red Sea. Traders must ensure they get piracy extensions in their policies. ICC (A), an all-risks form, covers piracy, including ransom, which is recovered under General Average. ICC (B) or (C) do not. However, there is a legal opinion that ransom could be recovered under the "riots" section of the Institute Strike Riot and Civil Commotion Clauses (SRCC). I suggest that cargo owners choose ICC (A) cover as courts have not yet tested the recoverability of ransom under "riots."

"The Dark Fleet is the biggest issue in the Black Sea. No International Group of P&I Club (IG Club) member will cover the dark fleet, so recovery for cargo losses would be impossible. Also, without a P&I, wreck removal, liability for pollution, etc., would go uninsured.

"Another issue is that some vessels switch off their transponders as they approach the area. Russian exporters may mix Ukrainian grains with Russian grains, but insurers or traders cannot know that."

"Imagine you are a trader," I said, "what traps should I look out for when I insure a cargo?"

"Most companies, even the big corporate trading houses, pay too little attention to insurance. Senior management must embed good insurance practices across the whole organisation. The CFO or the insurance manager may try to get the cheapest premium, but how about the coverage? What's the deductible? Have you covered heat, sweat, and spontaneous combustion? Is rejection risk covered? The corporate office should drive risk management and insurance.

"First, appoint a good broker and don't encourage brokers or underwriters who don't ask for copious information. Brokers should be fussy with details and fully understand the business.

"Second, do a benchmarking exercise. How does my insurance programme compare with my competitors? A good broker should do a benchmarking exercise.

"An all-risk policy will not cover rejection, seizure, or condemnation by food, health, port, tax, or quarantine authorities," he continued. "You require a rejection risk, which few people take. Insurers have little appetite for rejection insurance. There are specialist markets that write this class of business. The rates may be high, but at least attempt a small limit, start somewhere and cover rejection risk.

"What are the specific challenges for agricultural commodities?" I asked.

"Shortage is a big risk for any bulk cargo," he told me. "The shortage could be due to various reasons.

"If there are multiple receivers and ports, it's entirely possible that some excess delivery was made to a receiver in another port or your port.

"The draft survey may not reflect this as the tendency is to match the draft survey with the bill of lading. A draft survey method is not an exact science but depends on the condition of the sea, the swell, the wind, and the surveyor's experience.

"Another issue is moisture. Agricultural commodities should have less than a specific humidity level to avoid condensation in the hold. For soybeans, it is 14 per cent. For Chinese groundnuts, it may be as little as 4 per cent.

"And of course, you have this piracy and general average, theft, water damage through bad weather. These are the usual claims."

"There has been an increase in fraud by sellers and buyers over the past few years.

"An example of seller fraud would be when a surveyor fails to notice that a container has not been correctly sealed. When the surveyor leaves, the seller unplugs the seal, removes the cargo and puts some rubbish inside.

"There are three types of buyer frauds," he continued.

"The first type is where a buyer and seller have been trading for a while and build trust between them. The seller agrees to discharge shipments against a letter of indemnity, but suddenly, there is a dispute, and the buyer refuses to pay.

"The second type of fraud is the one-time fellow who places an order with you, forges the bill of lading or signs the bill of exchange, takes delivery of the original bill of lading, and disappears.

"The third type is imposter fraud, where someone pretends to work for a big company, shows industry knowledge, creates an email ID that resembles a corporate email ID, and gives the name of a first-class bank but with a fake account number and address. The buyer then intercepts or forges the documents, discharges the cargo, and disappears.

"Watch out for red flags. Go to a trade body like the Chamber of Commerce or the company to ask whether they know this email or this person or if it is fake. You should never enter today's market with an unknown buyer or seller."

"Are there things that you should particularly watch out for containers?" I asked.

"For general cargo like machinery, toys, and electronic items, containerisation is a better risk for insurance companies than shipment in break bulk. Still, because of heat-sweat issues, containers will have problems with coffee, cashew nuts, and grains. Containerisation has reduced losses but has not eliminated them.

"Damages, theft, pilferage, water damage, and piracy are common claims in containers and breakbulk.

"How is technology affecting the insurance world?" I asked.

"There is an issue with automated crewless vessels," Vish told me. "How will they reduce losses? Will the General Average come down? Will they encourage piracy? We need to see.

"Artificial intelligence will streamline claims processes. It can give you an online platform where claims and documentation are more straightforward. It can help underwriters generate proper premiums through data analytics.

"The sky is the limit for technology. Embrace it or be left behind."

"Do claims often end up in court?" I asked.

"Insurers in the US and Europe don't deny legitimate claims," he replied. "They will negotiate, but they won't deny. Most European and American companies have a strict Chinese wall between underwriting and claims to avoid the temptation for the underwriter to increase profitability by reducing the claims.

"If somebody files a case in a court in India, it will take 15-20 years before a judgment comes. By then, I will have retired from the insurance company and collected my bonus. So why should I bother? Compulsory arbitration would resolve this."

"Could you give me a pre-trade checklist for insurance?" I asked.

"Absolutely," he replied.

"The most important thing is to spend time on insurance. Don't go for the lowest possible rate. Identify brokers or experts. Benchmark your program and spend some time on risk engineering. Identify insurance companies with an excellent claims-settling philosophy.

"You should then consider your chartering philosophy and how you select a vessel. Do I go for the cheapest ship, or do I go for a good-quality one? You may save on freight today, but what if a 5-million-dollar claim is not payable?

"Look for any gaps in your coverage. Consider taking rejection risk insurance. It is costly but ask whether it is better to have it. Identify any unique exposures in your business and tell your insurance company about them."

"And for companies in general?" I asked.

"Companies should use insurance to protect their balance sheets. Large corporates often forget this and go for the cheapest premium instead of ensuring best-in-class coverage backed by risk management. As a consultant, I have always told my clients that insurance should be driven from the top to embed the right message within the organisation.

"I'll give you an example of a textile mill in India whose products were brand names. A new CFO joined them, saying, "This is not a low-lying area. We have a water shortage in this area. Why are you paying $50,000 for flood insurance? Cancel it." The board applauded the decision, but there was a freak flood the following year, and the company went bankrupt.

Protect yourself against anything which can ruin your balance sheet, even though the chances of that happening are rare.

8. PRICE RISK MANAGEMENT

There is a saying that commodity trading companies do not live on their margins. They live on price risk management.

I began my commodity career in 1978 with Cargill's sugar trading department in London. I worked there for a year before transferring to Minneapolis, where I kept track of the trading book and managed the company's risk position. The traders would buy and sell physical sugar, and my job was to hedge it. They would tell me whether they wanted the overall position to be long or short – and how long or short they wanted to be – and I would buy or sell futures to comply.

When I arrived in Minneapolis, the head trader told me he wanted me to day trade 50 lots – 2,500 tons. He explained I could be a maximum of 2,500 tons long or short during the day but could not carry the position overnight.

He added that he expected me to make enough money day-trading to pay the overheads of the entire department, an expectation that so shocked me that some forty years later, I still visualise where I was standing when he said it. I remember looking around the trading room at the half dozen or so traders and mentally trying to calculate how much they collectively earned.

I later learned that the previous year's sugar desk trainee had mismanaged the company's option position and subsequently left the company. The two trainees after me had more success. The first went on to become Vice-Chairman (effectively CEO) of Cargill. The second went on to become CEO of Viterra. I will leave you to judge how well I did in comparison!

Before arriving in Minneapolis, I had read everything I could find about trading. There wasn't much, but the little I found focused on 'beating the market'. Once I started in Minneapolis, I quickly understood that it wasn't the market I should beat but my own emotions, primarily fear and greed, but also pride – or, in this case, hubris.

I had to overcome my fear of entering a position and then keeping it when (as it often did) it began to lose money. 'Do I cut my losses or double up?' And I had to overcome my greed when I was making money. 'Should I take my profits now or wait – and at what point, if at all, should I reverse my position?'

I never made enough money day-trading to cover the department's costs, but it taught me a lot, first about price risk management and second about myself. My favourite book then was the 1974 classic *Zen and the Art of Motorcycle Maintenance*. I have more than once attempted to write *Zen and the Art of Sugar Trading*. Maybe it could be my next project.

Ralph Potter

The worst thing that can happen is when a trader thinks he knows something and disregards his rules.

I was blessed to have Ralph Potter as my mentor in my early years as a trader. He taught me everything I know about risk and helped me manage my negative emotions of fear, greed, and hubris.

He once famously told his assistant that if she saw him dancing around his desk singing "I'm a genius," she should immediately liquidate all his positions! (It happened more than once!)

A keen sailor, he also taught me that the time to trim the sails (or reduce the position) was when you first thought of it.

"Listen to your instinct," he told me. "With experience, you can feel if a storm is approaching. Don't ignore that thought. Don't wait for the storm to hit because it will be too late to get the sails in!"

Ralph is an ex-Green Beret, the American equivalent of the British Special Forces. He told me that being in the military taught him two things.

"First, a bad plan poorly executed is better than no plan. Second, you should only commit reserves to exploit and consolidate victory, never to salvage defeat. Don't throw good money after bad.

"The biggest mistake traders make is snatching profits," he told me. "There is a saying that no one ever went broke taking a profit, but that is a lie; people go broke snatching small profits that don't offset their losses. People often grab profits expecting to return to the market again at a better price. They may do, but usually, the market runs away, and they either must chase it or they don't get back in.

"A trader's greatest enemy is lack of discipline and succumbing to hubris – when you think you know more than everyone else in the market.

"The worst thing that can happen is when a trader thinks he knows something and disregards his rules. It can be when he has invested so much of his credibility – and so much of his personality – into putting on a trade, it makes it hard to exit. It's hard to change your mind. That's why you must have a risk point.

"The best traders are the ones who have unconventional vision and self-belief: to stick your neck out and have the guts to say, 'I am going to commit my company's money – or my investors' money – to make this trade.' It takes someone with exceptional self-belief. Most traders on a desk just want to keep their heads down.

"But you must take the risk. You must have the guts to trade. You also must have an absolute disdain for the opinions of other people. You don't have to tell everybody you think they are full of it, but other people's views mustn't sway you.

"There is a story of a trader who goes for a job interview, and the interviewer asks him what he considers his greatest weakness. "Honesty,' he replied.

'I don't think honesty is a weakness,' the interviewer told him.

'I don't give a s**t what you think," he replied.

"To succeed in the markets, you must have a well-developed sense of fear: it will keep you in business longer than brilliance. Brilliance can desert you in critical moments."

"Is there anything you would like to add?" I asked.

"Yes," he told me. "I would like to leave you with my three rules of trading:

"Have the guts to trade

"Have an absolute disdain for the opinions of other people.

"Have a well-developed sense of fear: it will keep you in business longer than brilliance. Brilliance can desert you in critical moments.

"Lastly, always remember that reserves are only committed to exploit and consolidate victory, never to salvage defeat. Another way of saying that is, "Don't throw good money after bad".

Charles Funnell

An FMCG company wants you to flatline. However, to be competitive, it needs the bumps – the ups and downs of volatility – to pick the right timing to cover hedges. It's a delicate balancing act.

Charles started his career as an inter-trade physical sugar broker in Paris before moving to Durban as the South African Sugar Association's export manager. He then spent a year and a half in the Philippines for Cargill before they transferred him back to Geneva as their structured trading manager.

After seven years with Cargill, he spent some time with Aisling, a commodity hedge fund, before moving to Dubai to head up risk management at Savola, the largest food company in the Middle East. In 2014, he moved to Schaffhausen in the German-speaking part of Switzerland as Director of Commodity Risk Management at Unilever.

"Moving to Schaffhausen and a large multinational suited me well," he told me. "Unilever has less trading appetite than a company like Cargill but is close to commodity markets.

"I enjoyed the broader range of commodities," he continued. "Until then, I'd done sugar and edible oilseeds, but I handled other things like dairy, cocoa, and some metals at Unilever. It was intellectually stimulating to learn new commodities and meet new people. I managed about eight or nine commodities for the company globally."

"What is the difference between a trader and a risk manager?" I asked him.

"The two roles are similar," he replied. "If you trade, you must know how to manage risk. Risk is at the heart of it all. You start with risk, and then off you go. To be a successful trader, you must understand and appreciate risk to create a positive and consistent P&L by mitigating the bad trades and maximising the good ones. It uses a more offensive approach.

"As a risk manager, you also focus on risk and reward either for hedging decisions or putting on a trading position. It is more of an approach to assess what can go wrong with either decision and put a plan in place to limit losses and capture gains. As a risk manager, you have a broader appreciation of market risk. It uses a more defensive approach."

"Okay," I said. "What's the difference between procurement and risk management?"

There's a big difference. The risk manager knows the commodity markets and appreciates risk. The procurement manager understands the process but often does not recognise or appreciate risk.

At Unilever, the risk management team was part of the procurement process, but the company separated purchasing procurement from risk management. It was sometimes difficult for a procurement manager to understand the risk manager. "

"To be clear," I asked. "When you're talking about risk management here, Charles, you're talking about commodity price risk management."

Yes. We weren't responsible for other risks, such as counterparty risk. That was the procurement manager's job."

Fast Moving Consumer Goods (FMCG) companies like Unilever are structurally short of commodities – they always need to buy them. I wondered if that forced them to trade the markets even if they didn't want to.

"As a risk manager in an FMCG company," Charles replied, "You look to mitigate price volatility. It is a very different mindset from a trader in a trade house who seeks out risk in price volatility for profit maximisation.

"The objective of a risk manager in an FMCG company is to provide as flat a price line as possible, so the business can lock in margins over the medium and long term while at the same time using the volatility in the market to make the company more competitive.

"An FMCG company wants you to flat line. However, to be competitive, it needs the bumps – the ups and downs of volatility – to pick the right timing to cover hedges. It's a delicate balancing act.

"Commodity risk management isn't just about beating an internal forecast. Nor is it about ensuring there's no inflation from last year's cost price. Inflation is the same for everybody. If wheat or sugar prices have gone up from last year, they have gone up for everyone.

"To look at it from a pure procurement mindset is missing the point that it's crucial to mitigate costs by buying at an opportune time, irrespective of inflation.

"Consumer companies must have a strategy and build governance around it. They must have a mindset as to what is making them competitive. Beating last year's price or the end-month forecasts is insufficient.

"FMCG companies trade the market by buying further forward than they would otherwise do when they think the price will rise. When they think prices will fall, they buy on a more hand-to-mouth basis."

Traders typically must make quick decisions on incomplete information. I suspected FMCG companies were not as fast-moving as the name implies. I asked Charles how quickly he could get senior management to make decisions.

"It is quicker and easier to get approval when prices are low," he replied. "It is difficult to convince senior management to put on hedges when the market is rising. It's challenging for FMCG companies to understand why they need to pay up – and why the price might not revert to mean. It can cause delay, and delay in an upward-trending market will mean additional costs. It can be challenging, but people trust you once you have a good track record. It speeds up the decision-making process.

"The challenge is often with the structure itself," he added. FMCG companies are heavy on people. It can take time to get everybody's buy-in."

I asked Charles how you could evaluate the performance of a price risk manager in an FMCG company. It's easy in a trading company – you look at the P&L – but a risk manager in a procurement function doesn't have a clear P&L.

"You can look at it in various ways," Charles told me. "However, you typically base it off a market average versus where you hedge. You can also look at it versus the cost of the additional inflation or deflation that occurred because you made those decisions.

"In all honesty, the area is ill-defined. We looked at it from different angles over the years, but there's no correct method because there's no P&L per se. You're trying to beat the market and to keep it all as flatlined as possible for the business.

"The rest is about whether you communicated well and involved the right people in the decision process."

I wanted to know the most challenging part of his role at Unilever. Was it getting the markets right, or was it explaining to his colleagues how commodity markets work? Charles told me it was the latter, getting the teams to understand the markets.

"People move around every three or four years in most FMCG companies," he said. "You start again each time someone new comes along. It can be frustrating to rinse and repeat, having built up a certain amount of knowledge and buy-in. FMCG companies like to move their employees between different roles and geographies. Traders tend to stay in their markets for many years.

"I think FMCG companies should look at more longevity in specific positions," he added.

After over seven years with Unilever, Charles established a consultancy company offering risk management advisory services to industrial clients in sugar, grains, and dairy.

"Isn't it difficult to follow multiple markets and be an expert in everything?" I asked him.

"The best traders and risk managers know how little they know," he replied. As Socrates famously said, "All I know is that I know nothing".

Joe Brooker

The more niche we become – and the further removed from the markets correlated with futures contracts – the more diversifying we become for the reinsurers.

Joe started in commodities as a market analyst for ADM, then moved on to ED&F Man and Platts. He has been with Stable since 2019. Somewhere in the middle, he took a year out to travel.

Rich Counsell, a UK farmer's son, founded Stable in 2016. He realised that hedging price risk was a complex, risky, and intimidating experience. He also realised that the futures markets provide an inadequate hedging mechanism for many agricultural products.

He looked at an insurance model and how insurance companies price contracts through actuarial data science – and wondered if the model would work in hedging agricultural products. He got in touch with the universities of Liverpool, Harvard and Lisbon and built out an academic bank of research. The company launched in 2019 with ten products working with farmers in the UK.

Stable works between businesses and reinsurers to offer put and call option contracts across 6 to 18 months. Within that, they must pay a percentage of the premium to their pricing partners – the PRAs (Price Reporting Agencies). The insurance companies take on the price risks but don't hedge them. They win on some and lose on others.

In 2023, the company became a fully-fledged insurer in Bermuda. The reinsurance companies take 95 per cent of the risk, with Stable taking

5 per cent, using their capital. Stable sources the deals worldwide and prices the risk.

When I spoke with Joe in 2023, the company had over 500 prices on their platform and offered hedging for protein cuts (beef, pork, and chicken), organic grains, lentils, pulses, fruit, and vegetables."

I asked him what the most challenging commodity was to hedge.

"We have written contracts for a Californian guacamole manufacturer," he told me. "It was challenging for our risk managers because avocados are highly perishable, and storage is limited. Most avocados come from Mexico, and the manufacturer relies on a narrow supply chain. It is sensitive to any kind of demand shift, supply shortfalls, or changes in customs regulations; prices can double in a week."

I asked Joe how the company prices the risk.

"Our data science team in London has built an algorithm that prices the initial premium based on historical volatility using traditional options pricing methods. The team prices risk mathematically, but we also have an underwriting team, including economists and quants. We then add commodity market knowledge, working with market experts. For example, we have an expert for each of the fruit and veg, nuts, dairy, proteins, and grains markets. We ask our market experts for their opinion. You could call it a quantitative and qualitative approach."

"How do you build a diversified risk book?" I asked.

"We offer a broad range of products across puts and calls," Joe replied. "It helps to balance the portfolio. We also diversify our risk geographically. We've got risks across hundreds of different markets, and there's time diversification within that.

"Some insurers already have exposure to energy products, but agriculture is a new risk for them – none ever had exposure to avocados! The more niche we become – and the further removed from the markets correlated with futures contracts – the more diversifying we become for the reinsurers. The insurers consider diversifying their risks and see Stable's risk pool as one aspect among their different books."

"Some of these markets are small and specialised. How do you deal with them?"

"There are a couple of things we can do to mitigate risk," Joe replied. We look at the market size and the competition within that market. Some of these markets are oligopolies. We also look at how the prices are reported for that market. The crucial thing is to understand who the contributors are to the price used as the settlement mechanism."

"What about counterparty risk?" I asked. "Some potential clients may be concerned that you're too small and you might not be able to honour the contract if there's a big market move. Is that an issue?"

"Our reinsurers have colossal balance sheets and set precise risk limits; we operate very clearly within those boundaries. We also limit our loss on any contract by selling call-and-put spreads, not outright options, so our potential losses are limited, especially with such a diversified book. By selling options spreads, not outright options, we limit our potential loss on any deal."

"Do you sometimes have to educate your clients on risk management?" I asked.

"Education is crucial," Joe replied. "It's often a question of language and terminology. Hedging can sound more complex than it is, so we work hard to simplify it all in terms of structure, language, and user experience."

9. BROKERS

People often confuse traders and brokers, but they are different animals. Traders act as contract principles on a commodity transaction. They run a price risk if they are not correctly hedged or a basis risk if they are hedged and the price of the physical commodity moves adversely relative to their hedge. (*Basis* refers to the price difference between a physical commodity and the futures market.)

A broker does not take any price risk but puts together a buyer and a seller for a commission. A broker's only risk is losing his commission if one or both parties to the contract fail to perform. His loss is limited to his commission, but so is his profit.

Brokers are the lubricants that keep markets working smoothly. They constantly look for win-win situations where buyers and sellers gain from a deal. Traders often do not have the time to call all possible sellers when they want to buy something, nor to contact all potential buyers when they want to sell something. Brokers do that for them. Brokers help to negotiate not only the price but also the contract terms. They must ensure that both parties agree on what they buy and sell.

As brokers are constantly in touch with market participants, they can quickly pick up on relevant news, views, and trends they can communicate to traders. Brokers are a source of valuable market information.

Brokers work for both buyers and sellers and should not favour either. The seller traditionally pays the broker the commission, but that does not mean the broker favours the seller.

A broker is not the same as an agent. A broker works equally for both the buyer and the seller and favours neither. An agent works for one party only. For example, a soybean producers' cooperative in Brazil may have a sales agent in China that represents the cooperative's interests in China and works to find buyers for its beans. Alternatively, a soybean crushing plant in China may have a buying agent in Brazil that works on behalf of the Chinese plant to source the best beans at the best price.

Different categories of brokers operate in the commodity markets, sometimes overlapping. One distinction is between a physical and a futures broker.

A futures broker executes an order on a futures exchange on behalf of a client. A physical broker puts together buyers and sellers in the physical (sometimes called 'cash') market.

Physical brokers tend to specialise in only one commodity: corn, wheat, sugar, or coffee. They can specialise and operate in a specific origin, such as Black Sea wheat or Malaysian palm oil. They can also specialise in a destination, say, wheat into Algeria.

Inter-trade brokers put together physical deals between trading companies. You might wonder why trading houses need brokers, but they do. (I was an inter-trade broker for over ten years.) One trade house may specialise in originating sugar from Brazil, but a different one might be good at selling sugar to Indonesia. Brokers can add value to that chain.

Kiran Wadhwana

As an origin broker, I keep my ear to the ground, and with my long-term relationships, I can get a good feel of the moves and trends in the local market.

I met Kiran's father, Narendra Wadhwana, when I worked for Cargill. He was the company's sugar agent in India, helping to put together deals with the STC, India's government-owned State Trading Company. The only trouble was that he was the agent for five different sugar trading companies. An agent usually only represents one company in a market or commodity. I have no idea how he managed to be an agent for five companies in the same commodity. But he did. Cargill was towards the bottom of the list, and as far as I remember, we didn't do a single business with India during that period.

I met Kiran for the first time at a sugar conference we organised in Singapore. We quickly took him on as our agent in India, and he kept us up to speed on all the developments there. Over the years, Kiran has become a family friend, and we keep in touch even though I am now out of the market.

The days of the STC are long gone, and India is now an active (more or less – sometimes less than more) free market for sugar. Kiran is an origin broker in the Indian export market for physical sugar. He is a middleman between a mill wanting to sell physical sugar for exports and a trader looking to export that sugar. He earns a commission on trades he puts together. I asked him why international traders needed origin brokers in addition to their own local offices.

"People move in and out within the big trading companies," he explained. "It means that most relationships are with the company and not with the individual – and they could be weaker as a result. An origin broker builds up personal relationships with suppliers over a long period.

"Origin brokers have a detailed understanding of what is happening in their procurement areas regarding crop prospects and industrial processing capacity. For example, have any mills increased capacity or added a refining end?

"As an origin broker, I keep my ear to the ground, and with my long-term relationships, I can get a good feel of the moves and trends in the local market – perhaps better than if a company has its own office.

"There is also the issue of counterparty risk. As an origin broker, I must know the financial condition of clients. I must evaluate the risk that they may default on a contract if the market moves against them.

"Do traders pay for you to bring the offers and to put the trade together?" I asked. "Or do they pay you for your market information?"

"It is a good question," he replied. "The answer is probably 'both'. In addition to broking, I also double up as a consultant for both local mills and international trading companies. Some take me on a retainer. I help domestic mills understand the world market and help international traders understand the local market.

"I send out a weekly report that covers crop progress, government policy, industrial capacities, and trading issues. I also cover ethanol policy; it is critical to the sugar market.

"Government policy is probably the toughest. It is also critical. India's government can't just look at one commodity. It must look at the total domestic food supply. We have such a vast population that it would be impossible for other countries to meet our needs.

"You could say that I am a bridge between the domestic and international markets, with information flowing in both directions."

"Are there many origin brokers in India for sugar?" I asked.

"Yes," he replied. "India has a sizeable domestic sugar market. Last year we exported about 12 million tonnes, while the domestic market is 27 million. Most brokers only work in the domestic market, although some double up and do exports. A domestic broker may not understand the export market. I am probably one of the few who works exclusively in the export market. I don't do any domestic broking.

"There are probably 15-20 brokers active in the export market. There is a thin line between a broker and a trader. Someone may be broking one day, and the subsequent day, they may be trading. I think I am the only one who only does broking. I do not trade."

"Could you describe a typical day?" I asked.

"I am lucky to have worked from home for the past 20 years," he replied. "It means there is no distinction between home and office life. It may sound good – and it is – even if it means that I work all the time!

"I get up at around 5 am, do my morning exercises and then read the overnight reports from London. I take this quiet time to check on the logistical and execution details of recent trades. I also do my administrative tasks.

"At around 8 am, I receive the overnight reports from New York. By then, my Indian clients have begun to contact me on WhatsApp, asking questions, exchanging market information, looking to buy or sell physical sugar, or checking on execution issues. I used to do everything by telephone, but it has now moved to WhatsApp.

"European clients wake up at around 2 pm my time. It starts to get busy as they are either looking for sugar or trying to keep abreast of any policy developments that may have occurred overnight in India. That continues until around 7 pm when the New York futures market becomes more active. I advise some Indian clients on pricing their export sales on the futures exchange. The moves in the flat price can also generate new physical business.

"My day ends around 8.30 pm. It sounds like a long day, but I don't have to commute. The line between home and office is, well, thin. I am a few years from retirement, and I don't have to put as much effort into my business to get the same result as I used to. I like that.

"What skills and experience do you need to be an origin broker?" I asked.

"An essential skill is getting on with people and managing client relationships," he replied. "To do that, you must like people and enjoy social interaction. You must also be willing to accept 'no' as an answer and realise that markets can be calm for extended periods.

"Working in India, I must keep a keen eye on government policy. We have a new policy every year. I try to understand the workings of domestic politics and anticipate what policy may be and how it might affect the markets.

"Perhaps experience is more important than any skill set," he continued. "Over my career, I have been a farmer, a miller, a trader, a futures broker, and a consultant. It has allowed me to understand both domestic and international markets.

"My grandfather started the family in the sugar business and founded ITC – International Trading Company – under which I still operate. He was a trader, but now I only do broking and consulting.

I had forgotten that Kiran had once been a farmer. I asked him to tell me more about it.

"When I finished my MBA in the US in 1985," he replied, "My father said, "Well, you have attended the best universities in the world. I will buy a sugar mill, and you will run it for me!"

The mill came with a 4,000-acre farm, and I became one of India's largest sugarcane growers. I learned the business from the ground up, even as a gentleman farmer."

"Out of all the hats you have worn," I asked, "Which is the one that has taught you the most?"

"My time as a gentleman farmer and miller helped me enormously," he replied. "If I had not had that experience, I would not have such a good understanding of the underlying issues in the market – nor would I have been able to have such a good relationship with the mills. You can only understand the psychology of a farmer if you have been a farmer. The same applies to milling. I did both for more than 20 years.

"The farm is still there but is in litigation with the government. The 1976 Urban Land Ceiling Act limits a farmer's land to 75 acres unless the farm is mechanised. Our farm is mechanised, and we are fighting the issue in the courts. Local people have encroached on the land. It is still in our name, but local people live there and farm it.

"The farm has a water issue. As the population has grown, the local government has diverted the farm's water supply to urban areas. The farm has become more of a liability than anything else.

"The mill is still there but has been closed for 20 years. We built and now run a school in the factory area. We opened two other schools in local villages – 1,400 students from nursery to year twelve. We also built a religious temple on the mill site for the local population."

"Which is the hardest job in your supply chain?" I asked.

"Farming is by far the hardest," he told me. "It is the most complex and risky part of the sugar supply chain. Although Indian farmers receive a fixed price for their cane, many other factors can affect their crops: climate, weather, and insect infestations (sometimes from neighbouring farms).

"New technology may make farming more accessible, but it remains risky and complex. Sitting here in an air-conditioned office is far easier than being in the fields."

"What is the worst thing about your job?" I asked him.

"When people default on a contract," he replied.

"There are two types of defaults. The first can result from an adverse market move; for example, if a mill sells you sugar at one price, the market price increases, and the mill sells the same sugar at a higher price to another buyer. Knowing your client and helping them manage their sales can reduce counterparty risk from adverse market moves.

"The second type of default can occur because of a change in government policy, for example, if the government restricts exports. I find the second the most stressful. It can result in huge losses for both millers and traders."

"Do you need different skills as a broker than a trader?" I wondered.

"The trader looks at a deal in terms of his bottom line – how he can make money from it. A broker aims for a win-win for both sides. When I sell sugar for a mill, I need to understand the miller's costs, their concerns and what other options they have. But I also know that the trader must make money. I tell the trader he must leave some money on the table for the mill, or he won't return to you next time – and vice versa. I am constantly looking to achieve a balance – that's what makes you a proper independent broker."

When I was broking, I found that I was always trying to keep people happy. Broking suited my personality as I tend to avoid conflict. Traders often find themselves in a conflict where they fight for their margin. I asked Kiran whether he thought that also applied to him.

"Very much so!" he told me. "I work to bring people together. I avoid conflict.

"Avoiding conflict is not just a question of personality," he continued. "It makes sense from a business perspective. The only raw material I have is my time. I must use it wisely. If you get into a conflict, you waste too much time trying to solve a problem rather than doing any productive work. So, if you can nip a conflict in the bud – not let it develop – you will have more time to do more deals while keeping your existing customers happy."

Kiran's brother works as a trader for an international trade house. Interestingly, in the same family, one brother is a trader and the other a broker. I asked Kiran how his brother's character differed from his.

"My brother is more of a risk-taker than I am," he said. "He has a higher appetite for risk.

As a trader, he may do business with a financially weak mill and take a chance on the counterparty to get a good deal. That is something I would fear doing. I prefer to have a financially strong counterparty and not get into a conflict over contract performance.

"My brother doesn't look at the physical volume of the business he does but rather the profitability of each trade he makes. I have a fixed commission per tonne, and I will try to maximise volume while ensuring that the counterparties are strong and that there is no risk of default.

"He takes risks that I wouldn't be willing to take. It is also a question of age. As you grow older, you become more risk averse. I am 5-6 years older than him."

"How does that affect your ego?" I asked Kiran.

"Markets have a way of beating the ego out of you," he replied. "It's the same whether you are a broker, analyst, or trader! We can all get things wrong. Humility is an asset. No one is always correct, and, in your career, you will get things wrong."

"Last question," I said. "What would your 20-year-old self think of you now?"

"Funnily enough, I recently asked myself that same question," he replied. "My 20-year-old self would never have imagined the path I followed. I was in the US when I was twenty, finishing my undergraduate course in Houston, Texas, and applying for an MBA at the University of Michigan, ANN ARBOR.

"There were six of us from India on the MBA course. Four stayed in the US, and two, including me, returned to India. I keep in touch with the four who remained in the US. They are all successful and certainly have more money than I have. So, if you judge success purely on money, they are all more successful than me.

"Religion plays an integral part in my life. As I mentioned, we built a temple on the site of our mill, and I am a trustee of the Akshardham temple in Delphi – the biggest Hindu temple in the world.

"The guru who built the temple, Pramukh Swami Maharaj, always said, "In the joy of others, I find my own." I have applied that motto in both my private and business life.

"So, when it comes to life quality and philosophy, I am satisfied with – and proud of – the life I have led. I think my 20-year-old self would be too!"

Indrek Aigro

You need to be more innovative as today's markets are such that business opportunities appear and disappear much faster than when I started seventeen years ago.

Torben Christensen founded Copenhagen Merchants as an independent broker in his basement in 1977. He quickly grew it into a Northern European grain brokerage company, mainly involved in wheat exports through the Baltic Sea. The company has six brokerage offices, mainly positioned according to exporting origins.

But Torben didn't just expand in grain brokerage; he also diversified into shipping and port terminals. Along the way, he became Europe's biggest trader in forestry biomass. Torben officially retired in 2016, but he's in the office three or four times a month, so it hasn't been a complete exit. Torben's son, Simon, took over the CEO role from his dad, and the Christensen family still own the company.

It's not just the company that has evolved. The broker's function is also changing. Price discovery, historically the broker's job, is less important now as markets have become more transparent. A broker's value now is in the intelligent delivery of market information, execution, and logistics.

Indrek joined the company in 2007 and is responsible for the company's grain brokerage activity. I asked him to tell me what that involved.

"If you ask a broker or a trader to identify themselves, they will reply that they are a corn, wheat, or beans guy. I'm a wheat guy. Wheat is close to my heart. I'm originally from Estonia, and when I joined the company, it was natural that I looked after the markets in the emerging Baltic States.

Nowadays, I'm responsible for brokerage overall. I still broker for a small portfolio of loyal clients, but my job mainly involves developing new offices, products, and markets. Our world is changing super-fast, and we must adapt to those changes."

While running our company's sugar brokerage, I found it challenging to manage the communication between the various offices in Thailand, India, Europe, the US and Brazil. I asked Indrek how he did it.

"It's challenging," he replied, "Especially given the time zones and cultural differences.

"We have around 30 brokers in six different offices. If everybody calls everybody even once a day, it's hundreds and hundreds of phone calls. You can't do that. You need to be more innovative as today's markets are such that business opportunities appear and disappear much faster than when I started seventeen years ago.

"We invest heavily in digital tools and have developed a platform – CM Navigator – for internal and external use, where we keep our bids, offers and vital analytical data. Everybody has access to it.

"It's like in sports when you train a football team to become perfect for a match, where everybody can read each other well. To succeed, we must have the right tools, people, and attitude."

The other thing I found challenging was managing individual competition between the brokers. I asked Indrek how he got around that problem.

"It is one of the core challenges," he admitted. "It is why brokerage companies tend to be small. It is a barrier which restricts growth. At some stage, brokerage companies often split up, and people go on their own. We see that happening a lot.

"Copenhagen Merchants is one of the few brokerage companies that acts like an organisation," he continued. "I would attribute this mainly to our culture and our values. We try to think with 30 heads but talk with one mouth. We do not cherish individual achievement; we cherish group achievement. Nobody in our company is valued according to what they do individually. Business often happens between different brokers or offices.

The more business transacted between brokers and offices, the better it is because it shows how our team benefits from the structure around them.

"We are getting into uncharted waters today because of our size. We don't see many brokerage companies of similar size, which means we cannot follow any given examples. However, we firmly believe that combining our digital platform and shared culture allows us scalability.

"Brokerage requires drive and competitiveness, but it should never be destructive. It comes down to the value set of people. I don't know if we have been lucky or intelligent, but when we recruit brokers, we place more weight on their value set than their skillset or the tonnage they have brokered in the past. They must be a cultural fit for us."

There have been many attempts to move physical commodity brokerage onto platforms, but none has gained critical momentum. I asked Indrek how he was progressing on that issue.

"I don't think any company is strong enough on its own to drive or disrupt the business," he said. "Still, we must stay on the frontline to see what is going on – which direction the wind is blowing.

"There are several reasons why brokerage hasn't moved online," he continued.

"The number of transactions is relatively small, and the number of standardised contracts is even smaller.

"There is always a lot of discussion about terms when you trade physical goods – load speeds, documentary instructions, etc. They often depend on the destination. Moroccan, Algerian, and Tunisian terms are all different.

"The contracts are significant – a cargo of beans or corn is worth tens of millions of dollars. It is not the same as buying a plane or train ticket.

"Nobody has been able to standardise contracts enough to digitalise them. Even if you take the most standard flows, say, Brazilian beans to China, it is billions of dollars of flow in a relatively standardised format. The number of contracts is small enough – and the contracts are big enough – not to incentivise you to click and do the business."

"Why does a market need brokers?" I asked.

"It's a good question," he replied. "The market needs brokers for different reasons now than twenty years ago.

"Historically, a grain broker gave you price discovery to tell you the value of your goods at a certain point and time. The broker also helped build trust between counterparts by saying that this is a good buyer; you can trade with them. Sometimes, the broker's function was to offer execution and post-trade services.

"Brokers must look in the mirror and ask what value they can deliver in five or ten years. Price discovery is no longer a broker's primary function. The markets are transparent, and anybody can find out the value of their goods. The execution services are becoming increasingly automated, both with blockchain solutions – where the ABCDs have invested heavily in Covantis – and AI.

"First, we believe that the primary function of a broker will remain the intelligent delivery of information. We have thousands of data points on prices, analytics, S&Ds, line-ups, freight, etc. Choosing the five relevant data points for a client and delivering them at the right time is a significant value-add.

"Second, people often look at a broker's execution service as passing on emails between buyers and sellers. However, that is not the core of the service, and it can be automated relatively easily. The core of the execution service is to avoid disputes and arbitrations. It starts with designing and constantly improving the contract standard to leave the minimum room for interpretation. It is about offering advice to counterparts in case of differing opinions and mediation to find a solution.

"GAFTA arbitrations do not take commercial interests into account. Sometimes, one counterparty needs the other one more than the other way around. We have access and visibility to the value of the continued trade relation in addition to the legal standpoint. Our execution service is more about consulting than just passing on emails.

"The third angle is visibility into freight and freight's visibility into brokerage. We have a multimillion-tonne trade book ahead, traded but not executed, plus we hear what the others are trading. We have relatively good visibility in the next six months' trade in certain areas. It offers some unique insights into the freight market and how to evaluate the freight rate correctly."

"You offer a kind of informal mediation service," I suggested.

"When we conduct the business and issue the contracts to both parties," he replied, "we take control of the execution service and the post-trade processes, starting with the vessel nomination and ending with payment. During this process, something often needs solving – big or small.

"The money is not made in catching the last quarter of a dollar per tonne in the port. The money is made by executing efficiently and minimising or avoiding demurrage. We try to control the process thoroughly and then give our opinion as a neutral counterpart in the transaction."

"What is your earliest point of intervention on the brokerage side?" I asked. "Is it ex-farm or ex-terminal?"

"We don't trade with farmers except in countries where farmers have 100,000-plus hectares and are also trading companies. Most of our business is FOB or C&F, but we also deal in rail cars. We sometimes trade containers, and we occasionally trade trucks. We do railway business in countries where rail dominates, like Ukraine and, increasingly, the EU. We previously brokered cargo and rail cars in Russia. It is a question of liquidity. If there is enough liquidity, we broker it.

"The domestic market is usually two-tiered in exporting countries like Denmark, Germany, the Baltics, or Romania. The farmer produces the grain and sells it to an originator, who then transports it to the port, loads it on the vessel, and sells it FOB to an international trader. In some countries, like Poland, it's a three-tier system, with the originator selling it to a local trader who loads it on a vessel and sells it FOB.

"The Northern European markets are over 90 per cent FOB business because the originators don't want to go to destinations. Their function is to identify their first liquid logistical point, usually FOB, and sell the grain FOB to a trading company.

"Sometimes, an end consumer will buy the grain and ship it directly to its destination, where the buyer distributes it to the local processors, feed compounders, flour mills, oil crushers, etc.

"We have recently seen a regionalisation process where global trading companies have lost market share because of compliance requirements and other issues. Some second-tier trading companies are becoming more assertive in specific destination markets. For example, some focus on West Africa or Iran, while others focus on wheat marketing in South America. Not everybody can do everything.

"Sometimes, a trader sells to another trader and then on again. We can see strings of six to ten companies before the grain is lifted and delivered to the destination. It varies."

As a broker, I found that I did the most business when the market was disrupted somehow, either by poor weather or a change in government policy. I wondered whether Indrek agreed that the market has less need for brokers when everything's going well.

"I would add three elements to this disruption," he replied.

"First, you need a healthy amount of volatility in the market. If the markets are flat, traders find it hard to identify trading opportunities. But too much volatility paralyses the business. Unfortunately, we are dealing with a growing amount of volatility in today's markets.

"Second, you need healthy prices. Ukrainian farmers are selling corn today for $85 ex-farm. It's unhealthy. We need a healthy supply chain. It is not sustainable if prices are too low. It starts disrupting the business. The markets are more straightforward for everyone if prices are not too soft and not too high, combined with healthy volatility.

"Third, wars, pandemics and weather disruptions are becoming more frequent. Traders analyse markets, but analytical thinking does little good when trends break. People trained to think analytically – to approach their markets analytically – might be disappointed if a black swan turns up.

"Apart from wars and weather, what is your biggest challenge?" I asked him.

"Recruitment is one of the biggest challenges for brokerage companies," he replied. "There is a global shortage of people. The younger ones are not curious about agribusiness and are more interested in consulting, finance, and start-ups. The problem is acute in Sao Paulo, where demand is growing fast. I hope your book stimulates young people's curiosity about our business."

Peggy Olde Bijvank

On an OTC desk, you must get to know every customer to understand what they're after and how to price it.

Peggy and I have two things in common. We both worked as physical commodity merchants at Cargill before moving to futures brokerage.

I started as a futures trader at Cargill and found it challenging to shift to physical commodity merchandising. I wasn't a good salesperson and didn't enjoy trying to convince people to buy what I was selling. It was not a problem that I had as a futures trader. The liquidity in a futures market is such that there is (almost) always someone willing to buy when you want to sell or sell when you want to buy.

I enjoyed being a futures broker. I built a small group of clients who trusted me to do my best. I never needed to convince my clients to do something. We discussed their hedging and risk strategies together, and I executed them in the market.

My later career move from futures to physical brokerage was quite a shock. I no longer had the futures exchange as a counterparty and had to search out a counterparty each time I had an order. It was no use having just one side of the trade; I had to have both. To do that, I had to have good relations with everyone in the market; it was not easy, as many clients had their preferred brokers.

After three years working as a vegoil merchant with Cargill in Amsterdam, Peggy moved into futures brokerage with the Natixis Bank in London. I told her that I had made a similar move because I preferred the intellectual challenge of the futures markets to physical commodity merchandising. I asked her if she felt the same.

"I moved to London partly for personal reasons," she replied. "Still, I saw it as a huge job opportunity to apply my knowledge of the physical commodities sector to a financial markets role. Natixis was setting up an agricultural brokerage desk for futures and options. They had people for coffee, cocoa, and sugar and took me on for grains.

"I enjoyed working as a physical commodity merchant," she continued. "Cargill has a fantastic culture with a strong entrepreneurial spirit. Cargill taught me to be entrepreneurial. I still benefit from all that today.

"I found the commercial nature of the job fulfilling, and I especially liked the tangibility of it. I could watch the vessels we had chartered arrive in the port of Amsterdam and then depart with the products you have traded aboard. I found it thrilling. So yeah, I enjoyed that.

"My first line manager was an accomplished salesperson. He taught me how to connect with clients and to have different approaches for different clients.

"At Cargill, I was a merchant responsible for their vegetable oil product line. My interactions with our clients were commercial and competitive. I had to understand what the market was doing and watch for whatever everybody else was doing. I had to follow inflows from South America and keep on top of crush margins.

"What was your role at Natixis?" I asked. "And, more widely, what is the role of a futures broker?"

"Unless they have been in the industry," Peggy replied, "most people don't understand futures markets or what a futures broker does.

"There are types of brokers: execution brokers and clearing brokers. The former provides access to the markets and executes trades for clients. They also offer market data and find liquidity.

"Clearing brokers process clients' trades after they have been executed. They hold the client's assets, guarantee the client's obligations and contribute resources to the default fund maintained by the clearing house.

These default funds serve to absorb losses from defaults and protect the sustainability of the future's markets.

Natixis was an execution and clearing broker.

"Although it was a significant change from physicals to derivatives, it was a natural evolution of my previous role. I was also involved in physical commodity financing.

"In 2008, one of our clients, a Brazilian sugar producer, built up a sizeable, short position in the market and couldn't pay his margin calls. The exchange asked the producer to reduce its net position, but they didn't. The exchange held the company in violation of its position limits and instructed brokers only to accept liquidating orders.

"Banks offer significant credit lines to clients, larger than a standalone brokerage house would. During periods of high price volatility, clients need enough credit lines not to be forced to reduce their positions. It is a natural business for banks to finance their clients, whether in the fields or the futures markets.

"This episode brought home to me the responsibility of the clearing member. It made me understand how well the system works and how vulnerable you are as a broker. It is a low-margin business where a client bankruptcy can wipe out your profits for years."

When I started as a futures broker, the commission on one lot of futures was $10 per side, of which we paid $2 per side to the executing floor broker. Over the years, the total commission slipped to $8 and then $6 per side. It is now around $1.50 per side for New York execution and clearing in sugar, but there is no floor brokerage anymore.

"It was challenging for brokers when the trading floors closed," Peggy said. "Clients had direct access to the markets via their office screens and often did their own trading. You could quickly lose contact with them. There were fewer points of contact.

"The more successful brokers understood they needed an edge. Some offered proprietary research. Others specialised in execution, for example, in arbitrage between raw and white sugar or between New York and London cocoa – the tricky stuff. Others competed with lower execution fees, looking to reduce their overheads.

I asked Peggy what she liked and disliked about being a futures broker.

"I liked dealing with many different clients in various sectors," she replied. "I had clients worldwide, from Brazil to Vietnam and Singapore to Europe. I had tradehouses, producers, and corporations as clients. It kept things interesting. I enjoyed socialising and networking, not just with the clients but with others in the markets.

"What I didn't like was that as a futures broker, you deal with a standardised financial product, which can be less attractive than dealing with shiploads of physical commodities.

"Also, as a futures broker, you don't necessarily get to understand a client's strategy. It's what I enjoy most in my current role, where we tailor and bespoke OTCs to individual clients' needs. To do that, we must understand their objective and their strategy. On an OTC desk, you must get to know every customer to understand what they're after and how to price it."

Peggy has worked in OTC sales with Lloyds Bank in London for five years. I asked her how her current position differed from a futures broker's.

"Futures contracts are standardised products," she told me. "They trade on an exchange and require daily margin calls. There's no counterparty risk as the clearing house guarantees them. The clearinghouse is the seller to every buyer and the buyer to every seller. If a counterparty defaults, the clearing house assumes the risk of loss.

"OTC contracts are not standardised but are bilateral and customised agreements between counterparties. They're not traded on the exchange and are often not subject to margin calls. You can customise the parameters of a swap, such as the quantity, the currency, the length, etc. They are always financially settled, whereas futures can be financially or physically settled depending on the market.

"The beauty with OTCs is that liquidity is not restricted to the volumes on the exchange as some market participants will warehouse the risk and not hedge them fully with futures. It means you can sometimes offer more liquidity to your client."

Peggy has had two extended career breaks for maternity leave. After her first career break, she took a one-year return-to-work programme with MacQuarrie Bank to get professionals like her back into the workforce. Still, she was back on maternity leave by the time she finished the programme.

"It's not how these programmes should work," she told me. "But hey, life happens." After another two years off, she applied for her second return role in commodity sales at Lloyds Bank.

"Those two breaks were a big disruption," she told me, "However, they were a positive for my career. They allowed me to do something new and have a different role in the industry. I went from a commodity merchant to a futures broker, from commodity finance to commodity sales.

"Looking back, I'm grateful for my different experiences, but maintaining a career is much easier than restarting one. There is a lack of returners programmes that offer viable re-entry at a suitable level. However, this is changing as the corporate institutions that provide them are beginning to realise they give them a competitive advantage in accessing talent.

"At Lloyds, I am one of the organisers of a pilot sponsorship scheme to support women's career advancement, matching female colleagues with senior leaders to drive diversity, equity, and inclusion. It shows you how sentiment has changed over the years. It would never have happened when I started my career."

"Last question," I said. "Why did you choose commodities as a career?"

"I did a master's degree in business administration from Erasmus University in Rotterdam. Unfortunately, their commodities programme didn't exist then. I decided to study business administration as it provided a comprehensive knowledge base in the field of business. It allowed me to study and work abroad, which I found very appealing.

"I completed internships at Siemens in Germany, Panasonic in Japan, and Shell in Amsterdam. I found those internships helpful as they helped me understand what I liked and disliked in a future job. I'd recommend young people to do as many internships in as varied a range of companies as possible.

"I was keen to work in a fast-paced environment," she continued. "When I saw Cargill's advertisement for graduate trainees, I just knew it was for me."

10. MARKET ANALYSIS AND DATA

As an analyst, I loved going into the cane fields and factories to talk to those who grew and milled the cane.

I remember once, in the early 2000s, visiting a cane mill in India. The country was (and still is) a significant driver in the sugar market. That year, the market was anticipating a good harvest and significant exports. The mill owner agreed with the market sentiment and predicted record exports.

One of the mill's cane buyers took me aside and said, "He's wrong. The cane is not there. Everyone says it is, but I can't buy any. The drought has had much more of an impact than anyone expected."

I asked him if it was a widespread or local phenomenon, and he told me that he had spoken to cane buyers outside his region, and they all reported the same thing.

"India's sugar production this year will be a few million tonnes less than expected," he predicted.

I did my research, talked around various mills, and decided he was right. The Indian crop was going to be much smaller than anticipated. We turned bullish on the world market price and sent a note out to our clients. That chance conversation helped seal our reputation.

But then, it wasn't entirely a chance conversation. As any agricultural commodity analyst will tell you, there is no substitute for getting out into the fields. Big data, satellite imagery, weather forecasting, and artificial intelligence play a role, but you must get your boots dirty.

The Grain Analyst

Analysts are not risk takers; they are risk calculators. They give you the odds, but they won't get involved in taking the risk.

I asked an analyst friend (who preferred not to be named) what skills she needed: mathematics, economics, politics, meteorology, agronomy, programming, and communication.

"All of those and more," she replied. "The job requires as many competencies as you can bring to the table. One essential ability is to know what's important and what's not. That comes with experience.

"The skillset an analyst needs has shifted over the years," she continued. "Sourcing information used to be critical as not all the required information was reported or available. It's the opposite situation today. We're flooded with information and immersed in big data. The tools that allow you to move with agility in this environment have changed."

When I was an analyst, we worked with Excel Sheets. I wondered how that changed in the ten to twelve years since I left the space.

"Don't be fooled," she replied. "There are still a lot of spreadsheets around. Excel is a fantastic tool with extraordinary editorial abilities. You can edit your numbers, move them around, and present them as you wish. However, it is an inferior tool for accurate data analysis. When we talk about big data, we're talking about big files.

"It's a matter of the data you work with, where it resides, and how you can access it. The concept is entirely different. The data now sits where it's well organized and automatically updated. You define the data you need and create an environment where it is kept, checked, and updated.

"You then create an interface to access this data and present it when and how you need it. The interface allows you to ask what you are interested in today: beans, corn, weather, crop conditions, energy prices? You bring what you need to your screen. You work with it and push it back up with your changes once finished. You completely lose the need for files. It becomes an application, a tool you can carry and access anywhere.

"How do the skills you need to be an analyst differ from those you need to be a trader?" I asked her.

"The two roles require two very different people," she replied. "Traders are risk takers, although they may not look at it as risk. Analysts are not risk takers; they are risk calculators. They give you the odds, but they won't get involved in taking the risk."

Commodities traded in silos when I started in the business; you traded wheat, corn, coffee, or sugar. Biofuels removed them from their silos and added new market complexity. I was curious how analysts manage the interaction between agricultural commodity feedstocks, fossil fuels, and politics.

"It's harder and harder to keep it together," she told me. "It's next to impossible. Ironically, it makes us more specialized and less aware of the full pie. We have specialists who closely follow the different sectors. Fifteen or twenty years ago, you could be a generalist and cover it all. But no longer."

"Can you get the information you need from the Internet?" I asked. "Or do your company's trading activities feed you proprietary information?"

"There is a degree of proprietary information," she replied. "Keeping in touch with buyers gives us a good vision of destination demand. It makes it easier to refine our demand estimates, particularly for grains where there can be significant variations. You must go there and talk to people," she added. "There's no substitute for it."

"How do we still get crops so wrong?" I asked her.

"Our climate is changing," she replied. "The weather is becoming more extreme and violent. If it rains, it rains too much; if it's dry, it's super dry; if it's hot, it's mega hot. It is a progression. Every summer, we set records. Every summer now is likely warmer than before, and the crops are sensitive to that.

"For example, we keep losing wheat crops late in the season. It never used to be the case. Wheat was one of the most resilient crops; it was tough to kill. In the last few years, several crops – a Russian, a European, and a US crop – have been decimated in the very late stages. These 32°C+ temperatures are very damaging for crops. Our models are not good at picking that up because it was never the case historically."

"What advice would you give a young person considering joining the business as an analyst?" I asked.

"Remain humble," she replied. "Agricultural commodities offer a challenging environment that's always changing, exposing you to all sorts of new things you need to learn. It's a wonderful space, but you need to be comfortable in waters that change all the time, that give you new challenges that force you to rethink things – and do it with other people as well."

Robin Shaw

You don't have to pay for your mistakes if you're an analyst. You merely have to say you got it wrong, that you're very sorry about last week's report, and then move on.

The first time I met Robin was in 1982, just after S&W Berisfords, the parent company of J H Rayner, had bought British Sugar. Robin hosted various sugar traders to a buffet lunch to celebrate the purchase, and I remember briefly chatting with him. I also remember that they had put enormous sugar beets on the lunch tables. It was the first time that I had ever seen sugar beet.

"Ephraim Margulies was the head trader at J H Rayner," Robin told me. "But he was more interested in cocoa than sugar. Everyone called him 'Old Man Marg'. He was a hard taskmaster. When he took over British Sugar, the then chairman was heard to say: "The next time he comes round here, we will switch off the lifts so that the bugger has a heart attack climbing the stairs".

"I remember once," Robin continued, "Our little sugar team were bullish, and we went to see Marg to ask him to extend our trading limit. He said, "So you think this market's got a bottom, do you?" "And we all said, "Yes, that's it. It's at the bottom." And he replied, "The only bottoms I've ever seen had holes in them." He was completely right. The market then collapsed. He was very, very clever."

"I had joined Rayner in 1980," he said. "It was a bitter experience which drove me to drink. I fled back to Sucden after five years, but Sucden had changed out of all recognition by then. And so had I. I had become an alcoholic. It was a hard-drinking atmosphere in London at that time. I don't know how we all survived. I only did, thanks to Alcoholics Anonymous.

"But why did you leave Sucden in the first place?" I asked. "You had been there for eight successful years."

"It was a pure misunderstanding," he replied. "Maurice Varsano had started trading coffee and moved me to the new coffee desk. He viewed it as a promotion. I viewed it as a demotion. I wanted to stay in sugar and left to go to JH Rayner in London."

"And you went back to Sucden in 1985?" I suggested.

"Yes," he replied. "Maurice had died, and his son Serge had taken over. It was all about Cuba and Russia. Serge had a genuine relationship with Mr. Krivenko from Prodintorg in Russia and Mr. Lezcano in Cuba. They liked each other, and they trusted each other.

"Serge was never a speculator. He didn't like speculating. He let us do it almost as a hobby. Sucden made money by doing big deals. We gave the Russians what they wanted: the safety of knowing they would get enough sugar to supply their domestic demand. We gave Cuba finance that kept them stumbling on."

"Colt Bagley, previously head trader at Cargill and Philipp Brothers, started physical brokerage in 1990," he said. "He came to Paris, and we had lunch. One of the head traders asked him who he had the best relationships with as a trader.

"He said, "What do you mean? We didn't have relationships. If we were cheaper, we sold. If we were more expensive, we didn't."

"No, no," she replied. "That's not how it works. Trading works through friendship. We genuinely became friends with the Russians."

It was in 1990 that I caught up with Robin again. He was by then a huge cheese in the market. I had just set up my little brokerage company and hoped to have Sucden as a client. Unfortunately, Colt Bagley's brokerage company pulled the rug from beneath my feet. He was in another league.

"I left Sucden in 1992," Robin continued. "I set up Czarnikow Rionda with Danny Gutman. We resurrected the name. It's a sombre story. We quickly made a lot of money. We thought we were clever, and then we were foolish.

"We lent money to Brazilian mills against future supply, but they didn't supply. We bought put options from a Chinese company, but they failed to honour the contracts when the market collapsed. Czarnikow Rionda went into bankruptcy in 2000, and I downgraded to becoming an analyst."

"But didn't you trade for yourself at one stage as an independent?" I asked.

"I sold my house in London and speculated with the proceeds. I learnt a helpful lesson: I am a lousy speculator. Robert Kuok once said that good speculators are born, not made. It is a question of character. To be a good speculator, you must be quick to change your mind. You must not be married to your opinions. Vain people don't make good speculators, and I'm rather vain. I think I'm right, and the market's wrong. Humble people make good speculators. Maurice Varsano always used to say that sugar is a school of humility.

Marex approached me, and I joined as a trader," he continued. "I proved for a second time that I was a bad speculator. But they kept me on as an analyst. Once I'd sold my house in London, I was practically destitute. I made much more money from houses than I ever did out of sugar."

It made me think of my grandfather on my mother's side. One of my earliest memories was catching a bus with my mother every Wednesday to Hastings, where her father and mother lived in a one-bedroom flat above a newsagent.

My mother's parents were constantly moving, and she attended sixteen schools before she was sixteen. She lived in cities as diverse as Buenos Aires and Buffalo in New York and used to tell me stories about living in vast houses with maids, cooks, and chauffeurs one day and the next day having to share a bed with her sisters when they moved the next day. Her parents were married in Manaus, Brazil, and he (and his father) made and lost fortunes in the rubber trade.

My great-grandfather was a sea captain. San Francisco awarded him the freedom of the city when he turned his ship's hoses on the fires that sprung up after the great earthquake in 1906. Her father finally lost all his money when the Argentinian leader Peron threw the British out of the country and nationalized the British-owned railways after the Second World War. My grandfather had put all his money into the railways and a British project to build the Buenos Aires underground system.

That's all I know – and, unfortunately, all I will know – about him. Even so, I still considered him a role model. When I left university, I had a choice between two careers: banking and commodity trading. I chose the latter because I thought it would be more exciting: I liked the idea of alternating between rags and riches, but I would have hated the reality of it. It seems that this was what Robin had done throughout his career.

"When I started in Cargill," I told him, "They put me on the futures desk in Minneapolis managing big positions. Everyone talked about beating the market, but I quickly learned it wasn't about beating the market. It was about beating my emotions."

"Right," he said. "And with one addition, a good speculator regards the market as his friend, something he loves. I used to regard the market as my enemy. I wanted to prove that it was wrong, and I was right. It was the wrong approach."

"What advice would you give somebody wanting to become a speculator?" I asked.

"Find out quickly if you have the right character," he replied. "And if you don't, get out quick. There is nothing sadder than seeing intelligent, hardworking people losing money and being swept aside by some brash young idiot who makes money. So don't fight that you may not be a good speculator. Learn about yourself."

I always felt that the job satisfaction of being a trader was terrible. If you get the market right, you either get out too early or too late, or you don't have a large enough position. And if you get it wrong, then you lose money. Robin agreed.

"It's just awful," he told me. "When my son left university, he was looking around, unable to decide about a career. I said, "Why don't you do my job?" And he said you must be crazy. You come home green every night."

"What's the difference between being an analyst and a trader?" I asked.

"You don't have to pay for your mistakes if you're an analyst. You merely have to say you got it wrong, that you're very sorry about last week's report, and then move on. The two emotions, greed and fear, that drive markets apply much less to analysts. You are not as emotional as an analyst. You look at the market in a more cold-blooded way and weigh it up more rationally."

Listening to Robin, I realized he and I have a similar trajectory. I started as a trader and became a broker and then an analyst.

"It's a bit like teaching," Robin said. "Those who can't do, teach. And those that can't teach, teach teachers."

"Now that you are an analyst and not a trader," I asked Robin, "Would you recommend your son today to go into commodity business as an analyst?"

"I think it helps to have been a trader if you want to be an analyst," he replied. "It is almost better if you've been a bad speculator because you can probably understand better what works. It would condemn him to ten years of misery, losing money as a speculator before entering that calm haven of analysis."

"But do you think you must have traded sugar to be a good analyst?" I insisted.

"It certainly helps," he replied. "The only thing that matters is what will push the price up and down. And if you've been a trader, you instinctively know it's the money. You follow the money. An analyst tends to get involved in intellectual conjectures and likes to prove a point or looks at it from an economic point of view."

"What is the hardest bit about being a sugar analyst?" I asked.

"It's judgment," he replied. "You can be crammed full of knowledge, but it doesn't help you if you've got more knowledge than the rest of the market. It also doesn't help you if you're right too early. You can lose as much money, or your clients lose just as much if you see the market six months too early.

"The other thing is that sugar fundamentals are quite a minor part of what moves the market. It's mostly the order flow and the macros, what the funds are doing.

"How did you get into commodities in the first place?" I asked him.

"I studied Russian and French at Oxford," he replied, "I was a Trotskyist by the time I left. I wanted to get to know the working class and got a job in a factory in Leeds, where I learnt that the working class didn't like me, and I didn't like them. I decided to get a proper job, and my father helped me get one in the City of London in vegetable oil brokerage. My father was a diplomat.

"I wanted to use my language skills and applied for a job with Sucden in Paris. At the time, the sugar trade houses never traded with each other – they concentrated on brokering government-to-government deals between exporters and importers. Vegetable oils were more about trading – and the various trade houses traded with each other. I had the bright idea that I could apply it to sugar. I went to Paris for an interview and got the job.

"At that time, everything was done at government tender. We were good at tenders. We had brilliant agents everywhere and were willing to put people on planes to be present at the tender. It gave us a kind of edge, especially if you had somebody on the inside telling you if you dropped your price by $2, you'd win. It was part of the bribery."

"I never won a tender as a physical trader at Cargill," I told Robin. He shrugged.

"Final question," I said. "Could you describe a typical workday for you now as an analyst?"

"I don't want to," he replied. "I'd get the sack."

Sacha Prost

AI will do the work for you and the chat box will answer immediately. It will take time to be 100 per cent reliable, but we will get there.

I was surprised when Agflow contacted me to ask if I would be interested in interviewing their new CEO, Sacha Prost. I have known the company for many years and, at one stage, have considered investing in it. James Dunsterfield, the company's founder, is an old acquaintance, but the company had so far failed to find its wings and take off. Would a young, dynamic, tech-savvy CEO provide the magic to make it fly?

"Agflow was probably launched too early – ahead of its time," Sacha admitted, "but it is now well-positioned to harvest its potential."

Although only young, Sacha is already a serial entrepreneur. Straight from school, he founded a fashion brand with his brother Nicholas, drawing on his family's motor-racing heritage.

"It was my first entrepreneurial venture," he told me. "I always had an entrepreneurial fibre through school, and one day, we came up with a clothing brand that transcended the glamour and values of Formula One and motor racing in general. It was a great adventure. You learn so much when you try to do things by yourself. Every step in building the brand helped me understand how businesses work and how I wanted our company to run."

A few years ago, Sacha set up a consulting company for digital marketing, acquisition, and business consulting projects. He worked for some private equity firms and began to make a name for himself in technology and private equity in the Geneva region. When Agflow's previous CEO left, a board member approached him for the position.

"I sometimes miss the glittering glamour of the fashion industry," he told me. "But I have always been interested and intrigued by agricultural commodities and how grains move worldwide. Being a complete freshman in the sector gave me a bit of an edge as the CEO of a data provider; I was able to see things a bit differently."

"How differently?" I asked.

"You question everything when you don't know anything," he replied. "Through that process, you identify things that work well and don't work. You look with fresh eyes at the areas that have the most potential. You must come in with a super-open mind and listen as much as possible, especially at the beginning."

I asked Sacha what his biggest challenge was so far.

"We've had several challenges," he admitted. "One was to revamp our pricing strategy entirely. It was the first thing I identified. CEOs have different backgrounds, but I consider myself a marketing person. I like to sell things. I believe I am sensitive to understanding what clients will be satisfied with. I won't relent until they are.

"I saw that our churn rate was too high, not because the product wasn't right, but because our pricing was skewed. I said, let's look at how we could do our pricing. We need to be entirely transparent about our pricing model because pricing should not depend on who the client is. You can't charge different people different prices for the same product. We revised the pricing model, fragmenting everything by product and commodity. If you are looking at soybean meal and only want tenders and quotes, you should pay for that. You shouldn't pay for the entire platform if you're not using it.

"We also had to improve our customer relations. You may have an issue with a product or a product that flops. It happens in business. We don't live in a fairy tale. But we must communicate correctly with our clients, listen to them, and understand their needs.

"Businesspeople often invest heavily in marketing the wrong product and ignore a more profitable product, quietly selling itself. You must identify and focus on the right products. We're in that phase now.

"There have been some tough choices, and we have had to let some people go, but the team must fit correctly. It's like a football team. Sometimes, it's not about having only star players. You need players who can play together.

"On the personal side, it has been challenging to understand what is essential in the data and what isn't. It takes at least 4 to 6 months to fully understand when people told me something had potential when it didn't."

I was curious whether Agflow added value to the raw data through proprietary analysis. Or did they only sell raw data?

"We are not analysts," he told me. "We stay as impartial as possible. We work with a network of more than 150 contributors and can give you a view of what the market is doing at a particular time and place for a specific commodity. Our methodology is our differentiator – it differentiates us from our competitors.

"We see a lot of new applications when it comes to our data," he continued. "Our clients, ranging from FMCG companies to hedge funds, are extremely fond of our data because they use it to build the best models. Using an analyst's price is like having twice the analysis if you're a hedge fund. We provide access to raw data through our API solutions."

"How are you using AI?" I asked. "It seems an obvious application."

"We are working on a chatbot that can prompt reports within our database," he said. "We aggregate many reports that our clients can access, but instead of reading them all, they can ask the chat box a specific question. We limit it to our database to make sure it doesn't hallucinate. It tells you where it obtained the information when it answers a question. It won't give you an answer if it doesn't have the information.

"I see a world where clients will have an app and be able to ask questions. We are working to be ready for that. However, the commodities industry is not as fast-paced as some other industries. Clients still ask for an Excel sheet emailed to them every day. We can still do that.

"AI won't give us data; our methodology will still do that. AI will help us acquire, clean, and deliver the data to our clients."

I was beginning to understand the company's direction of travel. If you wanted to know, for example, the cheapest source of oil seeds for your plant in Portugal, the chat box would give you the answer.

"Exactly," Sacha replied. "Instead of working your way through a table with different origins, delivery months, qualities, and price quotes, AI will do the work for you and the chat box will answer immediately. It will take time to be 100 per cent reliable, but we will get there."

Five Questions for John Stansfield

Could you share what you do today and your career journey so far?

My first foray into the sugar market was long ago at Louis Dreyfus when they told me to move from the Grain Department to Sugar. I was initially a grain analyst, covering UK wheat and barley. LDC asked me to sit on the sugar desk and learn about sugar. Somebody threw me the Kingsman report to read. It was my first introduction to the sugar market!

I've been in sugar analysis for around 30 years, working for various trade houses and hedge funds. I am now an independent analyst for Denex, a digital platform based in Switzerland. We aim to simplify data collection and provide more efficient ways of analysing the market. We cover agricultural commodities such as grains, oilseeds, and sugar.

How have information providers evolved over the years regarding what they offer?

Everybody's always been looking for the basics of crop analysis and trade flow data,

Data providers have moved downstream and now do more crop survey work. Your data provider now has a better handle on crops than in the past when only tradehouses had the complete overview of crop numbers. People can now access crop information more readily than in the past.

The provision of trade flow data hasn't changed significantly over the last twenty years. Going forward, I see room for a digital platform to consolidate trade flow data and make it more straightforward to assemble a consolidated trade flow.

We're trying to forecast crops, and I'm unsure how big data helps. You've got to get your feet dirty, get out on the ground, and try to understand acreage. That's where errors can occur. You don't notice the switches from one crop to another if you're not on the ground. Fundamental analysts have a critical role and will, hopefully, survive!

Did you ever trade?

It's a difficult question to answer as it depends on what you mean by 'trade'. If you work for a hedge fund, which I did, you provide trade ideas to a portfolio manager and then to a team of execution traders. There have been brief periods during my career when I have run a small proprietary book. It can be fun, but you can spend too much time screen watching. So, I've always stepped back, providing trade ideas for the execution traders or the portfolio manager. People not involved in the business struggle with the difference between a trader and an analyst. I think the best traders are also analysts. So, it's a merger of the two.

What's a common mistake people make when analysing the market?

They are not spending enough time understanding consumption. It's easier to follow crop numbers. Consumption involves a detailed analysis of monthly stocks, imports, and exports. It's hard work. The other problem is that people consume white sugar, not raw sugar; monitoring white sugar trade flows is more complicated than monitoring raw sugar trade flows. The key to success is to get to grips with the white sugar balance sheet, which flows back into a raw sugar balance sheet. It's been a massive issue for the last seven or eight years, with consumption falling in the developed world.

The challenge with consumption data is that an error can multiply through your balance sheet. A considerable demand shock, like COVID-19, can impact the quality of your consumption analysis. Consumption sets a good analyst apart from a poor analyst. The trade house analysts are often the best as they see the white sugar flows.

What advice would you give someone struggling to stay on top of market analysis?

I would advise them to continually look for new information and to stay on top of production, not just in the key countries, but in the top twenty producers.

Get out into the field, meet producers, and build relationships. One thing that has benefited me over the years is that the trade houses I've worked for have allowed me to travel. To understand production, you must get out there and meet cane and beet producers. The meeting at the mill is vital to understanding the market.

If you are a trader and expect your analysts to build a decent balance sheet, take them with you when you meet your clients in the supply chain.

My daughter Charlotte conducted this interview as part of the ECRUU series of podcasts.

11. PROCUREMENT

Although people often confuse the two roles, procurement is different from trading. Procurement focuses on acquiring inputs for operational continuity at optimal costs and quality, while trading centres on making profits through market transactions and speculating on commodity prices.

Procurement professionals acquire the goods and services a company needs to operate. The role revolves around internal supply chain management: identifying qualified suppliers and negotiating with them; managing transport logistics and inventories; budgeting and controlling costs; and ensuring procurement practices meet environmental, social, and regulatory standards.

Traders buy and sell commodities for profit. As we saw earlier, they take advantage of mispricing in the supply chain. They also take advantage of times when the market misprices the commodity's outright (flat) price. However, that does not mean that traders do not add value to society.

In his 1776 book, The Wealth of Nations, the Scottish philosopher Adam Smith wrote that an economy works best in a free-market scenario where everyone operates in their own interest. He argued that self-interested competition in a free market benefits society by making the market more efficient.

Traders and procurement professionals are similar in using market analysis to monitor market conditions, price trends, and global supply-demand dynamics to make decisions. They use futures and financial instruments to hedge and manage their price risks. They use market volatility to lock in forward prices or hedge.

Procurement professionals differ from traders because they can only buy, while traders can buy and sell. However, food processing companies are structurally short of the market; they must purchase commodity inputs to feed their factories and supply their customers. The quantity a procurement professional buys and when depends on how short the company wants to be.

Senior managers may put rules in place that allow a procurement professional to buy a maximum of one year forward, but they rarely stipulate when in the year they should buy.

Commodity prices usually move in anticipation of a situation, often solving the problem before it arises. As such, agricultural markets frequently trade 18 months forward. They are, after all, 'futures' markets; they trade the future, not the present. The one-year rule leaves the company exposed to price movements beyond that period.

One procurement professional I spoke with told me that procurement is about building long-term relationships with trusted suppliers. He argued that the mispricing that traders take advantage of is almost always short-term. Although that may be true, physical commodity traders must develop long-term relationships with suppliers and customers. Traders cannot trade without them. They are always careful not to burn bridges.

Lastly, I have spent many hours in meetings with procurement professionals at big food companies and was sometimes frustrated that they spent so much time setting their annual purchasing budgets. However, food processors must evaluate their employees' performance and set their KPIs. Beating a budget is often the best way to do that.

I will let them take up the story from here.

The Coffee Buyer

You need to understand and master the complexity of what you are buying. But you also need to be on top of how you communicate within the company.

A friend of mine is a coffee buyer for a roasting company. He agreed to participate in this project but preferred not to be named. However, his comments about procurement are interesting.

"Procurement is complex, with often competing goals," he told me. "I have social and environmental sustainability targets. I have quality, which is essential, and price and supply security.

"I must align my procurement targets to our business targets. I must deliver value for money when I purchase quality coffee, but I must also meet our business targets regarding the company's environmental and social goals. I don't feel that there is a conflict. Supply is a continuous challenge. What is the crop? How will El Nino or climate change impact production? Should we be concerned about political instability in some of our origins? We try to anticipate things, although we are not always successful.

"It must be challenging to set budget targets when the markets for coffee and freight are so volatile," I asked him.

"At least on our side, the company fully integrates the budget into the business. It's all about communication. We need to explain the environment so that targets reflect its complexity. Our responsibility is to present, explain, educate, and eventually influence the process. We need to have a seat at that table.

"The target setting is usually a good discussion if we adequately explain our context. It's a realistic discussion. We prepare. We're communicating in advance the potential impact market changes might have on pricing next year so that the targets do not surprise us.

"Do we challenge? Yes, we always do. But if we adequately prepare these discussions, the finance and business sides of the company acknowledge the complexity we're in."

"How has procurement changed over the years?" I asked him.

"It has evolved dramatically in the 20 years I have been in the sector," he replied. "Companies used to consider it a support function, but now fully integrate it as central to the organisation. Companies view procurement as a function that adds value."

"What advice would you give to a someone starting a career in procurement?" I asked.

"The "what" is essential in procurement," he told me. "You need to understand and master the complexity of what you are buying. But you also need to be on top of how you communicate within the company. You must share what procurement can bring to the table and demonstrate that it is central to the organisation."

Miguel Costa

My hair turned white on 24th February 2022. "Before the Russian invasion, Ukraine supplied 85 per cent of the sun oil imports into Europe

One of the great things about writing this book is that I met interesting people and learnt about different businesses. However, after more than forty years following the sector, I rarely encountered a company I had never heard of, especially one as big as Sovena. Shame on me!

Sovena Group is one of the largest Portuguese agribusiness holding companies, covering the entire value chain from the fields on the farm to the shelves in the supermarket with brands such as Oliveira da Serra, Andorinha, Fula and Olivari, amongst others. The origin of this group dates to 1871 when Alfredo da Silva founded Companhia União Fabril (CUF), and today, after many acquisitions, mergers, and divestitures, this family-run group is led by the fifth-generation descendant, Jorge de Mello.

The company has four interrelated business areas: olive oil, olives, vegetable oil, and biodiesel. It has also recently invested in healthy foods and snacks by acquiring Centazzi, owner of the brand Salutem. It has factories in Portugal, Spain, the USA, Colombia, and Angola and operates farms in Argentina, Morocco, Spain, and Portugal.

Oilseed crushing is still the company's core business. Miguel oversees the division from the company's headquarters in Lisbon. He is responsible for the supply chain for the group's commodities division, from production to refined oils for everything that is not olive oil: sunflower, soy, rapeseed, avocado, and speciality oils.

He describes his role as 'trading around an asset'.

"We are an industrial company with a trading arm to enhance profitability," he told me over a video call. "We look at the spreads between the different oils and sometimes arbitrage between them, but we don't take speculative positions on FOB Brazil or Argentina. If I cannot buy seeds in Spain or import them, I might buy them in France or Romania and exit those positions when I purchase the physicals to execute the cargoes to our plants."

"Sunflowers are our main commodity, but we don't have a futures market. The closest we have is the Six Ports* sun oil, the FOB Dutch mill for rape oil, and the MATIF for rapeseed.

"So, your primary objective is not to make money trading," I suggested, "but to keep your factories supplied and running."

"Yes," he replied, "but not at any cost. There is no point running a plant at capacity if we cannot earn a margin that at least contributes to fixed costs. We look at the market every day and calculate our replacement costs. What is the oil worth? What are the seeds? What is our margin? Can we lock in that margin by selling the oil and the meal to the domestic or export markets?

"Importing seeds doesn't make sense if we are not making $1 above our variable costs. Instead, we can import oil, refine it, and bottle it. I won't put seeds into the plant pipeline just because I have an asset to run.

"We are the brand leaders in Portugal, with around 45 per cent of the market, so we have a responsibility to meet our needs. We treat our private-label customers the same way. If we commit to delivering oil, we will do whatever it takes to ensure the customer has it."

Miguel began his career in 1996 with Continental Grain in Geneva, working on soybean execution. He had always wanted to be a trader, and Conti offered him a trainee trader position just before Cargill bought the company in 1999. Sadly, Cargill told Miguel he would have to stay in operations. He left to take a position in freight brokerage, hoping that some freight experience would help him reach his objective of becoming a trader.

"When Bunge opened an office in Geneva three years later, they asked him to join them, along with many of his ex-colleagues from Continental. He started on veg oil execution but moved on to the Black Sea grain desk, originating wheat, corn, and barley from Russia, Ukraine, Romania, and Bulgaria."

As mentioned above, Bunge has a toll crush agreement with Sovena in Lisbon. In 2007, Sovena sought someone to handle their soft seed crush operations in Lisbon. Miguel took the position and stayed with the company for four years before rejoining Bunge to manage their crush and food operations in Italy. He then accepted the challenge of building and operating the EMEA high oleic sunflower value chain from Hungary. He then rejoined Sovena in 2017.

I asked Miguel how he managed during and after Russia's invasion of Ukraine.

"My hair turned white on 24th February 2022," he answered. "Before the Russian invasion, Ukraine supplied 85 per cent of the sun oil imports into Europe.

"We obtained alternative supplies, mainly from Romania and Bulgaria. The resilience and the capacity of Ukrainian suppliers to work around different supply routes were unbelievable. Over the past three years, the country has done a fantastic job by exporting directly from their ports or via transhipment into the Danube into smaller ports or through Constanza or Poland.

"Unfortunately, I don't know whether they can continue doing that. You've seen the pushback from neighbouring countries, such as Poland, Romania, and Bulgaria, over Ukrainian imports. The farmers in these countries want to ban imports. It will become challenging if Ukraine cannot fully reopen its ports.

"Ukraine was once the leading producer of sunflower seeds. In the years leading up to the war, annual production increased from 10 to 17 million tonnes. It has since fallen back to 14.5 million. At the same time, Russia increased production to 18 million tonnes when it had always been a couple of million tonnes behind Ukraine.

"We also imported sunflower seeds from a project in Argentina where, with our local partners, we rent land and produce sunflowers. By leveraging our production and buying from third parties, we assembled around 50,000 tonnes of Argentinian seeds that we imported into Europe. That year, we did about 45 to 50 per cent of Argentinian seed exports.

"Today, we manage about 12,000 hectares of land with our partner on sunflower production. We are not farmers and don't trade the other crops in the field rotation. Our Argentine partner manages around 100,000 hectares, and we put sunflowers in that rotation.

"Argentina crushes most of its seed production, about 3.5 – 4 million tonnes, and exports the oil as crude or refined. We were interested in growing seeds near the port, south of Buenos Aires, and exporting them to supply our European plants.

"We only import seeds into our European crush plants if it makes economic sense. If it doesn't, we stop our plants and import oil. It is the same thing with Argentina but in reverse. If it makes sense to export seeds, we do, but if we get better prices, we sell them locally. We have done both over the past few years.

"We have tried to do some kind of toll crush agreement in Argentina to test if exporting the oil instead of the seeds would make sense. It's tricky as you're competing with the big grain groups, and they will not give you crush capacity for free. From an economic point of view, it's challenging to make sense of crushing at somebody else's plant.

"Our plant in Lisbon is at the port, and we have about 14 meters of draft. We can take Panamax or Capesize vessels, up to 100,000 tonnes. We have two crush plants on our Lisbon site, one dedicated to soybeans and the other to soft seeds. We also have another soft seed crush plant in Spain, near Cordoba and manage a 3rd one in north Spain via a JV with our partner ACOR.

"Soybeans are not our core business; the driver is meal production, not oil. We are a vegetable oil company. We have a toll crush agreement with Bunge on beans, where we manage the soybean crush plant industrially, and they manage the commercial side.

"We also partner with Bunge in rapeseed/canola crush, handled via Bio Colza, a joint-venture company. Bunge markets our rapeseed meal into the Portuguese market as it is mid-protein and closer to the soybean meal market, and we manage the oil flow. We manage 100 per cent of our sunflower operations.

"About 80 per cent of our meal production goes into the domestic market, but we also export to northern Europe. If I'm crushing at 100 per cent sunflower seed capacity, I must export meal as the domestic market is too small. It goes entirely to animal feed."

"What's your biggest challenge?" I asked Miguel. "What keeps you awake at night?"

"For the last couple of years, many things!" he replied. We deal mainly with sunflower seeds, so what has happened in the Black Sea over the past two years has been very worrying.

"Looking forward, the US elections in November could dramatically affect US support for Ukraine. It could be a game changer for the sun oil market.

"And in the long term, we are concerned about climate change's impact on agricultural production."

- Six ports are a cash assessment reflecting the value of crude sunflower oil loading on a FOB 6 ports (Rotterdam, Amsterdam, Antwerp, Ghent, Dunkirk, or Dieppe) basis for forward periods from the month ahead to twelve months ahead.

Sherif Abdeen

We are not traders. We are a manufacturing company. Our risk policy restricts the risk we can take, led by the treasury and the board committees.

When Al-Waleed bin Talal (who Time magazine called the Arabian Warren Buffett) cofounded Savola in 1979, he said he wanted the group to become the 'Nestlé of the Middle East. It is now one of the largest food companies in the region and has branded retail vegoils in Egypt, Saudi, Algeria, and Turkey. The group owns Panda, the largest grocery retailing chain in the Middle East. It has been investing in food businesses in the past couple of years, buying Bayara in spices and nuts and Al Kabeer in processed and frozen foods. Savola has a pasta business in Egypt and will soon go into snacks.

The company owns and operates two sugar refineries, one in Jeddah, Saudi Arabia, and the other in Sukna, Egypt, as well as a 160,000 mt sugar beet factory in Egypt with 20,000 hectares of sugar beet.

Sherif Abdeen is the company's Chief Strategic Sourcing & Supply Officer. He studied Economics at the American University in Cairo and joined Cargill in 2001. His first job with them was selling sugar locally to industrial users. He told me it was the most challenging job he had ever had as there were five or six millers all selling the same product. Cargill then transferred him to Geneva, where he spent a year and a half on the futures desk, surrounded, in his words, by the best traders in the business. He called his eighteen months in Geneva "the foundation of his career."

Cargill then sent him back to Cairo as a sugar trader before transferring him to their Dubai office, where he spent eight years. He joined

Savola in 2018, returning to Cairo and becoming the general manager for their Egyptian operations.

"I had four roles there," he told me. "One was to run the 850,000 mt refinery. The second was to run the company's Egyptian 160,000 mt sugar beet mill. The third was to manage beet production on 20,000 hectares of sugar beet. My fourth role was to manage the company's sugar risk for Saudi and Egypt.

"It was challenging in Egypt to compete with the state-owned and private mills, where everything is in local currency. Still, we were able to switch almost 100 per cent of our raw sugar imports into white sugar exports to manage the forex issue."

In March 2024, Savola promoted Sherif to his current position, overseeing sugar, vegetable oils, and wheat procurement for all of Savola's assets, including the two refineries. Savola buys about 2.1 million mt of raw sugar per year: 850,000 mt for Egypt and 1.3 million mt for Jeddah in Saudi Arabia.

"Have you ever run out of sugar?" I asked him.

"We have never had a forced shutdown," he replied. "However, we have had to reshuffle our maintenance programs. We have at least 21 days of maintenance each year. When the market inverses are significant, we can wash out (sell back) our prompt vessels and bring forward the maintenance period.

"Our warehouse capacity is about 350,000 mt between the two facilities," he continued. "We're not like other Middle Eastern refineries with massive warehousing, but we don't need it in our business model because we have a local market to trade. It helps us manage the pipeline more efficiently. We have a high market share in Saudi and Egypt.

"Both refineries run 90 per cent of the time at full capacity. Because of our size, we manage a vast pipeline. We used to buy one year ahead regardless of the spreads, with one or two monthly vessels for each, but we now manage the pipeline according to how we see the spreads moving.

"In 2020 and 2021, we had decent carrying charges and increased our stocks to the maximum. We saw massive inverses in the past three years and significantly reduced our stocks. When we do this, we risk running out of raw sugar if anything goes wrong with the next vessel.

"Still, we deal with top-notch suppliers, and it has never happened even though port congestion at load can cause long delays. Sometimes, vessels wait two months or more to load. However, we buy arrival windows, leaving it to the traders to take care of. We don't charter vessels.

"We have been lucky that the high white premiums paid off most of the inverses in the past two years.

"In addition, we always have the option to part ship with our other assets to manage the pipeline. It is more cost-efficient to buy separately for each refinery. However, we always maintain the option of a second-port discharge if something goes wrong with any shipment.

"We used to buy every shipment based on a two-port discharge, but it costs us more as Jeddah has a shallower draft, and we have to take a smaller vessel. In Egypt, the largest vessel we've taken was an 87,000 mt Panamax, although the draft can take up to 100,000 mts. The maximum we can take in Jeddah is 50,000 mt. The draft is shallow, but the authorities are currently dredging the port, and in the coming 18 months, we should be able to take larger-sized vessels.

"Do you buy exclusively from Brazil, or have you taken other origins?" I asked.

"Mercosur origins benefit from a reduced import duty into Egypt. However, as you get the import duty back when you export, we can buy from anywhere.

"Saudi Arabia has no import duty on sugar. When Indian raw sugar was at a discount to Brazilian raw sugar, we bought and imported four or five cargoes. The quality and the price drive us. These are the two factors that matter to us. So, whatever we find an opportunity, we go for it."

The world price of raw sugar is volatile. I asked Sherif how he managed to keep a stable refined sugar price for Savola's customers.

"The Egyptian local market is not completely correlated with the world market," he told me. "The country produces two-thirds of its consumption locally. Many variables impact the local price, including governmental sales of subsidised sugar through ration cards.

"The Saudi market is almost 100 per cent correlated to the world market, and the impact of the volatility is high. Most of our B2B clients in Jeddah buy on a premium basis, and we price them on a BEO basis. The customers take the price risk.

"We use various risk management tools, such as futures, options, and OTCs, for our B2C flat-price sales. We hedge and manage the price risk ourselves, and we price forward to ensure the visibility of our costs. In Egypt, we manage 100 per cent of our price risk ourselves.

"We export more from our production in Egypt than from Saudi Arabia's. We are talking about 7-800,000 mt of collective export program between both. We use all modes of shipment. We sell from Jeddah to Jordan, Egypt to Libya, and Sudan by truck. We also book containers and charter vessels.

"If you got bullish on the market," I asked, "would you price more than one year in advance?"

"No," he replied. "We have a rigid risk policy. We are not traders. We are a manufacturing company. Our risk policy restricts the risk we can take, led by the treasury and the board committees. It governs how far forward we can buy and limits us to a maximum of one year. We have a rigid approval process regarding how, when and who we buy from. The refineries are not in the business of speculation.

"It's the difference between trading and procurement," he continued. "Procurement is about the process. Trading is about position taking."

Michael Duspiwa

I see opportunities in terms of quality rather than quantity. For example, we have developed cattle feed that reduces the cattle's methane emissions. It's an excellent product.

Michael works for Fixkraft, a compound animal feed manufacturer founded in 1971. The company is Austria's second largest feed producer in volume – and the largest privately-owned one. The company has facilities in Enns, a port on the Danube River with railway access, and is close to a highway.

Michael got into the business by accident. He attended a tourism school, so he knows how to cook, but he always wanted to do something internationally. In 2010, he worked for six months in Ukraine as an intern in Donetsk, where he learned Russian. When he returned to Austria, he took a job with a small Austrian grain trading company looking for a Russian-speaking trader. He started with them as a junior trader in Russian origination.

"In my first months with the company," Michael told me, "I participated in a business trip to Morocco, even though I didn't know anything. The company had a client in Casablanca purchasing around a million tonnes of corn every year. He asked me what I thought of the market. I managed to give him an answer, but I thought, "Wow, it's nice that he asked me." In other industries, they look at you, see that you're new and have no clue, and then talk to the older guys with more experience. But no, he genuinely wanted my opinion.

"The company then sent me to Algeria to try to open some markets," he continued. "I also worked with Iran on grains and oilseeds. As you know, commodity trading is about contracts, and you don't see the physical grains. I thought getting a little bit closer to the goods would be nice, so after three years, I moved to an Austrian apple juice concentrate manufacturer, buying apples in Poland, Hungary, Romania, and Ukraine.

"It was interesting but different to the grain business. There was no forward business, no futures, nothing. If you offered a reasonable price, the trucks turned up at your plant. If your prices were too low, they went to your competitor. It made it linear. I missed the grains business, so in 2019, when the opportunity came up with Fixkraft, I grabbed it."

"How do the different types of animal feed vary?" I asked him. "Is pig feed different from cattle feed, for example?"

"Yes, absolutely," he replied. "Both in terms of nutrients and legal requirements. There are different legal requirements depending on the type of animal feed. For example, you can use GM soybeans for pigs but not poultry. Most of our feed goes to poultry, where we cannot use GMOs. For cattle, on the other hand, we are restricted to European-origin meals. I can buy Brazilian non-GM feed for poultry but must purchase European non-GM soymeal for cattle.

"It is diverse," he explained. "Non-GM European-origin meals would work for everything, but they are the most expensive option. You could use non-GM European soybean meal for pig feed, but you wouldn't sell a kilo because it would be too costly.

"We use Danube-soy-certified soymeal for laying hens. They require meals exclusively grown in Europe. Depending on the price, we also use some high-protein, mid-protein GM and non-GM soy. The price plays a role here. We use eight, maybe nine, different types of soya in our production. And we must keep them separate.

"Is your objective to obtain the right mix of carbohydrates and proteins at the best possible price," I asked. "Or is it more complicated than that?"

"There is the legal side I have already mentioned," he answered. "But there are some further issues, such as the permitted level of toxins. We need to track them, particularly in corn.

"Some farmers believe that they can do on the farm what we do in a compound feed factory by mixing their homegrown grains with soya. It does work. I'm not saying it's wrong, but they do not have the analysis. It's a natural product, and corn has different humidity and starch levels.

"Our customers often require specific feeds for their animals. There are so many factors in raising livestock. It's not just feed; it's also the water and the heating. We have harsh winters here in Austria, and with high energy prices, farmers may reduce the heating, which can affect livestock growth.

"We also look at the amino acids in the soya. We use synthetic amino acids to make the feed more easily digestible for the animals. And there it becomes a kind of rocket science.

"Do you have computer programs that help you?" I asked. "Is it something artificial intelligence could help you with in the future?"

"To a certain extent, yes," he replied. "We have a computer program that gives you the best mix for the best price. You enter the costs and the products available, and you press Start. It then shows you the cheapest combination for each breed of animal. However, there are certain aspects that the computer program does not measure. For example, we add sugar beet pulp pellets or apple pomace to our cattle feed. Neither calculates financially, but it is hard to quantify how much taste is worth.

"Artificial intelligence will struggle with customer needs. If one of our customers has a problem, we visit them and try to find a solution together. Sometimes, it's obvious, like increasing the heating or changing the air filter; sometimes, it is more complicated, and we may call a veterinarian to help.

"For cattle, we also need to analyse the farmer's grass. If the grass is dark green, it will have a lot of protein, and we can lower the protein in the compound feed. We must analyse the corn for pig feed if the farmer uses his own corn.

"How many inputs would go into feed for dairy cattle," I asked. "Five, ten?"

"Much more!" he replied. "And as I mentioned, we work with our clients to get the proper feed for them. We also do niche feed products, for example, for deer."

I wanted to know whether he hedged the price risk on his inputs.

"My favourite hedge is when we buy the raw material and sell the compound immediately," he told me. "In most cases, it is not possible."

"How I hedge depends on the product," he continued. "There are some products where I feel comfortable working with futures. Matif wheat correlates well with feed wheat, especially regarding new crops.

"It is more complicated for corn. Many German producers use Matif wheat to hedge their corn. They say it works for them. I have had bad experiences with Matif corn futures due to a lack of liquidity.

"Sometimes, I do physical hedges on corn. I buy corn delivered on a barge to my factory and sell it elsewhere.

"Soya bean meal is more complicated. In the last two years, there has been a poor correlation between Chicago and non-GM soy, and you could lose a lot of money. If the euro/dollar exchange rate is stable, it's easier for GM soy because I can hedge it on the CBOT. I prefer to keep my hedges in euros, so I use physicals to hedge, buying a delivered physical barge and selling the same quantity in the port."

"Do you sometimes buy full cargoes of soybeans?" I asked.

"We are unfortunately too small for that," he replied. "Our trading business is not that big. We sometimes buy a part cargo, maybe a hold of 5,000 tonnes, but it would be the maximum.

"How has the Russian invasion of Ukraine impacted your business?" I asked.

"My job was easy when I first started with Fixkraft," he told me. "Things started to get messy regarding availability when the Covid pandemic hit in 2020. Nobody knew whether the trade flows would continue, or the borders would close.

"In January 2022, I told one of my colleagues that the pandemic was over and we would enter a calm period again. The Russians invaded Ukraine a month later, and I realised the pandemic had just been a warmup. All hell broke loose. Price volatility exploded, and you couldn't buy anything. Suppliers didn't know if they could deliver. Nobody was selling.

"We had three contracts that specified Ukrainian origin. Our suppliers could have claimed force majeur because of the war. But everyone delivered. They executed the contracts even though they were at a lower price than the market. They said, "Please understand it's not easy, but we will deliver."

"One supplier told me he couldn't find truck drivers. He had the cargo in Ukraine but said males between 18 and 60 could not leave the country. Somehow, he found a guy who was 62 years old. They pulled him back from retirement, got him in a truck, and three days later, he delivered the cargo. These guys value their business relationships. I will not forget that. But I had never seen anything like it regarding volatility and market movements.

"Did any of your supply chains break?" I asked. "Was there ever any risk that farm animals wouldn't get enough to eat?"

"Many of our customers called us to ask if we could deliver," he replied. "And we said, "Yes, we can."

"We had a temporary challenge with mono-calcium phosphate. A raw material for mono calcium phosphate is only produced in Russia, as one supplier had his account frozen and couldn't deliver. We found other suppliers at a higher price. The market worked; we all managed, and the trade continued.

"How many countries do you buy products from?" I asked.

"The market is global, and it's a matter of how you define the origin. Our GM beans become soybean meal when crushed in Germany or the Netherlands. But the beans are from the US and Brazil. They are not of European origin.

"We do not use palm oil, so we don't import from Indonesia or Malaysia. We get amino acids and vitamins from China, which we buy from traders because we are not yet big enough to ship from mainland China. The goods might come from China, but our partners are German, Italian, Spanish, and Swiss trading companies.

"Indian soybean meal occasionally finds its from India to Europe. We get phosphates from Russia and Morocco.

"I would say we have business partners in about 30 countries. It is a truly global business.

I was beginning to understand that Michael had so many different inputs he could easily find a substitute in the case of a shortage or price spike in one of them. It effectively meant that the supply chain for animal feed was very flexible.

"That's true to a certain extent," he said. "Some inputs substitute well based on relative prices. If wheat is cheaper than corn, you use more wheat.

"But there are limits. For corn-fed chickens, 50 per cent of the feed must come from corn. Some of our feed comes with unique ingredients like sugar beet pulp pellets. We can't replace them.

"You can substitute sunflower meal with rapeseed meal, but to obtain a high protein feed, you need soymeal. You cannot reach the required amount of protein with a rapeseed meal.

"Some inputs you cannot substitute, like vitamins or phosphate.

The Netherlands is working to reduce its livestock numbers to meet its GHG emission targets. I wondered if Michael could see the same thing happening in other EU countries and how it would affect his business if it did.

"In general, we see meat consumption declining," he said. "But it will only have a limited impact on animal feed demand. However, it could result in a consolidation of the animal feed industry in Austria.

"I see opportunities in terms of quality rather than quantity. For example, we have developed cattle feed that reduces the cattle's methane emissions. It's an excellent product.

"Also, for animal welfare reasons, there is a trend towards slower-growing breeds, especially poultry. There is also a trend for animals to spend more time outside, where they grow more slowly. They need feeding for a longer time.

"What is the greatest challenge in your business?" I asked.

"To keep our production running," he answered. "We have customers who need daily deliveries. My worst-case situation would be if we halted production due to flooding, low water levels, border closures, etc.

"My second most significant challenge is price. Our target is not to always have the lowest price but to always have a lower price than our competitors.

"My third challenge is maintaining the quality of our feedstocks. However, we have long-term relations with our suppliers and trust them. We keep open communications with them and work together to solve quality issues."

12. WHEN THINGS GO WRONG

In 1980, while I was with Cargill in Minneapolis, the team sold a cargo of North Brazilian raw sugar to China for – if I remember correctly – October shipment. Poor weather delayed the harvest and slowed port operations, and the vessel sailed just after midnight on 1st November, missing the shipment deadline by one hour. We were out of contract terms, and the Chinese importers were no longer legally obliged to honour the contract.

The market had fallen significantly between the sale and the shipment, so it made commercial sense for the buyers to buy the sugar they needed elsewhere. After a complex negotiation, the team agreed to reduce the contract price of the cargo by one million dollars. We had failed to meet the contract terms, and reducing the price was less costly than reselling the cargo in the open market. I was shocked that a one-hour delay would cost a million dollars, but it was the price of maintaining a good relationship with a regular buyer.

In this case, the buyer had the law on their side; we had failed to meet contract terms. But what happens if a buyer or seller defaults on a contract because the price has moved against them? Arbitration is the first recourse. Courts are the second.

I will let the experts take up the story from here.

Swithun Still

The system can be ineffective if you're up against someone not acting in good faith. They're going to do everything not to respect the award.

Swithun Still is an old friend. I included an interview with him about grain trading in my *Commodity Conversations* book, *An Introduction to Trading in Agricultural Commodities*, and he kindly wrote the preface to *The New Merchants of Grain*.

I was due to meet him for lunch on a Monday at La Maison d'Igor, his favourite restaurant in Morges, Switzerland. It is a forty-five-minute cycle ride along the lake shore from my hometown of Lausanne. I knew Swithun would also want to cycle to our meeting, but a massive storm over the weekend had transformed Lake Leman into an ocean; white-crested waves were still crashing onto the shore. We compared notes during the morning and decided that I should take the train instead.

But then the sun came out, and I went on my bike. It was a fun ride as the storm had, in places, washed away the lake path, and I found myself cycling through foot-deep lake water. I got to the restaurant just as Swithun arrived on his bike.

Swithun had been president of Gafta, the Grain & Feed Trade Association, in 2019. The Association traces its history back to 1878 and has several roles, including education and training. Grain traders initially set it up to promote standard contract forms and provide an arbitration mechanism to settle disputes arising from these contracts. As much as 80 per cent of the global grain trade now transacts under Gafta terms and conditions.

I wanted to talk to Swithun about arbitration. He is one of Gafta's seventy-five (or so) qualified arbitrators. I wanted him to explain the role of arbitration when things go wrong. Perhaps more importantly, how should counterparties avoid things going wrong in the first place?

We had agreed that he would speak to me in a personal capacity, but he brought along a Gafta brochure showing the scope of their arbitration service. Between October 2020 and September 2021, Gafta's arbitration department received 310 claims. Over that period, Gafta awarded nearly four million euros under *125 Rules* and just over one million dollars under *126 Rules*. Arbitration is big business.

"Gafta 125 arbitration rules are used for most dispute resolutions under Gafta terms and are heard by three arbitrators", Swithun explained. "Gafta 126 Rules are for minor claims requiring expedited arbitration and involving parties agreeing to a sole arbitrator. Both have the right of appeal, in which case Gafta will appoint a Board of Appeal consisting of five qualified arbitrators.

"There are generally three exchanges at the first tier. There are the claim-submissions, then the reply-submissions by the respondent. The claimant then replies to the defence's submissions. The claimant will always have the last bite of the cherry.

"What frequently happens in complex cases is that there are rejoinder submissions and clarifications as to what's gone on. If the claimant introduces new evidence in his reply to the defence, then the respondent will frequently ask for the opportunity to respond to those new bits of evidence.

"It usually takes about three and a half months between claim submissions and the finalisation and closing of submissions. In the best-case scenario, the arbitration ruling takes four months, but more often, six.

"The arbitrators then assess any award, or quantum as it's called. The claimant may claim an amount, but the respondent will inevitably argue with the amount or say there's no valid claim. The arbitrators then convene over email and video conference to decide the merits of the arguments.

"All contracts under Gafta terms are as per English law, so the juridical seat of the arbitration is the law of England and Wales. It's not British law because there is no such thing. It is thus not Scottish law but the law of England and Wales.

"Sometimes, companies dispute the jurisdiction or deny they traded on Gafta terms, even if they have traded under Gafta terms previously. Sometimes, preliminary awards are made over jurisdiction or other matters such as *Time Bar*, where the respondent might argue that too much time has elapsed for the claim to be valid."

I asked Swithun the most common reasons for counterparties ending up in arbitration.

"They usually occur," he told me, "when someone defaults because the market price has moved between when the contract is agreed and when it is executed. If the price goes up, the seller may think twice about performing their contract – or try to find some way out of the contract. If the price goes down, the buyer thinks twice.

"It is especially true if the counterparties are not first-class buyers or sellers. If there's a price differential for a seller and he doesn't care too much for his reputation, he'll walk away and resell the goods. He knows it will go to arbitration, but it might take a year between the first tier and the appeal. If the award is defaulted, the defaulting party might simply liquidate his company, and the claimant might be chasing shadows when seeking to enforce."

"There have been quite a lot of arbitrations in the last year due to force majeure because of the war in Ukraine," Swithun continued. "There can be various reasons behind force majeure cases – and it is not always on the supplier side."

I asked him how a buyer could claim force majeure.

"Lots of reasons," he replied. "It could be because of export bans, war, strikes, extreme weather, or so-called Acts of God. Since the start of the war, traders of Ukrainian grain have declared Force Majeure because of the war. FOB buyers or CIF sellers have found it difficult or impossible to charter a vessel willing to go to the loading ports. There have also been cases where a vessel started loading but could not finish, or finished but could not sail."

I wanted to know how Gafta enforces arbitrations. "Is there a list of companies that have not honoured an arbitration ruling?" I asked.

"Yes, there is a list," he answered. "Gafta posts arbitration awards on their website and circulates them to members after the council meetings held three times a year – in January, June, and October. All members know when a company is a defaulter.

"Smaller companies may continue to trade with a defaulter, but multinationals won't. It's a no-go.

"And before you ask the question," Swithun continued, I don't know how many companies are on the list. I do know that many companies on the list are defunct. They disappear and often reappear with a new name, like a phoenix from the flames.

"The system can be ineffective if you're up against someone not acting in good faith. They're going to do everything not to respect the award."

Swithun told me he entered the grain trade in 1999 and did the Gafta Foundation Course in 2001. It is a week-long residential course where you learn the rudiments of contract types like CIF and FOB, Gafta procedures and all the various elements of the grain trade, such as superintendents and fumigation. In 2006, as its first student, he joined a six-module, two-year online course, Gafta's Distance Learning Programme. He then took a trade diploma exam, and Gafta invited him to become an arbitrator in 2008.

"You must have ten years' experience to be an arbitrator," he added. "I had just passed the cusp of 10 years. At the time of my appointment, I was GAFTA's youngest-ever arbitrator.

"I thought it would be an interesting second career – a paid hobby – and it was. I found – and still find – it fascinating to learn from the mistakes of others and see the things that can happen when simple mistakes are made."

"What sort of mistakes?" I asked.

"An example would be not giving notices on time – or not asking for an extension on a shipment period when a vessel is delayed."

"How do you find the time to be an arbitrator when you have a full-time job?" I asked him.

"It's a dilemma," he replied. "I didn't take on many arbitrations while working full-time, maybe one or two a year. But earlier this year, I was on a hiatus professionally and did several. I'm now trading again; fitting them in during the day is impossible. I do my arbitration work in the evenings and weekends.

"I think it's possible to do four or five arbitrations a year – maybe six at a push – if you are prepared to work evenings and weekends. It's challenging because you don't know how much work each one will involve before you accept them. Some arbitrations are open and shut cases; others are more complex.

"The other tricky thing is that it can take some time between my appointment as an arbitrator and seeing the first submissions. Arbitrations can be like London buses. None will come for a while, and then lots will all turn up at the same time."

I had one last question, perhaps the most important one: What would he advise people to be careful about to avoid ending up in arbitration?

"Know your counterparty," he replied, "Be aware that if you're buying from a supplier that is not first-class – or deemed to be first-class – you have a significant and often unhedgable risk if the market moves. Many counterparties don't hedge their transactions and find they can't perform if the market moves against them.

"One case I had was when a company defaulted on the purchase of wheat, claiming that the market price had dropped so much that they would have gone bust if they had executed their purchase. They called it "economic force majeure." We had to explain to them that there was no such thing – and suggested that maybe they should have hedged their purchase.

"If you've sold something and the market plummets, your buyers may try to find a way to extricate themselves from the contract – by hook or by crook, by fair means or foul."

Outside, the weather was still foul, and the wind had picked up. I took the road, rather than the lake path, back to Lausanne.

Alex Gedrinsky

To become an arbitrator, your peers must support and identify you as a respected individual who knows the business. You must follow serious training from your peers, older traders, and lawyers.

Alex began his commodity career in sugar but switched to cocoa when he joined Barry Callebaut after completing an executive MBA at Université Paris Dauphine. He was a senior cocoa trader with Barry Callebaut for about ten years in Zurich.

Barry Callebaut was – and still is – the world's number one chocolate producer and transformer. Alex went through the whole value chain with them, from cocoa bean production to the different transformation steps to the chocolate bar and liquid industrial chocolate. By trading all the products, he developed a deep understanding of the problems linked to the supply chain.

I first met Alex when he advised us on a consultancy project in East Africa. Since 2011, he has been an arbitrator for the FCC, the Federation of Cocoa Commerce, the cocoa market's equivalent to GAFTA in grain or the SAL or RSAL in sugar.

In addition to providing arbitration services, the FCC offers support services and education programmes, not only for traders. FCC members come from various stakeholders in the cocoa supply chain: exporters, processors, chocolate manufacturers, traders, brokers, warehouse keepers, and all other ancillary services. The FCC has about 200 members spread across 38 countries.

"The number of arbitrations varies yearly, usually depending on weather, market conditions, shipping issues, etc.," Alex told me. "Poor weather can lead to quality issues with the beans. It can also lead to defaults if the production is below expectations. An oversold crop can lead to disputes between sellers and buyers on the beans and the products. Depending on the years, I have anywhere from two to ten cases. In some years, I have none. Beyond arbitrations, we also have appeals to arbitration decisions."

I asked Alex what he saw as the primary role of an arbitrator.

"That's a big question," he replied. "The point of arbitration is to have respected members of the trade, not only in terms of people but also of organisations, to find a fair, timely, and economical form of dispute resolution as a service to parties who use our contract terms.

"You have two types of arbitration. Technical arbitration pertains to contractual rules, such as default, late shipments, or companies that have gone bankrupt and, in general terms, contract non-performance. It can also involve two entities that have a complex contractual agreement. They may ask the board of arbitration for their interpretation of the contract.

"The second type of arbitration is about the quality of the cocoa beans. Arbitrators will do a cut test to ascertain the quality of the beans. They may then ascribe a discount to the cocoa or reject it as unfit. While the FCC is not a grader of cocoa, it is essential for resolving a dispute, as it may determine specific problems at a given time from a particular origin. For products, the process of ascertaining quality is a little more complex."

"How do you become an arbitrator?" I asked.

"To become an arbitrator, your peers must support and identify you as a respected individual who knows the business. You must follow serious training from your peers, older traders, and lawyers. There's a whole language, behaviour and way of thinking that develops in this training.

"Then, once you are in the FCC or arbitration and appeal panel, the Council will periodically review you and your decisions. They might ask you to go for further training or check your standing.

There was one thing that has always bugged me about arbitration. Many arbitrators work for big companies, either traders or processors. I worried that an arbitrator from a big company could look after their company's interest rather than reach a fair result. I asked Alex how arbitrators deal with that issue.

"There is a spirit of the rules and the spirit of the law," he replied. "You should not be an arbitrator if you're not fair or looking for a good resolution. However, human nature is what it is, and yes, it has happened.

"But if you feel that the arbitration panel has treated you unfairly, you can go to appeal. It will bring a new tribunal with a new panel of arbitrators, sometimes with totally different views. I've been on appeal panels that have overturned decisions. Finally, if you feel the whole process has been unfair, you can go directly to the High Court of London.

I wondered about the role lawyers might play in arbitration proceedings.

"Parties to arbitration may take on a law firm to represent them," Alex told me. "A law firm will often try to use legal precedent to defend or claim innocence for their parties. Arbitrators prefer it when lawyers are not involved. It's quicker and cheaper. I have been in some arbitration cases where the legal costs were so high that they threatened a company's economic survival.

It's the role of arbitrators to tell the parties when to stop. There are rules. The claimant states his case, the defendant states his case, and there is room for rebuttals. The arbitrators then decide when to cease submissions from the parties unless they need more clarification.

"Like GAFTA, the FCC publishes a list of companies that fail to honour an arbitration ruling. Reputable trading houses will not trade with companies on that list – and the FCC will only take companies off the list once they fulfil their obligations.

I asked Alex what advice he would give to cocoa traders and buyers to avoid finding themselves in arbitration.

"Cocoa has the benefit of being a small market," he replied. "Most participants in the market know each other or know someone who knows somebody. People understand the contractual terms they're trading. The rules of contracts are available in French and English. The contract terms spell out the obligations of each party at each stage. As with everything in life, people should not enter contracts without knowing the rules.

"And they should be careful not to overtrade and find themselves in an unfavourable financial position where they cannot honour the contract. So, read the contract and don't overtrade."

My last question was about the qualities you need to be an arbitrator.

"Humility, an open mind, and the curiosity to listen to all the arguments from both sides," Alex replied. "You also need to have listening, writing and analytical skills, along with the ability to work in a team with your colleagues on the arbitration panel.

"Stubbornness is an attribute," he continued. "If something is not clear, you must go back and dig. Sometimes, one point can take a long time. You must make the effort necessary to clarify any unclear issues. You also need a sense of fairness – and the will to find the fairest solution."

But there was something I was still curious about. "Do arbitrators get paid?" I asked.

"Yes, they do. We are paid an hourly amount clearly stated in the arbitration and appeal fees and the arbitration rules of the FCC."

"I guess you don't become an arbitrator for the pay."

"You guess right!"

Brian Perrott

Emotion is a dangerous thing because it can make it more challenging to solve problems Commercial issues should all be solvable, however emotional they are.

Brian is Irish and partly grew up in Ireland. He studied law and politics at Galway University but moved to Cardiff to study maritime law. On graduating, he went to Holman Fenwick Willian (HFW) and, for a short period, to Middleton Potts, a famous commodity firm.

He joined Cargill in 1995, initially in Cobham, where Cargill had their UK offices, and then moved to Geneva, where he served ocean transport, sugar, and other areas. Brian loved his five years at Cargill but wanted to see if he could build his own practice.

Hill Taylor Dickinson gave him a partnership, and he slowly increased his client base before returning to HFW, where he had articled, partly because it was a more prominent firm. He has been with them for almost 20 years, and his business has grown significantly.

The nature of his work has changed over the years. Many companies now employ in-house lawyers. *I have had to adapt and change my product. I have had to expand and diversify my practice.*

Brian has had some challenging periods in his legal career. The first was the Red Bean Crisis when various trading houses had shiploads of soybeans sitting off China containing beans that someone had dyed red. It gave the Chinese buyers an excuse to reject the shipments, and the prices plummeted.

His second crisis was the freight crash when the time charter rate for Capesize vessels went from $200,000 a day to zero or minus dollars a day.

Brian had co-drafted the legal FFA document – the Forward Freight Agreement – with another lawyer and was much in demand when the forward market crashed. Everyone knew he had co-drafted the FFA contract and wanted him to tell them how to deal with it. He was overwhelmed with physical and futures freight work in 2008 and 2009. It was the only time in his life when he could choose which clients he acted for.

"I remember going to the Baltic Exchange during the freight market crash," he told me. "It was paralysis as everyone had their bank accounts frozen. The whole thing was surreal. The owners, charterers, interested parties and brokers had never seen anything like it. The freight market was on its knees. I didn't think so then, but in retrospect, I am fortunate to have experienced that unique period in market history."

I asked him how he coped with the stress.

"I remember sitting at my desk during the FFA crash and thinking I couldn't cope with the pressure. Every client wanted my urgent attention. Everyone's problem was unique and special. You just find great resolve, don't you? You cope. I had a good group of Partners and associates around me. There were long hours, long days.

"The freight crash was the closest I have come to burnout. You may have colleagues, but it's a lonely place because, ultimately, the buck stopped with me.

"As always, you must go back to people's backgrounds and experiences – to their childhood. I attended a strong, traditional Irish boarding school from eleven. My parents had been in England, and although I was born in Ireland, the other boys saw me as a Brit. I spoke like a Brit. If you survive that without too many bruises, you can survive most things."

Brian is the most active litigator in London in the commercial litigation rankings. I asked him if that meant commodity trading had more disputes and litigations than other professions.

"Yes, it does," he replied. "However, the statistics embrace commodities, shipping, and other pieces of commercial litigation. I have had something like 50 reported cases in my career. One case, for Cargill, went to the Supreme Court. We won."

Brian had a reputation at Cargill as a lawyer who solved problems rather than created them. I asked him if he thought some lawyers created problems.

"I come from the Cargill Academy," he said. "People at Cargill didn't enjoy disputes and didn't want them. They preferred to protect relationships but, at the same time, solve problems. I believe every legal issue, whatever the sector or subject, is capable of solution.

"Years ago, I was lucky enough to go on a mediation course where I saw the early benefits of mediation as a way of resolving differences. Mediation is a slightly more formal structure than a conversation. We ended up putting mediation clauses in Cargill charter parties, probably one of the first in the industry to do so."

"Do you think some lawyers create problems?" I insisted.

"Yes, I think some do," he replied. "Many colleagues are interested in solving problems, but lawyers sometimes respond to a client's passion and emotion. Emotion is a dangerous thing because it can make it more challenging to solve problems. It is why divorce can be so conflictual. Commercial issues should all be solvable, however emotional they are.

"Clients need to own a dispute and not leave it to the lawyers. Clients should remain invested and interested. The best clients remain interested, invested, and play a significant role in the solution."

"How does arbitration fit into all of that?" I asked.

"Arbitration is more hostile than mediation, which is a more informal affair. People regard arbitration as a gentlemanly form of court action. You are judged by commercial people you respect, and there is a sense that commercial morality will prevail. Contract interpretation is all about the words, but the context does matter. There's a belief that arbitration often provides a more commercial judgment than a court.

"One advantage of arbitration is that it is confidential. If there are embarrassing elements in WhatsApp or emails, they are protected. It's a less hostile forum. It's not open; you're not in the witness box in front of the court. I would argue that it should be mediation, arbitration, and court – in that order.

"Unfortunately, enforcement of an arbitration award (or judgment) can be a stubborn issue. You may win the battle but lose the war. Over the years, I have specialised in collecting awards, and we have recovered many millions on behalf of clients."

"Where do most problems arise within that agricultural supply chain?" I asked.

"They have changed over the years," he replied. "You have the classic quality, quantity, performance, and force majeure. New issues might be cyber-attacks and force majeure resulting from sanctions. Contract drafting is becoming increasingly sophisticated with cross-default provisions and termination clauses becoming increasingly common."

"What advice would you give a trader to avoid trouble?"

"Realise that you are both masters or mistresses of your contractual destiny. The words you use in your contract will dictate the outcome. I try to get people to realise the power and impact of words and to get it right at the beginning. It usually leads to a happier ending.

"Words are my commodity, and the words chosen will almost always dictate the outcome of a dispute. I spend an increasing amount of my time guiding clients appropriately."

"What would you say to a young law student to encourage them to get into commodities rather than something else?"

"I would say that international trade is fascinating. The best cases result from the buying and selling, the finance, and the shipping of goods. Without commodities, international trade, and shipping, the law reports would be a fraction of the size. Every area of the law seems to have been developed because of the business that we are in.

"I would tell young lawyers that they will have to work hard, and there will be challenges and pressures, but it's a wonderful area if you're interested in the law and the development of the law."

"Any final thoughts?" I asked.

"Personally, it has been a privilege to experience the highs and lows of the commodity market from a legal perspective. The characters I have met and the professional friendships I have developed have led me to conclude that this remains a people-centric business, where conversations lie at the heart of what I do."

13. SUSTAINABILITY

The UN's FAO defines a sustainable agricultural value chain as 'profitable throughout, has broad-based benefits for society, and does not permanently deplete natural resources.' A supply chain is not sustainable unless it is economically sustainable.

Boston Consulting Group once surveyed the fashion sector and found that 75 per cent of consumers felt that sustainability was 'extremely or very important' in their purchasing decisions. However, on closer questioning, only 7 per cent said that sustainability influenced their purchase decisions. More critical factors included low prices, quality, and convenience.

Sustainability is a prerequisite rather than a driver of purchasing decisions. Consumers expect and demand that everything they buy is sustainable. It is not an add-on, a nice-to-have thing. It is a prerequisite. However, because it is a prerequisite, consumers are unwilling to pay more.

The priority for most consumers in developing countries is to feed their families. Food is a significant part of the family budget. In Nigeria, for example, consumers spend 64 per cent of their income on food. Compare that to the UK, where consumers spend 8.2 per cent of their income on food. In the US, the figure is 6.4 per cent. Nearly all of us in the developed world could pay more for our food without impacting our living standards.

However, we are all products of our evolution. We may go to the supermarket to buy organic, certified coffee, but we purchase the two-for-one special offer supermarket's brand. After all, we have a family to feed, and our family comes before the planet's health or the safety and well-being of the coffee workers.

But there is hope in our selfishness. Our first responsibility may be the health and well-being of our families—the survival of our genes. However, we know that we must give farmers a living if we want them to provide us with the food we eat. We also know our genes won't survive for long if we don't look after the planet. As consumers, it is slowly sinking in that it is in our selfish self-interest that farmers continue to provide sustainably produced quality food.

There is a growing alignment of interests among farmers, governments, food companies, civil society, and consumers to ensure that food is produced sustainably, both environmentally and socially. Farmers want to protect their land; food companies want to protect their brands; and consumers and governments want to protect their health and environment. It makes for a powerful coalition for continual improvement. Things could always be better, but the world is moving in the right direction.

Tessa Meulensteen

Traders may now focus on the short term, but legislation will push traders to create greater visibility within their supply chains – and that allows for a vehicle to transfer more value.

Tessa leads the coffee work at IDH in Utrecht, Netherlands, developing strategy, aligning the different country teams and programs, and managing the global accounts.

She first approached me to talk about cocoa. She felt there were similarities between the coffee and cocoa supply chains, but that cocoa was a step ahead on issues like farmers' income and deforestation. I didn't want to talk about cocoa. I had started writing a book about it but found the politics too challenging. I asked her instead if she could chat about IDH and coffee.

But first, I had a couple of issues to resolve.

Tessa is a shareholder in Herenboeren, a Dutch organisation that brings local people together to run cooperative farms. She is a member of a 20-hectare farm on the outskirts of her hometown of Rotterdam. It is similar in size to the smallholding on which I grew up (and which I described in The New Merchants of Grain). My father could never make the farm pay, and I didn't see how she could. That was my first issue.

The cooperative's 200 shareholders employ someone to farm the land for them. She admitted that she has learned a lot since they began and that they produced little in the first three years.

"I don't understand how we expect farmers to farm when we put so much risk on their shoulders," she said. "I understand why it leads to a business model where you go for intensive production rather than the diversified model we're trying to do."

My father had done the same, moving into intensive pig production. He couldn't make that pay either.

I suggested the problem is that the price of food is too low as it does not cover the environmental and social costs of production. Consumers do not pay environmental costs like deforestation, social costs such as child labour, or healthcare costs from obesity or poor diet.

"I am aware that I can afford to pay more for my food and that other people might not be able to afford to," Tessa admitted. "We must also remember the amount of labour you need to farm. We all work on the farm. It's unpaid labour. Without that labour, we don't have the farm."

My second issue is that the cooperative farm's website promotes eating food produced near home. Transport contributes less than 5 per cent of the food supply chain's greenhouse gas emissions. I suggested we could do more good by importing more of our food from Africa or South America, where many people depend on agriculture for their living.

Tessa looks at the issue from a different angle.

"The big benefit of eating food produced close to home is the connection you build with the food production system," she told me, "Learning from that, understanding how much effort goes into producing food and therefore not wasting as much. It also encourages me to eat more seasonally and cook more creatively."

"I think the drive should not be around eating locally," she continued. "It should be around understanding that our food production system doesn't consider the externalities. That's what we need to change, and there are multiple ways of doing that – and this is one way."

I hadn't finished with my issues. I had a third one. The farm also raises cattle, pigs, and chickens. I asked Tessa how she could justify that in environmental terms.

"I would argue that a diversified farm includes livestock," she replied. "We have a 20-hectare farm. We use around 3 hectares for vegetables and fruits; the rest is for grazing. We have two cows per hectare because that's what a hectare can support. "You can produce beef in an environmentally friendly way, but at a much lower threshold than I would have expected.

"We try to have 250 chickens," she admitted, "with the idea that they graze in the orchard and eat insects. It's a natural system. The problem is we only have 70 chickens left because we also have foxes and birds of prey. We no longer keep the chickens in the orchard as they don't survive there. There is an ideal picture of how livestock and crop production can work together, and then there's reality."

I wanted now to turn to IDH. I have known the organisation for some years and am a fan. The organisation is firmly grounded in the reality – not the theory – of food production.

Tessa told me that IDH is a not-for-profit organisation whose stated aim is to transform markets. IDH doesn't implement projects on the ground. Instead, it works in coalitions with the private sector or public-private partnerships to drive change. IDH views its strength as collaborative– bringing people together – rather than in advocacy.

"It's big, right," Tessa told me. "Better jobs, better incomes, better environments. We try to find the interlinkages. Farmers can double their incomes by cutting down the forest, but that's not necessarily what we want to advocate. Or we can say that farmers should invest in climate-neutral production, but how can they do that if they don't even have the money to eat?"

I told her that raising farm incomes by increasing production through more land, better crop varieties or fertiliser can drive prices down and do more harm than good. It can lead to increased deforestation and push prices lower. It can be counterproductive. I suggested that part of the problem is that we want to raise farm incomes long-term, but the market price depends on short-term supply and demand.

Tessa told me that it is easier to do in supply chains like coffee, where there is a potential for quality differentiation. The larger roasters like Nespresso are building long-term relationships with their suppliers, emphasising quality and supply security over price. Protecting their brand means they must make 100 per cent sure there's no child labour or environmental damage in their supply chain.

"I tell my friends that if they want to have a relative certainty that things are progressing," she told me. "Their best bet is Nespresso. Or if you are out of home, Starbucks. There are good models in your local store, but you must ask the right questions and choose carefully. Some amazing quality coffees don't take farmers' incomes into account. Nespresso and Starbucks have done a great job, but there's typically more value in their supply chains than in your seven-in-the-morning, I-just-need-to-wake-up coffee."

"Over time, we're going to see more sourcing based on relationship more than price," she told me. "Traders may now focus on the short term, but legislation will push traders to create greater visibility within their supply chains – and that allows for a vehicle to transfer more value."

I harbour a perhaps naïve view that coffee is more a victim of climate change than the culprit. I asked Tessa if she agreed.

She did. "Climate change is a bigger threat to coffee than coffee is to climate change, "she told me. "But I am a bit hesitant. I am concerned that coffee is driving climate change in some big producers such as Brazil and Vietnam – through input-intensive farming systems, where the quantity of fertilisers and agrochemicals used impact water quality and biodiversity."

Before joining IDH, Tessa worked in the private sector with Unilever's Ben & Jerry in the quality department in a factory. I asked her about her experience there.

"I learned a lot there." she told me, "Most importantly, I learned how difficult it is to do things. It is much easier to sit outside and tell people what to do.

"My job now is great, right?" she continued. "I can sit on the sidelines and tell people they must improve farmer incomes, but it's incredibly complex to achieve. Saying this is what you must do is very different than being on the inside and trying to change it there.

Her comments made me think about that great quote, sometimes attributed to Einstein and sometimes to the US baseball player Yogi Berra,

"In theory, there is no difference between theory and practice. In practice, there is."

Tessa has a degree in anthropology and an MSC in sustainable development. She told me that the MSc taught her to think about cost-benefit analysis in environmental issues.

"It helped me a lot," she explained, "On a personal level, I learned more working in the Ben & Jerry's factory. It shaped me more than the Master's, which was relatively within my comfort zone. I would advise people to step outside their comfort zones to move beyond theory to practice. It will make a difference."

My time was nearly up, but I had two more questions.

"What advice would you give to your 18-year-old self?" I asked.

"You don't have to conquer the world tomorrow," she replied. "You can listen a bit more, learn more, take your time, you'll get there".

I then asked her if she would have listened to that advice.

"No way," she answered. "No, never."

Nicko Debenham

Farmers need a living income that allows them to pay their workers, send their children to school and attain grades that give them a choice in the future.

Nicko comes from a horse-racing family where all the children went into racing. He broke his collarbone in the US, came back to the UK to repair it, and met his wife in London. He took her back to the US, and they got engaged there, much to the horror of both her parents and his. His future father-in-law decided to take him under his wing. He told him he should own horses, not be paid to ride them.

His future father-in-law had worked as an expat in Nigeria for 35 years, and he sent Nicko to work for a family friend, Chief Bakare, in Ondo State at the heart of Nigeria's cocoa production. It was a chaotic period because the government had privatised the cocoa board under an IMF structural adjustment program.

The Bakare family began trading, buying cocoa and selling it to Europe. They built a processing factory. Nicko worked for them for about six years and then moved to an old-fashioned London trade house, trading everything from tallow, gum Arabic, and sesame seed. He brought cocoa to them and set up a business in Nigeria and Cameroon. The company owner wanted to sell the cocoa business to Amajaro. Nicko was unhappy because he felt it was his business and should have a share in the new enterprise.

He left and set up my own business, originating cocoa from Nigeria, Cameroon, Ghana, and the Ivory Coast. It worked well for five years, but it was the era of bank consolidation, and his bank facilities dried up, and his capital base was too small. He went to work for Armajaro, staying there for twelve years, setting up traceable supply chains across Africa, Asia, and Latin America, mainly Ecuador and Peru. By the time he left to join Barry Callebaut in 2014, 85 per cent of Armajaro's cocoa was sustainable – and the company was the largest trade house in cocoa.

Nicko worked for Barry Callebaut for eight and a half years as head of sustainability, with a mandate to turn the company from a laggard to a leader in sustainability. He stayed with Barry Callebaut till December 2021, when he set up his own company, Sustainability Solutions, working with government entities to help producers raise the cocoa price to a level that generates meaningful value for farmers.

"To solve child labour and deforestation," he told me, "you must first solve smallholder poverty. I also work for commercial companies on sustainability, helping them comply with all the new regulations and build a social value strategy."

"Could you tell me about these new regulations?" I asked.

"There is a saying that Americans invent, Chinese copy, and Europeans regulate," Nicko said. "Europe is a printing machine of new regulations."

"We have recently had CSRD, the Corporate Sustainability Reporting Directive. We now have EURD, the European Union Deforestation Regulation. The next one is the biggie, the CSDDD, or the Corporate Sustainability Due Diligence Directive.

"The EUDR regulation covers seven commodities: soy, cattle, palm oil, timber, cocoa, coffee, and rubber. It targets deforestation, but they've sneaked other forms of illegality into the regulation. CSDDD means that companies must perform due diligence on everything in their supply chains – and prove they have done it. We expect the CSDDD will be passed as a directive in 2024 and transposed into national law by the Member States by 2027.

"EUDR entered into force on 29th July 2023 with an 18-month preparation period before its application on 30th December 2024. It relates to deforestation generated since 31st December 2020. The EUDR uses the FAO's definition of forest, which is half a hectare of 10 per cent cover of five metres of trees or higher. If a forest existed before December 2020 and no longer exists, then that's deforestation.

"Among the seven commodities, cocoa and coffee present the most significant challenges as they rely most on the EU market. More than 60 per cent of global cocoa production enters the EU, much of which is processed and reexported. The figure for coffee is between 25 and 30 per cent. The statistics for palm and soy are less than 10 per cent. Europeans can choose where they buy their palm or soy, making it easier to conform to the regulations.

"If traders want to ensure that their coffee and cocoa are not devalued – if they want to bring it into the EU – they must conform with the regulation."

"Will the cocoa sector be able to do that?" I asked.

"Cocoa is a product consumed by children in rich countries and grown by children in poor countries, often in abject poverty. It is an incredible product that everyone loves, but it is emotive because of poverty and child labour. In addition, Ivory Coast and Ghana have seen massive deforestation over the last 20 to 30 years.

"NGOs and the media have targeted chocolate brands on these issues for 25 years. The brands and the supply chain companies have had to stand and defend themselves. They have developed sustainable supply chains, collected data, and done the due diligence. The cocoa companies look at EUDR and say, "Yeah, it's a bit of a pain, but we can do this.

"The EU is simply asking for the sector to collect data. To do that, you download an application on your smartphone and survey the farm. While there, you ask the farmer about other forms of possible illegality. You make sure you understand the risk of that farmer not having the right to farm that land, illegally using his children on the farm, not paying labour, using forced labour, or having other issues with labour rights. It's not that difficult. You then follow the coffee up the supply chain. It's perfectly possible.

"If I'm correct and there's a two-tier market, traders have the incentive to take the necessary steps to achieve that higher end of the two-tier market. That's the motivation. Most people view it as an opportunity, but some are digging their heels in. They haven't yet seen the light."

I wanted now to ask about child labour. I had heard that some children over twelve don't attend school in the Ivory Coast because their parents don't have the required registration documents. And if they can't go to school, they work for their parents on the farm.

"Sadly, national child labour monitoring and remediation systems are not solving the problems," Nicko admitted. "The solution would be for governments to establish rural infrastructure development with schools, electricity, water, and registration of every rural resident, including their children.

"In the absence of government action, companies undertake remediation activities. A company may pay for birth certificates for unregistered children so that they can attend school. Other companies may supply school kits; a child can't go to school without a school uniform or rucksack. I mean, who the hell decided that? You're telling me I can't bring my child to school just because they don't have the right coloured shirt or pair of shorts. It's ridiculous, but that's what you're up against.

"Farmers need a living income that allows them to pay their workers, send their children to school and attain grades that give them a choice in the future. The only way you'll get there is for farmers to have a decent income and for communities to have electricity, water, and communications with schools, health centres, etc. The first thing you've got to solve is income, but the second is rural infrastructure."

Derek Chambers – the famous cocoa trader – once told me cocoa farmers were just as poor or even poorer when he retired than when he started his career 40 years earlier.

"The challenge we all face," he said, "is that if you optimise the outcome from a farm – and achieve the capacity and capability of trees on that farm – you should be able to double or triple its production. If farmers did that, the world cocoa price would be not even half what it is today; it would be a quarter.

"It's about transforming the agricultural policy in a country to obtain a more balanced mix of crops. It's as much about teaching farmers not to grow cocoa as it is about teaching farmers to grow cocoa. But it needs to be backed by government policy. Neither Ghana nor the Ivory Coast are self-sufficient in food. Maybe their governments should use the tax from cocoa exports to subsidise the production of vegetables, chicken, pork, etc."

I asked Nicko if he had any final messages for traders and food companies.

"First," he replied, "if you're a brand company and cocoa is your core raw material, you must be stupid if you haven't learned that you're handling a hand grenade with the pin out. Cocoa has everything there is that can go wrong. Child and enslaved labour, deforestation, abject poverty, and even potential corruption are all wrapped up in a parcel of cocoa. And that's why I say, for God's sake, don't let go of that pin. Run your business correctly, do your due diligence and do what you should do.

"Use digital technology to understand and engage with your supply chains and capacity. Work with your partners in the supply chain. There is a massive opportunity if you do that.

"We are moving to a world where people need to pay a fair price for a product which provides a livelihood for the people who produce it. Is it a human right to be paid a fair price or get a fair income for doing a job? It's going to be a debate, and it's going to happen. Historically, with all these issues, the companies that lent into it and tackled it first came out of it best.

"Lean into it, identify how you can make a difference and tell the great stories around it. It's what I call proud marketing."

Melanie Williams

Although certification isn't perfect, it has had a beneficial effect. It allows concerned consumers, NGOs, and commentators to ask questions about the provenance of commodities.

For the past half-century, non-governmental organisations (NGOs) such as Greenpeace and Oxfam have played a positive role in alerting public opinion to the damage we are inflicting on our planet and our fellow human beings. Over time, the NGOs developed a strategy of naming and shaming food companies into cleaning up their supply chains.

Agricultural commodities have historically been defined by physical properties: weights, moisture content, foreign matter, broken pieces and other physically verified attributes. Suddenly, consumers began asking commodity traders to address the social and environmental issues in their supply chains and to verify traits they had never verified in the past.

The food supply sector had long argued that it was the role of the governments in producing countries to implement social and environmental standards: no child or slave labour, no deforestation, minimum pollution, etc. It quickly became apparent that many governments — especially in developing countries — could not do this effectively – or at least to the standard now demanded by consumers and NGOs.

The food industry was unsure how to react to these new demands and turned to outside participants for help. Gradually, a range of voluntary sustainability standards and certification agencies emerged, stepping in to fill the role that governments, traders and food companies were ill-equipped to play. The trade houses and the NGOs, most notably WWF, supported and encouraged these agencies.

At Kingsman, we were involved in developing these standards, particularly in the biofuels sector. When I retired, I was briefly Chairman of Bonsucro, the certification scheme for sugar cane. During this period, I often turned to Melanie Williams for advice.

Melanie has a PhD in chemistry from the University of Cambridge. For the past ten years, she has worked as an independent sustainability consultant, helping companies implement sustainability schemes and write standards for some schemes themselves. I asked her to talk me through what certification schemes do.

"Certification schemes develop sustainability principles and standards containing specific requirements that can be audited for compliance," she explained. "They train and approve auditing companies to carry out independent audits within the supply chain and certify the people and companies who pass those audits.

"Although certification isn't perfect, it has had a beneficial effect. It allows concerned consumers, NGOs, and commentators to ask questions about the provenance of commodities. It has brought the issues of deforestation and people's rights to a broader audience. It allows consumers to choose more sustainable products.

"ISCC (International Sustainability and Carbon Certification) was launched in about 2011 and is the most significant, meaningful, and influential of the EU-approved biofuel sustainability schemes. It has since expanded into food, feed and materials.

"There are also single commodity schemes, such as RSPO, Bonsucro, and RTRS, and schemes targeted at higher value food commodities, such as Rain Forest Alliance. (The ITC Standards Map gives a good idea of the scope of the different schemes.)

"The EU is trying to reduce the number of certification schemes," she continued. "They are bringing in a registration requirement that excludes schemes without third-party auditing. However, auditing companies are developing their own standards for responsible agricultural practices and supply chain traceability to comply with the EUDR (The EU Deforestation Regulation)."

"Only a small percentage of agricultural production is certified," I argued. "Many importers (China, MENA) don't care about certification, which makes it difficult for certification to gain critical mass. Is the certification industry losing momentum?"

"It is a problem," she replied, "But the developed world can only control its own production and its imports. There will be more developments, such as the CSDDD (Corporate Sustainability Due Diligence Directive), which will require companies who operate in the EU to assess the risk of their suppliers impacting human rights or the environment. It applies to agriculture and other sectors, too. These types of measures should boost the demand for certification."

"Food companies often leave certification logos off their retail packaging," I said. "I never understood why."

"Some don't want the schemes to gain recognition as this increases the risk that suppliers will ask for a premium," she replied. "Others don't want to reduce the visual impact of their corporate logos, or they think too many logos will confuse consumers."

"Traders often argue that certification reduces trading opportunities and substitution," I said. "Does it result in a less efficient supply chain?"

"The world is moving towards shorter supply chains in general," she replied. "Mutual recognition of certification schemes increases flexibility, but inevitably, there will be more friction."

"How can we be sure that production comes from certified farms and not their neighbours?" I asked.

"Geolocation data helps, and some providers offer services to interpret satellite data to show, for instance, land use change. You can prevent other types of fraud with scheme-wide or national databases that track transaction volumes between operators."

"If you were the world's dictator," I asked, "What measures would you take to deal with deforestation, declining biodiversity, and global warming?"

"I would educate and support the world's women," she replied. "It would lead to a more just society and population stability. Better decisions happen when politics and business are mixed with an equal representation of both sexes and with people from different backgrounds."

"Are you optimistic or pessimistic about the future?" I asked.

"I am optimistic that we will overcome the challenges of climate change, mainly with new technology, but some changes in behaviour too."

Five Questions for Anita Neville

You are the chief sustainability and communications officer at Golden Agri-Resources (GAR), the world's second-largest palm oil producer. You've been with GAR for eight and a half years, but before that, you were ten years with Rainforest Alliance. What made you move?

I worked for ten years with Rainforest Alliance and seven years with WWF. It was a long stint, and I was ready for a change. If you're a communicator from the NGO community, you usually end up in a Nestlé, a Unilever, or a retailer, but brands and sales don't motivate me. I'm motivated by how we grow things and how farmers farm.

I am the most city of city people. I grew up in Brisbane, but my father was a quintessential Australian who loved the bush. When we were kids, we were always off camping somewhere out West. He was always dragging us off to state forests and national parks. It spurred my love of the natural world and the environment. I'm a product of the 1970s when national forests were still working. I saw land used productively and managed for its environmental values. I believe my father is to blame for where I ended up.

Several former Rainforest Alliance and WWF colleagues have moved into corporate roles. It's a good thing. You need an intersection between not-for-profit organizations, business, and government. You need them to mix and blend so that they understand each other better.

I was in Singapore in September 2015, and a friend suggested I talk with GAR. I did. It seemed like a great way to do what I love but in a corporate environment. It ticked all the boxes. My family agreed to move, so it all worked out.

I'm also a board member for the Roundtable on Sustainable Palm Oil, but you look at certification differently when you're a business.

When you're the standard system designing principles and criteria, you should ask yourself how the system drives continuous improvement for the whole sector. Unfortunately, it too often becomes, 'How do you lift the top – the ceiling?'

The big difference for me coming to GAR—and why I joined—is that people will hold the company accountable for the weakest link in its supply chain, the smallholder. As a business, we must lift the industry's floor with us. It's what certification should be doing, too.

We're asking, "Is this about lifting everyone or improving the top two per cent?" If it's the latter, it's of no use to us. Lifting the floor is critical to us as a business and industry and to Indonesia as a country.

Is there an issue with certification in that producers pay for it, making smallholders worse off?

I was perhaps atypical, even in Rainforest Alliance, but I've never agreed that certification suits everyone. Working in the corporate environment, I see how expensive it is for smallholders.

I share your concern about cost. Who pays? It is challenging because most certification systems don't break 20 to 30 per cent of global production. The FSC is the most successful at maybe 30 per cent of global timber production.

I want to see smallholders improve their production practices. I want to walk them to the door of certification on the assumption that a standard system represents the best agricultural practice. But we should give them the right to choose. Do they go through the certification door and commit to a lifetime of paying an annual audit fee and all the things that come along with that? Or do we help them to behave appropriately, regardless of the certificate or the piece of paper?

I don't believe certification systems have developed well for smallholders. You end up with a big gap between the certified and the uncertified, the latter making up the lion's share of global production. It doesn't seem to be the right solution. Certification is excellent for many things, but I don't think it's the only tool we should use.

Regulation is stepping in to do what certification hasn't done. We see that with the EUDR and ISPO (Indonesia Sustainable Palm Oil), the country's national sustainability certification scheme for palm oil which will become mandatory by 2025. There is no easy answer regarding what's better, certification or regulation.

I'm looking for a buyer who is prepared to pay the actual cost of commodity production, with all the externalities internalized into the price.

Now, let's go back to your job. Do you spend your day on sustainability or communications?

In some ways, sustainability is communications. I spend much of my day trying to inspire, negotiate with, convince, and cajole people into doing things they may not want to do. Or to act faster than they feel comfortable with.

Sustainability is also about translating sustainability jargon into business speak. It's essential to step back and translate external demands so the company can understand, absorb, and make informed decisions. Then, you must translate back out from inside the business to external stakeholders and explain why you're doing what you're doing at the pace that you're doing.

I feel I'm communicating all the time. But it's probably about 70 per cent on sustainability and 30 per cent on communications.

Before joining GAR, I spent over 20 years working in international environmental NGOs. I'm well-versed and battle-hardened in the campaigning and political world of the environment. I take my responsibility for sustainability seriously.

Judgment should focus on GAR's actions in the field. What are we delivering? Are we meeting our commitments? If we're not, are we explaining why we're not in a legitimate, understandable, and acceptable way?

I'm proud of what GAR is delivering. Could we be faster? Could we do more? Sure, of course. But over the last nine years, we've delivered on our commitments to a deforestation-free supply chain and the transformation of our suppliers. We're working hard on climate change and reducing our carbon emissions. Our CEO is a great advocate for that work, and I'm proud of the part I've played in getting him there.

We have previously worked with external NGOs on some environmental or social issues. We collaborated with Greenpeace to develop our approach to high-carbon stock areas. We've worked with OFI, Orangutan Foundation International, on orangutan conservation and training our staff on the estates and communities on zero harm to wildlife.

We prefer to work with local groups and organizations rather than international NGOs. We aim to build Indonesia's local capacity to advocate for its environment and social issues.

Palm oil is the most environmentally sustainable vegetable oil, yielding five times more than sunflowers, six times more than soybeans, and ten times more than coconuts. Why aren't these statistics reaching the broader public?

Those are just numbers. Numbers lack emotional appeal. It doesn't matter how productive palm is compared to soy or rapeseed; you lose the argument whenever somebody posts a video of an orangutan in a devastated forest on social media. People regularly post videos from 2013 as if they were happening now. No, it happened ten years ago. It is terrible that it happened, but things have greatly improved in the past ten years.

We must put a human face on palm oil because the stats won't help us. We've done that in a limited way at GAR, given that we don't have the marketing budgets of a Unilever or a Nestlé. We've seen people wake up to the reality that you can produce palm sustainably. Millions of people here in Indonesia rely on the crop, directly and indirectly, for their livelihoods. It can be a force for good.

But it is hard to get people to listen to those good news stories when they are so attuned to the negative.

In the late 1980s, soy was the big bad, but it didn't last long. The NGOs quickly pivoted to palm, partly because soy fought back, but palm didn't. It's a cultural thing. A lot of plantation owners did a Southeast Asian thing and put their heads down, ignored it, and hoped it would go away. And so, in the vacuum created, the only narrative that stood was the NGO narrative. We're slowly winning. It's slow because that narrative is so entrenched now.

But we won't win with those numbers you give, even though I use them all the time. We'll win it based on human stories with an emotional connection and by delivering on the promises the palm sector has made around decoupling production from deforestation, protecting wildlife, and reducing carbon emissions.

We've taken the approach within GAR to ask how we can get into the inboxes of the people who matter the most – customers, our financial backers, and shareholders. We've done that. Once we talk to people directly and put facts in front of them, they get on board with the idea that palm can be sustainable.

Taking that to a broad public communication has been more challenging, partly because no one wants to hear it from us. Still, we see some influential journalists finally getting the message.

It can be challenging to combat fake news; how you react depends on whether it is a lie or an interpretation of events. If it's a straight-up lie, it would depend a bit on where it was published and who was repeating it. But, honestly, it's like Whack-a-Mole.

You must decide whether it is essential for you to challenge it. Challenging everything would be exhausting and time-consuming and would not give you much. You'd be spending all your time doing that and none of your time establishing your narrative.

When I joined, GAR was in a similar situation, consistently playing defence. We decided to stop reacting to every little thing about ourselves and the palm sector and to take control of our own story. We framed that around the implementation of the GAR Social and Environmental Policy. If it didn't have a connection to that, we ignored it unless it was an egregious lie. It has stood us in good stead and given us consistency in our narrative, which we underpin with data.

We've continued to progress. We report on what we're doing, how it's going, and why it's stalled in some instances. This has built credibility and confidence in the business. Our people know what our narrative is. They know what to talk about if they are challenged. It's about empowering our employees to feel they can speak up and have pride.

Could you just give an example of what GAR is doing to improve the livelihood of your smallholders?

We employ nearly 100,000 people across Indonesia, most working on farms or in factories. We provide early childcare facilities (BPAs) and medical centres for our plantation workers, funding and running them in buildings on our estates. We have more than 340 early childcare centres, with over 770 carers serving in the region of two and a half thousand children, from babies through to the age of five, after which children in Indonesia move on to primary school.

We are working on how to improve the performance of these early childcare centres. We want to empower the women who run these centres to take over some financial management and improve their skills and abilities to become small business managers.

Many children in our BPAs failed to meet essential developmental milestones, such as the ability to sort from small to large, recognize colours, or stand on one foot – fundamental things. By introducing measures like regular height and weight checks, scaling up our caregivers on some basic educational requirements, and connecting them with our health clinics and volunteer services, we now address maternal and child health-related issues around stunting and malnutrition, a problem in

Indonesia. Doing this can fundamentally change the direction of these children's lives.

14. TALENT MANAGEMENT

Talent management is an area where I have often struggled. Working as an independent broker, I focused my attention and energies on my clients, not on my small team. As the company grew and we expanded into analysis, biofuels, and conferences, I had to spend more time looking inward rather than outward.

I had no training or experience in talent management, and the little I found was geared more towards big multinationals rather than small companies like ours.

A friend lent me a book about team management written by a business school professor. In the first chapter, he explained how to build a team for any new project. "Choose one team member from your company's departments: marketing, research, IT, manufacturing, accountancy, and legal affairs, etc." My problem was that I was the only person in many of those departments. I quickly abandoned the book.

I had difficulty recruiting people when we were in France. French law forbade me from advertising open positions in English even though all our reports were in English, and the company's working language was English. However, the bigger problem was that French people preferred the security of a big company. Young French people like to join a big organisation and stay there for an extended period. Job security is paramount.

In 2006, we moved to Lausanne with its two world-class universities, top business schools, and a young international and entrepreneurial population. I was over the moon. We quickly built first-class teams in our various activities, preferring to take graduates, post-graduates, and PhDs directly from university.

But then we ran into a different problem: retaining people once we had trained them. We were in a period when hedge funds were expanding aggressively into agricultural commodity trading. Hedge funds (and sometimes trade houses) headhunted our young people as soon as we had trained them. Our little company soon earned a reputation as a training school for the Swiss commodity trading industry. It was a good thing, but it was still difficult to manage as we always had to maintain a pipeline of fresh talent.

I quickly learned that teams do not manage themselves. I remember coming to the office one day and finding myself the only one there. Annoyed, I began calling around and discovered that I had, separately and without noticing, given everyone the day off – all for good reasons! I quickly put reporting structures in place so that not everyone reported to me.

We also had to put in structures for career development and remuneration, with team leaders and department managers all contributing. Once a company gets to a specific size, it can no longer leave it to one person (in this case, me) to decide salary increases, end-year bonuses and promotions.

There was the issue of recruitment. Most employees have no idea how expensive it is – in time and money – to recruit staff. Retaining existing staff is much more efficient than recruiting new people. And yes, we tried everything to make the process more efficient, using external consultants and headhunters. Even so, recruitment remained a permanent challenge.

Despite our best efforts, we realized that our brightest young people were outgrowing our little company; providing them with a structured career path was challenging. That was one of the reasons we finally sold the company to S&P Global. Many of our ex-employees remain with S&P Global in increasingly responsible management positions.

One of our longest-serving employees, Liz Silver, often reminded me of the curse, "I wish you, staff!"

Sometimes, I felt that having staff was a curse. Still, it was one of my greatest joys to see people develop professionally, becoming experts in their relative fields and taking more and more responsibility in the process. It is possibly the thing I miss most about the business.

Julian Stow

Most people misunderstand what a headhunter does. They look at it from the candidate's point of view and think that a headhunter can magic them up a job. But that's not how it works. It is the opposite.

I first met Jules at a conference where he mentioned that his father was a freight broker and a director of the Baltic Exchange. Jules told me that the only career advice his father gave him was not to go into shipbroking. He followed his advice but still focused on the city, sending over 300 application letters to various banks and brokerages, hoping to become a foreign exchange trader. He told me he had found a copy of one of the letters the other day and was shocked at how punchy, pushy, aggressive, and arrogant he was at 21!

Having failed to become a foreign exchange dealer, he joined Czarnikow as a trainee sugar trader. After an initial period in London, Czarnikow sent him to Singapore, where their office handled Queensland's sugar exports. After a few years in Singapore, he moved back to London, where he looked after Czarnikow's Moscow office, but from London.

In 2004, ED&F Man offered him a job to return to Singapore to manage their Asian trading book. He accepted the position and spent four years with them before joining Barclays Capital as a derivatives trader in Singapore and London. The bank ran into difficulties in copper and wound down its commodities business in 2012. He moved to Standard Chartered, but they, too, wound down their trading business after he had been with them for three years.

He took a position in London with Oak Capital, where he began to take an interest in quantitative trading, doing a lot of work on calendar spreads and relative value. He left Oak Capital to set up his own business, running and designing systematic trading strategies for small hedge funds. The systems struggled during the Trump years when many historical patterns broke down. He then ran into Covid and lockdown.

"I had a long hard think about what I wanted to do," Jules told me. "I was in my late forties and realized I no longer wanted to trade. I think it is an age thing. Trading is stressful, but you only realize how stressful it is when you stop.

"A headhunter friend asked me what I enjoyed about trading – what excited me. I was shocked to realize that I couldn't think of anything!" Jules joined his friend as a headhunter.

Commodity traders are like soldiers, usually relatively young. I asked Jules what advice he would give traders when they got too old to trade.

"I am lucky to have somehow solved that puzzle," he said. "I have just turned 50, and I now see CVs from friends and former colleagues my age. The funnel narrows as you swim towards the top.

"I think older traders need to identify which aspect of their job they genuinely enjoy and then orientate themselves in that direction. If, like me, they decide they don't want to do it anymore, I suggest they consider moving on to something else.

"It might sound negative, but it isn't. It is incredibly positive. Traders, particularly physical traders, are great entrepreneurs. Trading is an entrepreneurial business that you must look at holistically. Every time you do something, you must ask how it will affect other parts of the supply chain.

"So, my advice would be to see what business you want to be involved in and start it! You have the skills you need, so decide which niche interests you.

"Apart from experience," I asked, "what skills do you need as a headhunter?

"Emotional Intelligence and the ability to empathize – to listen and not just hear what people tell you. You can never have a bad conversation, even if it eventually comes to nothing. The more data points you have, the better. Each talk is a data point. A big part of headhunting is joining those dots.

"We are all different, so it is a matter of making the most of your skill sets. I am an affable guy, and I enjoy chatting with people. That's my thing. Other headhunters may be more quantitative and analytical. You don't have to be a particular person, but it is a people business. You can't rub people up the wrong way – you wouldn't last long!

"Most people misunderstand what a headhunter does. They look at it from the candidate's point of view and think that a headhunter can magic them up a job. But that's not how it works. It is the opposite.

"The hiring clients drive the process. They contract us on a retained or contingency/success basis. If a client doesn't retain us, we will at least want exclusivity. It doesn't look good on me if I am the fifth headhunter to call a candidate about the same position.

"We will sit with the client to work out what skills and experience they are seeking. There will sometimes be a job description, but the HR department often writes job descriptions with only an arm's length idea of what is needed.

"I prefer to sit with the head of the desk or with the person to whom the candidate will ultimately report. I need to understand the firm's culture, the team dynamics, the essential skills, and the nice-to-haves. We will then assemble a list of candidates and approach them to see if they will move.

"I think of a candidate list as a colouring book that hasn't been coloured in. My job is to colour it in – to provide the information you don't see on a CV that might not naturally come out in an interview. I sometimes feel a bit like a priest. Candidates tell me stuff they wouldn't tell colleagues or competitors. I must treat it in confidence.

Jules' description sounded like what I used to do when broking physical cargoes. He brokers people – but it is similar.

"Your analogy of a broker is a good one," he told me. "I happily chat with people all day long with no objective other than to try and find out what the employment market is doing – who is moving where, which firms are doing well – that sort of thing. When you were a broker, and someone came to you with a cargo to sell, you would already have a short list of potential buyers. The same applies to me. When a client approaches me with an open position, I already know who might fill it."

I was interested in finding out how a headhunter gets paid.

"It varies between firms," Jules told me. "The employer generally pays a percentage of the first-year compensation package, including a signing-on fee if there is one. We prefer to concentrate on a few high-paying positions and do them well rather than doing many smaller ones."

Could you describe a typical day?" I asked him. "How does it differ from being a trader?

"I never looked at my diary when trading unless I was travelling somewhere," he replied. "I knew when the market opened and closed, and that was enough. My working life now is divided into half-hour chunks. I spend most of my day speaking to people via video conference or telephone.

"Technology has set me free as I can now work between home and the office, but it is easy to get holed up and become a technology prisoner. It is essential to meet people in person, even without a specific reason. The best conversations I have are with people I meet for a coffee where there is no agenda. There is no substitute for face-to-face discussions.

"I do my research. I constantly work to broaden my network, turn my second-level contacts into first-level ones, and learn about new markets like energy, power, and gas."

"Are ag traders different from metals and energy traders?" I asked.

"I prefer to divide the market between derivative and physical traders," he replied. "Physical agricultural commodity people are a breed apart. Energy guys have a confident swagger – and more of a dangerous look behind their eyes!

"Most physical traders are social. They must be able to get business done with their clients – real people. Most derivative traders don't deal with people; they just deal with their market screens or OTC brokers. And any OTC broker will tell you they aren't treated like real people!"

I had two further questions. The first was about the opportunities for women. The commodity business has a reputation for being male-dominated. I asked Jules if that was changing.

"Yes, it is," he said. "First, companies are under pressure to employ more women. Second, women look at commodities differently than in the past. It is a bit of a snowball effect. More women are applying to the sector because it is becoming less male-dominated. The more women join, the more women want to join. It is self-reinforcing.

"There are three 'buts'," he added.

"The first is that the process will take time. Finding women with the experience required to fill senior roles is sometimes challenging. It will change as women work their way up the ranks.

"The second is that women are sometimes less flexible geographically than men. We still have some way to go before it becomes the norm for men to give up a job to follow their partners to another country. Some women may be more reluctant to move countries if it means their children must change schools. It is becoming less so, but men may prioritize their careers while women may prioritize stable family life. Geographic flexibility is essential in our business.

"The third follows from the second – women may be more risk averse than men when changing jobs. We had a recent search where a woman was the best candidate by far, but she decided not to take the risk of jumping."

Jules moved around a lot during his career. My last question was: "Knowing what you know now, would you have done anything differently?"

"No," he replied. "I have enjoyed every bit of my career – admittedly, some more than others. Each experience has given me a different point of view and insight. I am lucky.

"I am not one for looking back and wishing I had done something differently. It's gone. It's happened. Move on. In saying that, I realize I am more of a trader than I thought. Don't beat yourself up over past mistakes. Learn from them and look ahead for new opportunities."

Romina Morandini

People realize this is a team game, and you need everybody in the chain to execute their part to the best of their abilities.

Romina is originally from Argentina but has worked in more countries than anyone I know – Argentina, the UK, Brazil, the Netherlands, Switzerland, Chile, and Canada. She spent the first ten years of her career with Shell before moving into ag commodities, first with Cargill and then EDF Man, Noble, COFCO, and Bunge. She has since moved to natural resources and mining.

Having worked in energy, moved to ag commodities, and then to mining, I was interested in whether ag companies presented specific challenges in managing talent.

"Yes, I think so, more and more," she replied. "Given the food element component, agribusiness is more global than the other sectors you mention – not in every role, but in many roles. You need a global mentality from a supply chain perspective and an interest and understanding of geopolitics and economics. I see that in pockets in other industries where I worked, but one of the things that I miss from agribusiness is the daily global conversation.

"That's on the positive side," she continued. "On the opportunities side, agribusiness companies, in my experience, are less structured regarding career opportunities and management. I have found that other industries provide better career visibility. The ag business has an incredible career to offer. Still, I believe it has not done as much as it could to market what it can do for people's careers, particularly those with a talent for an international perspective."

"Did the different ag companies you worked for have different cultures?" I asked. "And to what extent does the CEO set the culture?"

"Each of them has a distinct personality that partly depends on size," she replied. "In a company as big as Cargill, for example, the heritage, not the CEO, shapes the culture. I experienced its culture as robust and well-defined. The other companies I worked for had more of an entrepreneurial flair, and the culture was somehow more linked to the personality and approach of the CEO.

"The CEO plays a role in fine-tuning a company's culture, but it has more to do with its history and whether it grew organically or through acquisitions. People often define culture as 'the way we do things around here'. I find culture plays a crucial role in successful integrations after a merger. A strong culture that aligns with a company's strategy is a considerable asset and challenging to replicate.

"What about managing all the different types of professions in the ag supply chain?" I asked. "Is that a challenge?"

"It is the same in the oil and mining or consulting industries. You need a wide variety of different profiles and skills. I know that people in the ag industry like to say they are unique. They are unique in certain aspects of what their roles require. That is true, but not necessarily in the diversity of skills needed to succeed in an industry.

"What I think is different in ags, at least in my experience, is the stardom of the trader. The trader used to play a protagonist role. I think it's starting to subside a little. People realize this is a team game, and you need everybody in the chain to execute their part to the best of their abilities. I started to see a more conscious recognition of corporate functions during my last years in agribusiness."

My next question was about compensation. Traders get royally compensated, but operators don't.

"Ag trading companies tend to pay quite competitively," she replied. "Their people are generally well-paid compared to similar roles in other sectors. From a human perspective, the challenge is that people do not necessarily compare themselves with what they would earn in the market. Instead, they compare the different job families in the internal ecosystem.

"That can create some internal friction, but it's the same with other industries relying on different kinds of top-notch technical talent. The rainmakers can be highly paid, but they also assess and carry the risk and eventually make the call. It's probably more acute in the trading industry, but I think it's an accepted fact."

Romina had mentioned that trading was becoming more of a team operation – a theme running through many of my interviews. Women tend to be better team players and networkers than men. I asked her if she thought that the future of trading was female.

"I don't know if the future of trading is female," she replied. From a demographical perspective, the future and present of work is becoming more female. Industries that don't consider women forego a big part of the equation. In my time, there were very few female traders – maybe one out of ten. You must be outstanding to be a female on a trading desk. The ones that made it were exceptional.

"Other sectors have been more active or at least more visible in being inclusive, not only on gender. Agribusiness will, unfortunately, miss out on a lot of talent if they don't become more proactive. However, having been in other industries for the last five years, perhaps that is already happening."

"How can agribusiness attract top-quality candidates, both male and female?" I asked.

"We haven't done as good a job as we could around marketing," she said. "That is slowly changing, particularly in Geneva, with SuisseNegoce and the MSc in commodity trading. People are getting a better insight into the industry and what sort of a career path that could lead to.

"I see the difference as Gen Z comes into the workforce. Without going into the stereotypes, mental health, the work/life balance, and the ESG impact are all important. Gen Z has different priorities, and purpose seems to play a significant role in how they select their future employer."

Romina currently works for an engineering company that, through acquisitions, is going from 1,100 to more than 5000 employees. I asked her how she aligned and managed the different cultures. I was thinking of Bungie's acquisition of Viterra.

"It's been an intense ride," she replied, "We are still putting it together. Aligning culture is a long, long road. From a communication and engagement perspective, we've done much work making the cultures explicit, but there's no magic wand. It will take us a couple more years, and it requires everyday effort and leadership to set the right tone, which I believe we have done. These last few years, working intensely on Mergers and Acquisitions and integration will be one of my career highlights.

"Remuneration is one of the critical pain points of integrations and acquisitions. You must ensure you hold on to the critical talent. Before considering strategy, you must look at the people and skills you can't afford to lose."

I had seen on Romina's LinkedIn profile that she had recently completed the FT Board of Directors program. I asked her what she had learned.

"The course put a lot of focus on how people dynamics make or break a board," she said. "The most important takeaway is that board members must be vested in the company and not just be there for the public recognition side of it.

The other thing I learned is the sheer complexity of it all – the number of challenges a committed board and executive team faces is no joke. You must be agile and active in scanning the environment to determine where the next risk to the company might come from.

"Can conflict be a good thing?" I asked.

"There is a perception that conflict should be avoided and that we should behave and be friends," she replied. "I don't have that perspective. Conflict can be positive if you split the problem from the person. I know it sounds easier than it is, but you need creative tension; if there's no tension, there's no creativity, and groups gravitate towards group thinking.

"Conflict becomes problematic if it turns into institutionalized friction. Permanent friction and unresolved conflict create an unhealthy environment."

"What about pessimism and optimism?" I asked. "Do you need a pessimist in every team?"

"I think you do," she replied. "You need a mix. The same goes for extroverts and introverts—or any other personality trait. You need a mix of different personalities to challenge, again in a healthy conflict, yourself and your team. You need it in trading, but you also need it in any business decision."

And my last question: "What advice would you give your 18-year-old self?"

"Don't take life so seriously. Focus on what is essential in the long term. Things will eventually sort themselves out."

Beatriz Pupo

Younger people do not necessarily want to earn more money but want a better lifestyle. And most important, they want to feel that they're working for a company that shares their ethics and vision and does good in the world.

I first met Bea when she joined our Brazilian office as a trainee ethanol broker and analyst. Born and raised in Santos, the biggest port in South America, Bea, in true Brazilian fashion, grew up near the beach.

She relocated to our head office in Lausanne in 2009, where she joined our rapidly expanding biofuels desk. After four successful years there, she resigned for personal reasons to move to Montreal, Canada. We didn't want to lose her, so we took what at that time was a brave decision to ask her to stay with the company and work from home.

She remained with us as an analyst after Platts acquired the company in 2012 and moved back to Brazil with them in 2017. She is now one of the company's leading biofuels analysts and manages a three-person analytical team spread across the globe.

Although biofuels account for only five per cent of world road transportation fuel, they consume a significant quantity of the world's crops – more than 40 per cent of US corn production and 50 per cent of European rapeseed production. They play, therefore, an integral role in the ag-supply chain.

But that is not why I wanted to reconnect with Bea. I had recently stumbled across one of her posts on LinkedIn and was intrigued to read that she wasn't posting about biofuels but about mental health. I asked her over a Zoom call why she had become interested in the subject. "It's a tricky one," she replied. "It's between, 'Do I hide away or talk about it and expose my vulnerabilities.' I took the decision a while back to talk about it."

"I battled with depression for a good part of my life as a teenager and young adult." she continued. "People don't speak about depression as society tends to class it as a weakness. You don't hear people talking about it at all, right? However, my own experience shows that the more I let myself be vulnerable, the more I talked about it, and the more I could develop as a person and a professional. "I'm not saying," she said, "that we need to be sharing everything about ourselves in places that are not meant for that, but the more I allowed myself to be human, the more I developed. And as I developed, I realized that I could use my voice as an advocate to eradicate the stigma of mental health issues."

As part of this book project, I have interviewed more than 50 ag-supply-chain specialists over the past year. It has been a joy and a privilege to share their experiences and enthusiasm for their roles, especially among the younger generation.

However, I am sad to write that one or two of the people I interviewed were exhausted – not thriving, merely striving to survive. They tried to be positive and enthusiastic, but I saw they were making a great effort to be. I thought of Stevie Smith's poem, Not Waving but Drowning.

"Burnout is a big issue everywhere," Bea told me. "It is an illusion to think we can be high-performance people all the time, both at work and home, with our family and friends."

"I have learned that vulnerability and resilience go hand in hand," she explained. "The more I allow myself to be human, open, and curious to deal with the complexities of life, the more grit I develop. My North Star is the idea that we can all be role models in our day-to-day interactions, contributing to a better world, one action, word, and thought at a time. "

"I feel privileged to use my voice and story to amplify the importance of normalizing discussions and creating safe spaces to address these topics."

"Being in the corporate space for the past ten years, in a high-pressure environment, has taught me many things, particularly after dealing with burnout myself. Having lived this experience, one of the key things I learnt is that the perception of our self-worth can be distorted by overly identifying with our professional selves. It is linked to burnout. Exploring a more holistic, conscious approach to well-being and life-work balance can help individuals flourish and escape this 'enmeshed' state."

I asked Bea what she meant by 'enmeshed' state."

It is a psychological term," she explained, "to describe a situation where the boundaries between people become blurred, and individual identities lose importance."

"I recently read appalling stats," she continued, "that 69 per cent of people say their manager has more impact on their mental health than their therapist or their doctor—and it's equal to the impact of their partner. Another study shows that 70 per cent of employees said that their work defines their sense of purpose.

"It can be particularly challenging at work when your reputation becomes your identity. It's dangerous because you forget who you are, your values, and what you want. When I coach, I see many people who don't know their values anymore and don't know who they are.

"They need to recharge, but they don't know how. It can be simple, right? It can be anything. It could be going for a hike and looking at the ocean. It could be dancing. But knowing who you are outside of work and what lights you up is important. Linking your personality and identity to your job can be dangerous, but it's a common problem."

I suggested to Bea that it's a more common problem for men than women, particularly when men reach retirement age. I have friends whose entire identity, status, and social life have been built around their jobs. They lose all three when they stop working.

"It happens to any gender," Bea argued. "I can see that retirement might be more challenging for men than women. However, women have an additional problem because they are under pressure to perform at work and home. Most household duties and responsibilities tend to fall on women. Gender equity must start at home. I feel women suffer more than men because they have that added pressure to be the best at work and home. They must also be the best caretakers for their kids, partners, and older family members. "

"Research shows, for example, that women do a lot of unpaid work just supporting their colleagues mentally, which men don't usually do. That that can also be tricky."

I asked Bea what advice she would give to a team leader to ensure the mental well-being of their team. What things should a team leader watch out for regarding burnout?"

"As you know," she told me, "I have only recently taken on a leadership position. It's very new to me, and I'm still learning. I try to be a role model. I know I can be unrealistic with work expectations, but I also tell my team that taking time out and having more than just their work is essential. "

"As a leader, I try to walk the talk," she continued. "What are you doing as a leader? Are you showing your team that you take care of your mental well-being? If you do, it will hopefully have a trickle-down effect.

"I try to make sure that people are comfortable telling me as their boss – or their peers – if they're not feeling well – that a meeting is not essential or that a piece of work can wait another day. I tell them that they should not prioritize work; they should prioritize their well-being."

I explained to Bea that all this is relatively new – and quite alien – to me. Growing up, my father always told my brothers and me, "Business before pleasure." His words have stayed with me over the years. I am of a post-war generation where a man's principal role was to provide for his family and ensure economic well-being.

I told Bea that I felt that, at least in Europe, mental well-being is now more critical than economic well-being. "

"Generation Z, the 20-to-35-year age group," she explained, "has different priorities to previous generations. Younger people do not necessarily want to earn more money but want a better lifestyle. And most important, they want to feel that they're working for a company that shares their ethics and vision and does good in the world.

"Managers and leaders have this power to shift culture. I have the luck and privilege to work for a company that recognizes the importance of well-being in the workplace," she added.

"Retaining the workforce has become a priority," she explained. "The younger generation is not necessarily concerned with working 9 to 5 and having a stable job and salary. They want more from life. Of course, it is a privileged group of people who can make that decision, but I see it with all the younger people in my team."

I was coming to the end of my time, but I wondered to what extent Covid and working from home had changed people's attitudes to work.

"Did Covid make people realize that there is life outside the office," I asked her. "And was it positive on people's mental health?"

"I think there was a decline in people's mental health during Covid," she replied. "Being in isolation, having to rethink everything, how you carried on, meant you had to reinvent yourself in many ways. "

"On the plus side, working from home gives you the liberty to control your time, be flexible and know when you must do a little more or a little less. This liberty is not something that people will quickly give up. You can see this now as many companies try to get employees to return to the office. They are confronted by their people who do not want to.

"We should also return to diversity and inclusion, she continued. "Working from home is terrific for me as a parent. It gives me the flexibility to have quality time with my daughter. It has done wonders for my mental health. "

"But there is another reason. Letting people know they can be in charge of their time and are trusted to do the work they must do is fantastic. It's invaluable. It's empowering."

"Are you working from home in Santos now," I asked her.

"Yes, yes," she replied. "I go to the office occasionally, but my team is not there. My whole team works remotely. I go to the office if we have conferences, meetings, or client engagements. I prefer to work from home, but I must be careful to contact colleagues and stay connected even though I'm not attending the office."

"That's it," I told her. "Those are all my questions."

"Aren't you going to ask me what advice I would give to my 18-year-old self?" she said. "You ask everyone else."

"Okay. What advice would you give your 18-year-old self?"

"Meditate and cultivate deep self-awareness," she replied. "It will transform your life and your relationship with the world."

"It sounds like good advice for everyone," I told her. "Not just for 18-year-olds."

Kona Haque

I have enjoyed every minute of my career in commodities and have no desire to switch to another industry.

Kona joined ED&F Man in May 2014 as Group Head of Research, responsible for the company's commodity and macroeconomic research team (including Volcafe coffee). She previously worked at Macquarie Bank, responsible for agriculture and soft commodities research for seven years. Kona spent four years as Senior Commodities Editor / Economist at the Economist Group.

She has also worked for a shipping consultancy as Director of Bulk Commodities and spent four years at Metal Bulletin Research, specializing in base metals. She also worked as an economist for a grains market information provider and with the United Nations in Rome, Italy. Kona has an MSc in Economics from the London School of Economics and a BSc in Agricultural Economics from Reading University.

I asked Kona why there are so few women in commodities.

"Commodities as a sector generally seems to do a bad job attracting women," she replied. It could be due to perception – commodities are essentially "raw materials" for processing, which some may see as a place for engineers or heavy-lifting personnel, which tends to be male-oriented.

"But within the commodities space, I would say that metals and energy are even more skewed towards men than the agricultural or softs sector. Ags have a softer image and, in my biased opinion, are better able to attract females.

"But there are areas within commodities that are well represented by women – such as Finance, HR, operations, and Research. At any rate, times are changing, and I've never seen the commodities sector so keen to employ women as I have now. It is only a matter of time before the balance improves here, too."

"Do you think being a woman has held back your career?" I asked her.

"Not at all," she replied. "I joined the sector 25 years ago when investment banks were just beginning to build their commodities desk in anticipation of the bullish trend following the rise of Chinese demand for energy, metals, and food. At that point, the search was on for anyone with a good background in commodities – which I had. Since then, I have always tried to be the best version of me, as a commodities employee, that I could be, which in turn gave me recognition and allowed me to compete with other men on a level playing field.

"So even though I would typically miss out on male-oriented after-work drink ups, golfing networks or what have you, I strived to build value by outperforming my peers during work hours, for example."

"Is travel a factor," I asked. "Women may be less safe than men going out to get business, particularly in developing countries?"

"Developing countries are not inherently unsafe," she replied. "Local knowledge is essential, and we have many female colleagues in our origin locations. A good company will never force you to travel to dangerous places, and we counsel all staff to take precautions when travelling on business.

"Inevitably, when women get married and have families, travelling far and often becomes less easy. It is not unique to commodities, though – it's across businesses. To solve this, the government and companies must develop solutions enabling mothers to travel more often knowing they have reliable alternative home arrangements during their absence."

"I have the impression that women tend to work better in networks rather than confrontation," I said. "Do you think the way the commodity trade is evolving will result in more women traders?"

"Commodity trading doesn't always have to be confrontational!" she replied. "And some women are pretty good at it anyway – it depends on individual personalities. I've yet to come across a role in commodities that is genuinely gender specific. In many traditionally male-oriented roles, women can be as good as men (if not better).

"The challenge is to get women to apply for those roles. At ED&F Man, we've been actively trying to boost women's applications at all levels. We train hiring managers on unconscious bias and promote the idea of commodities as a career to our employees and the young people we mentor.

"We have set up a Women's Network to encourage women to aim high at ED&F Man and in our wider industry. Commodity companies need to be more active in recruiting at an early stage. Some universities, for instance, offer excellent courses in commodities, which have opened the field for women and provided a strong talent pool."

"Final question," I said. "What advice would you give a woman looking to enter commodities?"

"I would say go for it!" she replied. "I have enjoyed every minute of my career in commodities and have no desire to switch to another industry. Commodities are real, tangible, and international. The sector is influenced by changing politics, weather, and economic trends, so there's never a dull moment. None of this is gender specific; if you are good at what you do, women from all countries and backgrounds should join the sector.

"Women should look for a company willing to invest in people and ideally find a mentor/sponsor. It's important to be open-minded and confident in your abilities (and not a shrinking violet), as there is a lot of scope for moving around the industry and flourishing. Teams with a good gender balance are known to be high performing, so if the commodity industry can boost the intake of women, can you imagine how far it can go?"

15. PROMOTING THE SECTOR

While researching his 1979 book *Merchants of Grain: The Power and the Profits of the Five Grain Companies at the Centre of the World's Food Supply*, Dan Morgan had considerable difficulty obtaining information from what he described as 'shadowy and unknown' grain-trading companies.

He quoted a US senator describing grain merchants: 'No one knows how they operate, what their profits are, what they pay in taxes and what effect they have on foreign policy – or much of anything else about them'.

When Dwayne Andreas became CEO of ADM in 1974, one of the first things he did was to eliminate the company's public relations department. He once famously said, 'Getting information from me is like frisking a seal'. In 1976, the French magazine L'Expansion called Louis Dreyfus 'a commercial empire of which one knows nothing.'

None of the trading houses was more obsessed with secrecy than Bunge. Dan Morgan wrote, 'Bunge was a private company about which nobody knew, and nobody could speak. To Bunge officials, public relations meant keeping Bunge out of the limelight.'

But why were the grain companies so secretive back in the 1970s? Dan Morgan wrote,

'The companies stay in the shadows most of the time. Perhaps it was the ancient nightmare of the middleman–merchant that made them all so secretive – the old fear that in moments of scarcity or famine, the people would blame them for all their misfortunes, march upon their granaries, drag them into the town square and confiscate their stock.'

The world is a different place today. All the sizeable agricultural commodity companies are present on social media and actively engage with

NGOs on issues related to environmental sustainability or human rights. Public Relations and Communication professionals now play a significant role in the agricultural supply chain. But what exactly do they do?

I contacted a friend in the sector who, although asking not to be named, sent me a job description she had recently prepared for an opening in her company's communications department. It read as follows:

- Combat misinformation on issues like environmental impact, sustainability, and food safety.

- Shape the sector's image and manage relationships with stakeholders, including farmers, traders, investors, regulatory bodies, and the public.

- Educate stakeholders about market dynamics, pricing mechanisms, and the factors influencing supply and demand.

- Maintain and enhance the company's reputation and brand by highlighting its commitment to sustainability, showcasing initiatives such as reducing carbon footprints, promoting fair trade, and supporting biodiversity.

- Ensure internal teams are aligned and informed about company policies, market conditions, and strategic changes.

- Stay abreast of changing regulations.

- Establish the company as a thought leader by participating in industry conferences and contributing to academic and industry publications.

- Craft tailored communication strategies for different cultural and regulatory environments to build strong global relationships and expand market presence.

- Form partnerships and collaborations with other companies, research institutions, and non-governmental organizations to enhance the company's capabilities and reputation.

She added the following note:

"PR and Communications professionals in agricultural commodity trading navigate a landscape filled with challenges, such as market volatility, misinformation, and regulatory complexities, while seizing opportunities presented by sustainability initiatives, digital transformation, and global outreach.

"Through effective stakeholder engagement, crisis management, market education, brand management, and internal communications, PR professionals help to stabilize, enhance, and grow the agricultural commodity trading industry, ensuring its continued contribution to global food security and economic development."

I couldn't have put it better myself!

Nicole Marlor

There will always be people who criticize the ag commodity sector.

As Cargill's European Lead of Media Relations and Crisis, Nicole has helped me interview various Cargill people for my books. I asked her if she would allow me to interview her for a chapter on communications and was delighted when she agreed.

It took a few months to connect, but I eventually caught up with her while on holiday in France. We talked by video conference as I sheltered from the pouring rain on a hotel balcony. It was the only place in the hotel where the WIFI worked well enough for the call, and even then, the call dropped out a couple of times.

Although Nicole now lives in the UK, she grew up in Minneapolis, where her father worked for Cargill. She studied Public Relations and Communications at St Mary's University of Minneapolis and worked for nearly six years with General Mills. She joined Cargill in 2006 and moved to the UK in 2014.

"I always knew I wanted to follow a career in communication," she told me. "I was a good talker and quite persuasive from a young age. I was always better at communications than science and math, and I enjoyed it.

"My dad worked at Cargill for 30 years and had a successful career with the company. I learned about Cargill growing up, but I went to work for General Mills when I left university. General Mills is a CPG (Consumer Packaged Goods) company, and I joined Cargill because I wanted to be on the end-to-end supply chain side of it. I don't come from a farming background. It was more of a family thing."

"What are the specific PR challenges that Cargill faces?" I asked.

"Cargill is a multi-function company operating in multiple sectors and countries," Nicole replied. "There will always be challenges regarding communications and PR, whether with our license to operate or different needs in different countries.

"Social media presents multiple challenges. It makes communicating easier, but PR was easier before social media. I'll give you an example. Before social media, you could issue a press release, say, in the UK, for a UK audience. You can't do that now. Everything goes global. Issuing a press release in Europe doesn't mean it will stay in Europe. Someone can tweet about it, and then I can get a call from a journalist in Brazil who's unhappy with something.

"It's true for any company but especially for Cargill as we operate in many different sectors and geographies. It is one of my biggest challenges as a PR professional for Cargill. But it's a good challenge because it keeps things interesting."

When I talk with friends about the agricultural commodity sector and explain how it works and what it does, somebody always says, "Well, of course, you'd say that." Having failed to disprove the message, they attack the messenger. I asked Nicole how I should respond when that happens.

"It's a question we deal with all the time," she replied. "The way we combat it is to be transparent about what we're doing regarding challenging topics like sustainability or trading. We are more open now about market dynamics from a global perspective than we have ever been. We tell our positive stories and are transparent about the more complex issues.

"We continue to educate. There will always be people who criticize the ag commodity sector. There will always be people who criticize Cargill because we're a big company. We will always be a target.

"Unfortunately, no matter how much you educate, how many media releases you send, and how many good things you share, there will always be people who will be sceptical of the sector. But I think that's true in any industry.

"It doesn't discourage me, but I see internally it gets many people down," she added. "Maybe I've been doing it too long that I'm used to it. Like I said, I also enjoy it."

"Do you spend more time defending or promoting the sector and Cargill?" I asked.

"It's probably 50/50," she replied. "However, I don't look at it as defending; I look at it as educating. I spend most of my time educating and promoting.

"Because of our scale, we're always going to be a target, but because of our scale, we're feeding the world. Some people will attack us because we are a big company in big ag. They often assume that we're hiding something when we're not. Other people look at it like, 'Oh, you're feeding the world. Cargill is a great company putting food on the table.'"

"Do you respond to every negative tweet and article?" I asked.

"Our general policy is not to engage on social media," she replied. "We won't get what we want by responding to everything.

"We struggle when there are negative articles about us because our management wants to respond and correct. I spend a lot of time reminding leaders that this was a negative article, but here is what we're doing that they didn't write. Here's what you can be proud of Cargill doing, and here's what you can share with our employees.'

"We spend a lot of time internally responding to negative articles, but we do not react externally unless there's something inaccurate.

"It is the difference between PR and communication," she continued. "In PR, you communicate primarily to an external audience, whether social media, journalists, or the public. In communication roles, you're looking at a different audience, primarily the company's internal stakeholders, so employees."

"So, on the communication side, you respond to negative articles internally by communicating with your stakeholders," I said. "But on the PR side, you don't respond to negative articles. You just keep educating and promoting."

"That's correct," Nicole told me. "There isn't a way to respond externally. If we did, I would spend 24 hours a day, 365 days doing that, as there are a lot of negative articles out there.

"We try to educate journalists, but a few will always be sceptical. They don't understand, and they don't want to understand. We will only spend time working with journalists if they are willing to listen.".

"When does PR turn into lobbying?" I asked. "After all, you're communicating with politicians, lawmakers, the media, and the public."

"We have a government affairs group within Cargill," she replied. "It is not my role. However, we work together to invite politicians if we are inaugurating a new factory or something.

"It is a fine line. PR has a sales element, as does lobbying. You try to ensure that people have a positive view of your company. It all comes down to integrity and ethics and ensuring you're being honest about what you share."

"Over the last couple of years, increased volatility has led to an increase in trading house profits. Have you faced criticism because of these higher profits?" I asked.

"We're a privately held company and have stopped releasing our earnings publicly," she told me. "However, it is true that volatility from weather events or political conflicts makes for a more profitable trading environment.

"We continue to see criticism on this issue. However, Cargill and other food trading companies don't set food prices. Supply and demand set prices. What Cargill does is help minimize the supply disruption arising from events such as COVID-19, the war in Ukraine, the vessel attacks in the Red Sea, and poor weather. We work to make connections to ensure that the supply chain remains resilient. We add more value when markets are disrupted."

I was intrigued by the 'crisis' part of Nicole's job title. As my friends know, I tend to avoid conflict and hate crises.

"Personally, it drives me," she told me. "Crises are one of my favourite parts of my job. Few people enjoy a crisis, but I find it challenging in a good way. I think of it as an opportunity."

"What advice could you give a company on how best to manage a crisis? I asked. "It could be an accident resulting in environmental pollution or personal injury, or the reputational damage from the discovery of child labour or deforestation in the supply chain."

"The first thing is to ensure that you have the right people sitting at the table," she answered. "If there is a crisis, you've got someone over here and someone over here, and people don't know what the right hand and the left hand are doing. You must have a proper team in place and ensure that everyone knows who the lead is. It is critical.

"Once the team is in place, ensure you get all the information. I need you to tell me what's happened, where it's happened, how many times it's happened, who it's happened to, who's involved. I need to know everything to be able to assess the situation.

"The rule in a crisis is 'communicate, communicate, communicate,' but that implies internally, not necessarily externally. It depends on the situation. You must never come across like you're hiding something. But there are instances, say with the death of an employee or an investigation into a human rights issue, where you've got legalities. Sometimes, there are only certain things that you can say.

"It's critical to remain calm. You see so many people in a crisis flailing around, and it won't do any good."

"Are women better communicators than men?" I asked.

"I probably would have said yes to that question ten years ago," she replied. "Now, there are a lot of outstanding male communicators, maybe because they've had great women media coaches. No, I'm kidding.

"There's an element of communication where you must feel comfortable taking risks and trusting your instincts. It is a quality that both men and women have. So, no, I wouldn't say women are better communicators. I would say they're different communicators. Women tend to talk more;

they share their feelings more. But that's not necessarily a good thing in a role like mine."

"If somebody was thinking about a career in PR and communications," I asked, "would you recommend they study it at a university or learn it on the job?

"In a complex company like ours, you will need some formal education in the field. I recently hired someone with a political science background, but she had previously been a communications manager at an agency and had some experience. You can either do a course or gain experience in an agency. You don't necessarily need a full unique degree in it."

"What advice would you give to your 18-year-old self?" I asked.

"Trust your instincts. Be bold. Don't be afraid to challenge and take risks."

"Is there anything you wanted to add?"

"I never thought I would say it," she replied, "but agricultural commodity trading is one of the most exciting fields in PR. It is so interesting, but many people know little about it. There's so much opportunity, especially for women. PR is one of the most exciting fields that you can be in in the trading space."

Maryana Yarmolenko Stober

It's easier to have a career as a professional woman in this industry than ten or 15 years ago, but it's not equal yet. Things are changing, but the speed with which they are changing is not good enough. Too slow.

Maryana was born in a small Ukrainian city in the Ternopil Region, Ukraine, and did her first university degree at the Ivan Franko National University in Lviv. She completed her law degree at Lund University in Sweden and then worked in a law firm in Ukraine before joining ADM in Switzerland in 2010. She covers various corporate legal issues – M&A, joint ventures, competition, commercial and trade – and is the lead lawyer for one of ADM's business units.

As part of her job, Maryana manages legal and trade matters for the company's leadership team in Ukraine. After the Russian invasion, she supported the teams there to find new export routes, establishing internal policies on bomb shelters, and looking after refugees. In addition, she handled Western European matters resulting from the invasion: force majeures and supply chain disruptions.

Maryana is a member of WISTA, the Women's International Shipping and Trading Association, present in over 50 countries with over 5,000 members globally. She is president of the Swiss chapter, where she works with the board on strategy and PR, promoting the association within the sector and communicating with our members.

Individual WISTA members pay a membership fee of CHF 300 per year, but more corporations are joining to support women in leadership. WISTA had some of the biggest trading houses as members. The Swiss

Chapter has around 100 members and is probably as large as those in larger countries like France, Germany, or Norway.

In 2023, WISTA commissioned PWC to report on the number of women in the Swiss shipping and trading sector. She kindly sent it to me before we talked. It found that, on average, women compose about a third of Switzerland's total shipping and commodity trading workforce and hold around a quarter of senior leadership positions. These numbers are slightly higher than the global average and suggest that the industry is above the Swiss average and ahead of other sectors.

"These figures are almost too good to be true," she told me. "I'm not saying they are incorrect – they are correct. However, we saw that the companies that participated in the survey were those most interested in gender equality. "

"The survey included questions from employees and employers, but it was challenging to get employer feedback—only companies devoted to the topic filled in the employer side. We will have another project with PWC later this year to dive deeper into the numbers."

"If these numbers are correct," I asked, "Are you satisfied with a third of the workforce and a quarter of the senior leadership positions? Or would you aim for 50 / 50?"

"We would like to aim for higher," she replied. "A survey by the IMO (International Maritime Organisation) found that the percentage of women in the shipping industry is 29 per cent worldwide. That number includes seafarers and women on board vessels where there are fewer women than men. Most of the shipping and commodity trading jobs in Switzerland are office jobs. We see no reason why more women could not be in these jobs. So yes, we would like this number to be higher, more than a third and much closer to a half."

PWC didn't look at pay. I told Maryana I thought it essential to see if women only occupied low-paying positions or were underpaid in similar positions to men. I asked her if this was something that WISTA would look at in the future. She replied that they didn't look at it for two reasons.

"First, pay is a sensitive and confidential issue in Switzerland," she said. "We felt we would get even fewer responses if we asked direct questions about pay. Second, new legislation in Switzerland will require companies to self-audit and report on pay equality between genders.

"But we did ask about the different perceptions of gender equality. We asked, for example, whether employees felt that their companies promoted women at the same rate as men, paid them the same as men, and gave them equal opportunities for development and decision-making power."

"Individuals, not HR departments, answered these questions, and the perceptions differed between men and women. Only a third of women considered they were paid the same as men at their workplace, but two-thirds of men felt women were. On the perception level, most men thought that employers treated women equally to men in pay and promotions, but most women disagreed."

The PWC survey found a low employee awareness of diversity and inclusion priorities in their companies. I suspected things were changing, but I wondered if they were changing enough."

"Things are changing," Maryana told me. "It's easier to have a career as a professional woman in this industry than ten or 15 years ago, but it's not equal yet. Things are changing, but the speed with which they are changing is not good enough. Too slow.

"The PWC report mentioned a World Economic Forum estimate that if we continue at the current pace, it will take more than 100 years to close the gender gap.

Many women in commodities work in support functions like operations, HR, and communications; there are few women traders. I asked her why.

"Women can do trading jobs exactly like men can," she answered. "At WISTA, we refer to several studies that say that women are not risk-averse; they just tend to face consequences when they take risks.

"Modern trading is more around teamwork and networking than in the past. There is less room to make independent, risky decisions. Trading has become more structured, meaning women can easily enter trading roles.

"Historically, trading was seen as a job that required you to be plugged in all the time – on weekends, evenings, and vacations. Men have more possibilities to do this than women.

"Since COVID, trading companies have started to give their employees more flexibility. It's okay to work from home; it's almost okay to work part-time, and it's also okay to switch off during vacation. I believe we will see more women traders with this new normal.

"Working from home has become customary since COVID. Companies will lose good people if they are unwilling to give this flexibility."

"My ambition for this book was for women to make up about a third of the people I interviewed," I told Maryana. "However, I struggle to find them; when I do, they are reluctant to be interviewed. I don't understand why."

"It's interesting," she replied. "Maybe it's because you want to interview people in senior or mid-level positions, where only a quarter are women.

"I understand that you struggle to find women for the interviews because we also find it challenging to identify senior women for our events. It's not that women don't want to come and share their experiences with other women. They do want to come. We never have a problem when somebody says no, but we have trouble finding them.

"In your case, it is also maybe because of how society works – and the education in the last 50 years or so – that women tend to pass on opportunities. Women may feel they must be 100 per cent ready for the interview – to be perfect, more perfect than men. It's something we talk about a lot at WISTA. Women may feel they don't have the time to prepare and pass on the opportunity, while men would just take it even if they are not ready."

"Last question," I said. "What is the most significant thing you learned with WISTA?"

"That when you have a project or an idea you are passionate about and know how to execute it, you can do great things."

Five Questions for Florence Schurch

Please tell me about your role as Secretary General at SUISSENÉGOCE.

My role is to promote Switzerland's shipping and commodity trading sector by working with local and federal authorities and communicating on the industry. Another critical role of the Association is to educate the next generation by providing training courses to prepare young people and adults for entering the industry. We do not engage in commodity trading. My team comprises individuals with expertise in communications, politics, government, human resources, and training courses.

I spent five years at the Swiss Embassy in Washington, two years with the Swiss Consulate in Germany, and 11 years with the Geneva government in public affairs. I joined SUISSENÉGOCE in February 2020, attracted by the challenge.

When the executive board interviewed me for the position, I told them that I had worked as a lobbyist for the Canton of Geneva, promoting the Geneva economy. However, I never encountered anything from the shipping and commodity sector on my desk.

While preparing for the interview, I Googled the names of the companies whose directors were interviewing me. I didn't know one name. I thought, "Why doesn't such a significant industry communicate? Why isn't anyone in government or authority aware of the added value of all these companies?" Since my first day in this position, it has continued to surprise me how little people know about an industry that is essential to everyone's everyday life.

Why does the shipping and trading sector need SUISSENÉGOCE?

The Executive Board has assigned the Association three missions.

The first is to monitor regulations, maintain communication with the authorities, and promote the sector's interests. Swiss politicians don't usually interact with individual companies; they meet with associations. SUISSENÉGOCE plays a vital role by liaising between politicians and merchants, addressing any challenges members may have.

Second, the Association plays a significant role in education and training. There are many shipping and commodity trading houses in Switzerland, and they are not here only because of the banks. They are also here for a well-qualified and multilingual workforce.

It is partially thanks to the Master of Science degree in commodity trading offered at the University of Geneva and the educational and training services provided by SUISSENÉGOCE. The Association holds the EDUCA label, a Swiss standard for adult education. It means that the government can send us unemployed individuals for training. Thanks to our courses, we take pride in helping unemployed people secure employment in the trading industry.

In 2020, the Swiss population voted in favour of the Responsible Business Initiative (RBI). The ordonnance came into force in 2022 and requires that companies provide reports on child labour and metals and minerals originating from conflict zones. Over the past three years, the Association has organized training courses and workshops where we invited the Swiss government to explain what they expected from the companies.

Third, there is our role in communication. When interacting with the media, the Association speaks on behalf of the entire industry rather than a specific company.

Is shipping a significant industry in Switzerland?

Swiss companies operate 22 per cent of the world's vessel fleet. There are two million seafarers in the world. It means that Swiss companies employ 400,000 seafarers. It's a lot.

The seafarers work all year round, bringing us everything we need. They transport over 90 per cent of the goods and commodities traded internationally. They are under attack from pirates. Hostile countries take them hostage.

We can support seafarers by talking about them and reminding people that without them, they wouldn't have the cup of coffee they drink in front of their computers. They wouldn't even have a laptop or the clothes they wear. The cotton would still be sitting in a warehouse somewhere.

Journalists have been calling us recently about the attacks on shipping in the Red Sea, worried that they will cause delays and make things more expensive. But what about the seafarers? No one is interested in talking about their safety and well-being.

Do you spend more time defending the sector or promoting it?

Proactively promoting the industry is a crucial aspect of the Association's mission. I tell our members to avoid being defensive in their communications and adopt a more proactive approach. We must demonstrate the value that commodity merchants add.

People listen to the dogs that bark the loudest. It's a challenge to counter misinformation. Brandolini's law, also known as the bullshit asymmetry principle, emphasizes the effort required to debunk misinformation compared to the relative ease of creating it. Refuting misinformation can be time-consuming and resource-intensive, making it challenging to address an issue effectively.

People have moved on by the time you have corrected the information; it's too late. That's why it is more important to promote the industry.

The past few years have been characterized by volatile markets due to factors such as insecurity, wars, and sanctions. Countries have shown a willingness to secure their supply of commodities by purchasing them in advance. Additionally, wars have disrupted supply chains and contributed to market instability and inflation. These challenging times have highlighted the expertise of commodity merchants in navigating these complex situations. We were never short of coffee, wheat, gas, or electricity.

Climate change has also impacted commodity markets, leading to reduced crops and higher prices. Price increases are primarily driven by scarcity rather than increased profits for merchants. Higher crop prices can also lead to higher financing and operating costs for merchants, potentially reducing their margins.

Don't forget that wheat prices rose after the Russian invasion of Ukraine, but they have since fallen. Wheat is now cheaper than it was before the war. However, if you go to the store or bakery, bread is still as expensive as it was when prices increased just after the beginning of the war.

What advice would you give to your members?

Communicate, communicate, communicate, promote the sector, promote the industry. Explain the use and the necessity of what you do for everybody in everyday life. Always be willing to talk to the media and always tell the truth, even if you may be unable to tell journalists everything.

Paul Chapman

Most of the headlines and books on commodity trading glorify and revel in the scandals. They do a disservice to the industry as they don't reflect how it operates today.

I have a confession: I am a terrible listener. I always have been. At school, my mind would drift off almost as soon as the teacher began the lesson. At university, I abandoned most lectures in favour of reading in the library. And now, when I watch a movie, I find myself reading the subtitles rather than listening to the dialogue.

My daughter is a massive fan of podcasts. For as long as I can remember – which at my age is not long – she has been trying to convert me to them. She wants me to shift my blog conversations from text to audio. I have tried, but somehow it doesn't work for me. (Call me old fashioned, but I prefer the written word.) I want to listen to podcasts, but I always find my mind drifting, just as it did at school. What shall I have for lunch? Does that girl like me?

There are some excellent podcasts on the commodity sector that I have failed to listen to. Luckily, Spotify has found a solution for people like me: they provide a text version. It's not perfect, but it does the job. I can now binge on podcasts, catching up on the episodes I have missed over the years, even if I read rather than listen to them.

Paul Chapman's HC Group podcast is one of my favourites. He has produced a weekly podcast for the past four years and recently celebrated his 200th edition. It is quite a record. Over the past three years, I have conducted over 100 interviews for my book and blog, and I am exhausted!

I asked Paul how he found the time to do the podcast in addition to his day job.

"Typically, I have a half-hour to an hour chat with potential guests beforehand," he told me. "We develop the primary arc of the conversation. I don't like scripting or going into too much detail.

"The actual podcast takes an hour to record. I do a draft edit and send it to a lady in Finland who does the fine edits. All in all, end-to-end, it's probably a three-hour process. But then I've had a lot of practice. The first few episodes took a lot longer."

Although Paul can't capture all the data, his podcast has about 25,000 monthly listeners. He is nearing a million downloads and has had some 300,000 listeners. A core audience listens to every episode, and many people dip in and out depending on the topic.

"Most other commodity podcasts are short market updates," Paul told me. "Ours are more extended discussions. One advantage is that, as a recruiter, I can ask stupid questions. I can say I don't understand something and ensure everyone's on the same page.

"Ultimately, everything comes down to people. We talk about talent at some point in every podcast. The success of a hedge fund or trading house depends on how good their people are and the culture that they build."

"HC Group is a global search firm dedicated to the commodity sector and the people within it," he added. "Our podcasts are an extension of the culture of the business."

Paul joined HC Group after university and was celebrating his 20th year with the company when I spoke with him in June 2024. He joined the company in London as a desk researcher on the European gas and power markets, and, in 2007, he put his hand up to go to Houston to take part in the US's booming energy market.

The company started focusing on agriculture in 2010, with ADM as one of its anchor clients. At that time, the leading ag houses were diversifying into other areas of the value chain, so much of their work was outside of trading in areas such as animal and human nutrition.

In 2018, Justin Pearson, the company's co-founder, was keen to move on. Paul and his colleague Damian Stewart bought the business from him and are now co-owners. The firm was then down to about 24 people. With luck and judgment – luck being the markets coming back and judgment being that they made some significant changes to get the business back on its feet – they're now 85 people in six offices.

"At HC Global," Paul told me, "we do everything a top-tier standard search firm would do, but we only focus on the commodities sector. That focus gives us a competitive advantage over other, more generic search firms. We understand the roles and better assess candidates' skillsets and fit. We have an established network and brand within the market, so we are typically already connected within the candidate community, and they trust us. It also means we can be true advisors to our clients."

I was keen to turn the conversation back to the podcasts. I have sometimes struggled to find interviewees for my blog and books. I asked Paul how he did it.

"Most of our guests come from recommendations from our network," he answered. "Overlaid onto that is an odyssey of personal interest. What do I find exciting? What are the current themes that need addressing?

"It is sometimes challenging to find individuals not overly controlled by communications departments. We look for guests who can provide a balanced, in-depth view rather than just advertise talking points.

"People are sometimes reluctant to participate for fear of revealing strategies and information. There's a historical culture in that you don't want exposure, you don't want to be in the media, and you don't want to talk openly about anything for fear of giving your competitors insights and information. There's a feeling there's a downside to discussing how much money you're making. You face political and cultural headwinds in the commodity trade."

Another thing that I struggle with is to find women willing to be interviewed. Again, I asked Paul how he did.

"I try to find a balance between men and women," he answered, "but it's a function of demographics. Women make up about 30 per cent of the workforce in the sector but occupy only 20 per cent of the senior positions. I try to do better, but the demographics of the podcast probably reflect that reality."

"What have you learned since you began the podcasts?" I asked him. It is a question that people often ask me about my blogs.

"I feel less confident about everything now than before I started the podcasts," he answered. "It takes work and research to understand markets. I've learnt how complex and nuanced everything is and how people quickly jump to shorthand, heuristic judgments.

"Let's take the energy transition. We've done episodes on critical minerals with issues around child labour, unsatisfactory working conditions, and corruption. You hear companies like Apple say that they want this and that, but they ignore some of the complexities. Regulators ignore the trading community when it comes to battery minerals. They don't engage traders.

"If you want to affect energy transition and get to the heart of sustainability, the commodity sector is the place to do it. Other sectors, like the technology sector, are terrible for the environment, but they've managed to hide the material supply chains they rely on. Trading houses and traders receive the blame.

"A senior banker recently told me his bank's risk committee would drop a commodity trading house if it got fined millions of dollars for an infraction. At the same time, Google regularly gets billions of dollars in fines, and no one has a problem doing business with them.

"The stock market typically values companies with a trading arm at a discount," he continued. "Trading is innately hard to understand. It overlays with the desire of the sector to go under the radar. Most of the headlines and books on commodity trading glorify and revel in the scandals. They do a disservice to the industry as they don't reflect how it operates today.

"When you see a headline that a trading company made billions of dollars trading European power, the public perception is that the energy traders have been gouging us. The reality is they have been solving problems.

"The worry is that there's intensive pressure on governments to intervene, particularly in the ag markets. Without a free-trading commodity market, you would have increased volatility, sharper price spikes, and higher inflation. It is a real challenge for the sector. In a more volatile world, will we lose the functionality that allows markets to address issues in solving problems in space, time, and form?"

I asked Paul if the sector's negative image discouraged people from joining it.

"When I first joined the sector," he told me, "the top companies such as Cargill had the pick of the litter of the best schools in the US. The top students now go to investment banks, hedge funds, and technology companies. A lot of that has to do with the low returns over the last decade. It has resulted in a talent bottleneck at the junior executive level. Everyone's feeling it.

"The sector has some real challenges. It's not promoting itself. It's not attracting the best and the brightest. And it hasn't done so for some time."

"What is the solution?" I asked. "What should the sector do to promote itself better?"

"I did an MBA at Rice University in Houston," he answered. "We had classes on equity trading but not commodity trading. Few universities teach how commodities flow around the world. All top universities should have classes on it."

Which leads nicely into the next chapter!

16. EDUCATION

Little formal training was available when I started in the commodity business. Companies preferred to take their graduate recruits directly from university. They would teach them how commodity trading works and train them to think in a certain way – to learn the company's culture. I didn't realise how lucky I was when I accepted a graduate job offer from Cargill, a company I had never heard of and knew nothing about.

Years later, as we were building our conference business, we were often asked to hold training programmes for new entrants into the sector. As a trial, we did tack on one or two after our various conferences, but we never mastered the art.

The first challenge we failed to overcome was that attendees had different experience levels, and we struggled to find the right balance between beginner and advanced. The second was that the courses were time-consuming to prepare and give. The third was that our business is international; it is expensive for employers to send their young teams halfway across the world for a two-day training course.

We abandoned the idea and instead decided to concentrate on our reports and analysis, hoping that new entrants would pick things up and get to understand the business by osmosis. However, I made a mental note to myself to write an elementary introduction to the sector when I retired – something I achieved in 2016 with *Commodity Conversations*.

I admire people who provide training and university courses to young people in our sector. In this chapter, I introduce you to four wonderful people helping train and educate the next generation of agricultural commodity professionals. The future is in good hands.

Eliane Palivoda Herren

Commodity and shipping are a broad space incorporating many professions: audit, trade finance, legal, inspection, shipping, risk, and compliance – middle, back and front office.

We may have struggled to recruit and retain key personnel during the 2000s, but we were not alone. In the mid-2000s, commodity trading companies in the Arc du Leman, from Geneva to Montreux along Lake Geneva – including Lausanne, approached the GTSA, the Geneva Trading and Shipping Association – now SUISSENEGOCE – with the idea of starting a training scheme to increase the supply of young talent.

SUISSENEGOCE worked with the University of Geneva to set up in 2008 the Master of Science, Executive Diploma and Executive Certificate in Commodity Trading. The programme is now on its 16th intake and has over 1,000 course alums.

I spoke to Eliane Palivoda Herren, the Executive Director of the master's programme.

"This year," she told me, "33 students from 15 countries are in the programme. Of those, 27 per cent are Swiss, 55 per cent are European, and 18 per cent are non-Europeans. The average age is 25 years.

"The programme is for young people with a bachelor's degree. The University is open regarding bachelor's degrees. We have had students who've studied finance, management, accounting, law, international relations, and all the scientific backgrounds such as mathematics, chemistry, physics, etc. We have someone from a naval academy. We often have people with a shipping degree, mainly from Greece."

I asked Eliane whether winning a place on the course was challenging.

"It's a two-step process," she replied. "A committee initially selects the best candidates based on their academic results. Those candidates then go through a second phase, applying to companies linked to the commodity trading industry, such as commodity trading, shipping, inspection, and audit companies or banks, for a traineeship.

"It's not easy to find a traineeship, but we help. This year, we had a record 170 applications, of which we initially selected 100 candidates."

"So, out of the 100 students you selected for the course this year, only 33 were hired by a company?"

"The companies invest time and money in their trainees," she told me. "Most stay within the company, so it's worth it. I know people from the first three or four intakes still with the same company. Companies hire again year after year. Some companies have graduate programmes but still take trainees from our programme."

"Do all the graduates end up in commodity trading and shipping?" I asked.

"We want our students to have an overview and transferable skills they can use in many different areas and businesses," Elian replied. "Commodity and shipping are a broad space incorporating many professions: audit, trade finance, legal, inspection, shipping, risk, and compliance – middle, back and front office. The sustainability aspect is essential. Energy is not just oil and gas. It is electricity, whether wind, solar, or hydro. We teach all the aspects of the business."

"Who teaches the course?" I asked.

"We have professors and PhDs from the University of Geneva or other universities, and we have a few professionals. We have experts who are professionals coming from the commodity industry.

"It's a one-year course. It was initially 18 months, then it became two years, but we have shortened it to two semesters of classes. The traineeship runs over a year, and it's up to the company to decide whether to employ the student when he finishes his courses or wait while he writes his thesis, usually in the third semester. The course is a 90-credit program under the European Credit Transfer and Accumulation System."

I asked Eliane how a potential participant could judge whether the course was right for them.

"Our program tends to attract students interested in a master's degree with an academic and a practical side, students interested in what's happening in the world and how geopolitics or the weather affects commodities. It also attracts students who are interested in the environment.

"It is an intense program because you need to be 100 per cent at the office when you're at the office and 100 per cent at the University when you are at the University. It's every weekend for a year. Students know that presence is mandatory. There's no recording. There are no online courses; students need to be present. We explain this clearly, so nobody is surprised. We never had anyone say that this was not what I had expected. I'm dropping out. We never had that.

"And as I said, it is a two-stage process. When the companies interview potential trainees, they are also looking for specific skills, more and more soft skills."

"Women make up 42 per cent of the class this year," I said. "Do you know the percentage in 2008 when you first started?"

"In 2008, 31 per cent of our students were women. However, we have had years – 2015 and 2020 – when the percentage dropped to 5 per cent. Commodities and shipping remain a male environment, but you would have a similar situation in other sectors, sometimes the other way around. If you go to psychology, 80 per cent of the students are women, and 20 per cent are men.

"I never had a woman come to me and question whether the program is for her because she is a woman. I never had that question. The sector offers so many opportunities, whether you're a man or woman, I don't think there is any constraint."

"Anything you want to add?" I asked.

"Yes," she replied. "The course is constantly evolving to adapt to the changing market conditions. It is not the same course now as in 2008!"

Wouter Jacobs

Growing up in a big port makes you aware at a young age that there is another world out there.

Wouter is the Executive and Academic Director of the Erasmus Commodity & Trade Centre in Rotterdam. The Centre runs two commodity programmes: a commodity elective on their MSc course at the Rotterdam School of Management and a part-time executive programme in commodity trading.

He has never traded commodities and has spent his professional life in academia with a master's in science in spatial planning and economic geography and a PhD in management with a thesis on the political economy of port competition between Rotterdam, Dubai, and Los Angeles.

"If you grow up in Rotterdam," he told me, "you live with the port, the cargo, and the ships. It is the DNA of the city. Growing up in a big port makes you aware at a young age that there is 'another world out there'.

"After my PhD, one of my first commercial projects was studying the relationship between business services and the port economy. I talked with bankers, insurance companies, and lawyers and learned about the white-collar jobs in maritime trade, shipping, and port operations. They introduced me to commodity trading as the business that makes things move.

"A whole world began to open to me, and I could see everything come together. I began to ask why I hadn't known about this world before – why had no one taught me any of this? I saw a great opportunity to swing my academic career in a new direction. I love to teach and research. I wanted to transmit my intellectual fascination and newfound awareness of the commodity world to my students. I realised we needed educational programmes on commodities, so I designed and set up our executive program, which is, let's say, an MBA light."

Local merchants founded Erasmus University in 1913 as the Netherlands School of Commerce, offering business and maritime trade courses. The Rotterdam School of Management was founded in the 1970s, inspired by American business schools, and now ranks among the top ten in the world in economics and business. Erasmus was a humanist scholar from Rotterdam and was among the first scholars to travel to other European universities to learn and share ideas.

The executive program is a leadership program for young professionals with eight to twelve years of experience in the commodity space. It does not focus on operational trading skills but on learning to navigate in times of uncertainty. All businesses are exposed to uncertainty, but the commodities business is especially so.

The course has four core modules where participants learn to understand the driving forces behind the commodity markets: geopolitics, sustainability, risk and compliance, and technology and innovation.

"As part of the leadership program," Wouter told me, "we confront our participants with real-life situations. We teach them what people expect from their leaders regarding ethics, values, culture, and courage.

"We don't try to teach participants how to trade – they already know how to trade or are familiar with trading. However, the programme is not only for trading companies. We have participants from commercial, functional and risk roles in banking, inspection, and shipping.

The executive learning course consists of a three-and-a-half week physical, full-time class exposure spread over six months and three locations, starting in Rotterdam and moving to Denver, Colorado, with the JP Morgan Center and concluding in Singapore. Average class sizes are 12 to 14, typically about 40 per cent of women. Companies sponsor their employees to undertake the course and meet their costs.

"The business school also offers a commodity elective for MSc students. Everybody in the business school follows their own MSc programme. They can pick their verticals, such as supply chain management, which includes finance, marketing, strategic management, etc. They also need to choose horizontal electives.

"Our commodities elective is one of the most popular in the business school. About 60 of our 400 students choose it each year. We dive into the mechanics of the commodity business and the culture. What does it take to be a trader? We tell them they won't become a trader just like that. We also tell them that trading is not for everybody, but plenty of opportunities exist other than trading. Trading companies need analysts, operators, finance, et cetera.

"We want to transmit to them that there is a mechanism – commodity trading – in the world economy that is poorly understood but impacts their daily lives. We teach them how it works and explain the skills they need to succeed in the business. It's an enormous eye-opener for them. We bring in outside practitioners to share their experience as it's not a business you can learn from a textbook.

"Sustainability is an essential element of our business school philosophy. We look at how to measure and monitor sustainability and guide sustainability into future leaders' strategy, taking a more systemic, planetary boundaries approach.

"We also look at the moral and ethical questions that crop up. There is sometimes a conflict between the trader and his company. A trader might want to do a deal to maximise his P&L, but a company will take a more comprehensive view to ensure the trade complies with all the regulations. It will also want to protect its reputation and brand.

"At the same time, we emphasise that hunger for commerce, risks, and adventure drives and defines the business culture.

"In 2023, we launched the Erasmus Commodity & Trade Centre (ECTC). We formalised our activities into a dedicated centre within the Erasmus family. Our mission is to nurture ideas and talent for tomorrow's trade. We do this through education and applied research and by building a community and an international learning platform. As I mentioned, merchants founded Erasmus University, and an endowment from industry partners enables us to achieve our mission and ambitions."

Scott Irwin

Great traders must be nimble enough to know when they're wrong and change their positions. I don't think there's any way to teach that.

Scott is the Laurence J. Norton Chair of Agricultural Marketing, Department of Agricultural and Consumer Economics, University of Illinois at Urbana-Champaign. He is one of the most respected academics in agricultural commodities globally. In 2023, he published a book, *Back to the Futures*. I asked him what prompted him to write it.

"The book's purpose is to be an entertaining way to learn about commodity futures markets," he replied. "It has a serious teaching purpose, but it's wrapped in, hopefully, entertainment that keeps the reader moving along."

In the book, Scott describes his two attempts to trade in grain futures markets. The first was in August 1981 when, as a graduate student, he thought the market was overestimating yields. The second was more recently when he believed the market was overestimating acreage. He lost money on both occasions. I asked him what he had learned from those experiences.

"The first was hair raising, a near-death for my graduate school experience. It taught me that I didn't have the nerves to be a trader. I was stupid to take those kinds of risks as a graduate student – it was insane. But it was a good lesson to learn without getting bounced out of graduate school. It taught me to stick to what I'm good at. I am pretty good at academics and research, but I don't have the stomach to carry that financial risk. I'm just not built that way."

"If you'd made money on that first trade," I asked him, "would you have persevered and tried to become a trader?"

"It was the classic newbie trader story," he admitted. "I made enough money in the first few months to be dangerous. I got blown out. I had considered buying a seat on the old Mid-America Commodity Exchange. Had I not been blown out, I may have done that. However, the odds of that happening were low.

"I started trading again in 2010. First, I became a principal in a small firm providing real-time yield forecasts for US corn and soybeans. I believed it could give me the edge a trader must have to succeed. Second, my father passed away in 2009. Our family still had a substantial farm operation, and I inherited the corn and soybean marketing for our farms back in Iowa, working with my mother. It forced me to be closer to the markets on a day-to-day basis.

"Third, I believe that trading makes me a better teacher and a better researcher. It gives me a quicker awareness of emerging issues in the markets. My motivation was to have skin in the game, but not so much that you get flayed! So, yes, I trade now a little, but only options."

"In your book, you describe how your father repeatedly tried to beat the markets but failed. What was he doing wrong?" I asked him.

"I believe he made a series of errors that most farmers repeat," Scott replied.

"The fundamental purpose of hedging is to manage your risk and reduce the fluctuations in your revenue over time. However, most hedgers work their positions selectively, looking to pick up some gain and extra return. Farmers aren't unusual in this regard. They want to manage the risk exposure of their crops and livestock, but they don't understand that you must have an edge to be successful.

"It's hard for farmers psychically because they're so connected to their crops. They have an intimate knowledge of what's going on in their fields. It leads them to believe they have an edge about what will happen with supply. There is a maxim: don't get caught looking out your back door. It was always a big problem for my dad.

"As a farmer, you compete in an incredibly sophisticated, billion-dollar business where your opponents are more sophisticated than you. You must understand who you're trying to beat.

"If you're going to play the game, you must be prepared for the ups and downs. Even if you're beating the market on average over time, you will have significant drawdowns and big gains. Hopefully, a few big gains offset your losses.

"I don't think my father had the mindset to understand the overall purpose of what he was doing and how difficult it was to win the game of selective hedging.

"Since my dad died in 2009, I do the marketing with my mom, who will be 88 in a few days. She would have made one heck of a good trader. Her instincts about the markets are better than mine. A good trader has an intuition that I can't describe and a personality that can deal with the ups and downs. She has both.

"You must also have a short memory to survive if you are speculating or selectively hedging. We've made some big mistakes in our marketing, but my mom always moves quickly onto the next opportunity.

"My dad wanted so badly to hit the highs. It's a terrible mentality to win in this game. If we do a great job marketing our corn, we'll get a better price of 20 or 25 cents a bushel than our neighbours. It doesn't sound much, but if you do that for 20 years, man, it adds up."

If Scott's mother was a better trader than his dad, it raises the question that has been bothering me throughout this book: why aren't there more women traders in the market?

"Almost all US universities are now majority female," Scott told me. "Still, as far as agricultural commodities are concerned, I'll be lucky if I get 25 per cent females. It is a puzzle to me that I do not understand. I see it changing, though, slowly. More and more females are going into grain merchandising, but it's still not the 50 per cent it should be."

"What makes a good trader?" I asked him.

"To be a good trader you must have an above-average ability to collect and process information.

"Equally important is the right kind of psychological makeup. Probably the best typology for a trader I've ever seen is in the book *Superforecasting: The Art and Science of Prediction* by Philip Tetlock and Dan Gardner. It is one of my favourite books of the last decade. Being a trader is not necessarily the same as being a forecaster, but this book is about people who make predictions. A trader constantly makes predictions.

"A good trader must have a Sherlock Holmes brain – an insatiable curiosity to dig into the facts and understand relationships – and not necessarily believe what everybody else thinks. It's not a normal personality, the ability to believe in your own skills and attributes. But to be a great trader, you must have that kind of Sherlock Holmes personality.

"Great traders must be nimble enough to know when they're wrong and change their positions. I don't think there's any way to teach that. Great traders are super intelligent people, but they also have the drive and psychology to take that cognitive frame of mind and implement it into trading.

"The Super Forecasters Project suggests that only one to two per cent of people have the potential to be super forecasters or super traders. These are rare skills."

I asked Scott about his University's courses in agricultural marketing.

"We offer three courses at the undergraduate level," he told me. "The first is a popular freshman-sophomore course on agricultural marketing. We also provide junior-senior classes on commodity price analysis and commodity futures markets. And then we have the commodity futures markets course, looking at the markets and how you hedge and speculate in them.

"We also offer three courses at the graduate level. One covers time series econometric applications in commodity futures markets. We have a second one that covers traditional supply and demand and trade policy in agricultural markets.

"And then, we have a unique and fantastic course in our PhD program, a one-semester seminar course where students read as much cutting-edge literature as they can in a semester. It's kind of the jumping-off point for students doing dissertation research.

"Last question," I said. "What advice would you give a young person looking for a career in agricultural marketing?"

"First, get as much academic training as possible," he replied. "We have recruiters constantly engaging with the students at the undergraduate level. We never have enough master students for the market demand.

"Second, while you're getting that training, do as many internships with grain and trading companies as possible to find out if you have the profile for the business.

"Third, I tell my students to start following the markets and the daily market narrative. Get engaged in what I call the everyday market conversation.

"Fourth, read as much as you can. I tell my students to start with your book, *Commodity Conversations*. I then ask them to read *The Economics of Futures Trading* by Thomas A. Hieronymus, followed by *The World for Sale* by Javier Blas and Jack Farchy.

"I'm honoured you placed me at the top of that list," I told him.

Five questions for Ivo Sarjanovic

If I remember correctly, Ivo, you always wanted to be a teacher. How did you end up as a trader?

I have always had a vocation for teaching. Although I pursued accounting in Argentina, my focus lay in economics. I commenced a PhD program in economics at New York University, but unforeseen circumstances thwarted its completion. Consequently, I returned to Rosario and embarked on a career in trading. I have no regrets about this shift; I perceive striking parallels between the intellectual rigour of market positioning and the pursuit of scientific inquiry. Moreover, it proved to be a prudent economic decision

Nevertheless, I always intended to return to teaching upon retiring from trading. Lacking a PhD, I am more akin to an industry practitioner—someone equipped with experience to impart rather than a purely academic figure. I enjoy teaching, but it is more of a hobby.

Some of my colleagues at Cargill affectionately dubbed me 'the Professor.' In collaboration with a colleague, Dave Buchanan, we established a Grain Academy within Cargill. Although I am uncertain of its current existence, it was an exceptional program complementing what you learn in your daily roles.

Cargill's culture weaves teaching into one's responsibilities, eliminating the dichotomy between work and education. In addition to learning technical tools, it fosters an environment rife with brainstorming, diverse perspectives, and open forums for discourse.

I've always viewed trading as an intellectual challenge. As a follower of the philosopher Karl Popper, I find his ideas particularly applicable to trading. Your game plan serves as a hypothesis you present to address the problems you encounter in the market structure. Subsequently, you test this hypothesis through the mechanism of profit and loss. Profit validates it, whereas a loss falsifies it.

Could you talk me through your current teaching activities?

I have been teaching at the University of Geneva since 2008 and recently became a fellow at the Erasmus Commodity Centre in Rotterdam. Additionally, I instruct a class on Agri-commodities in the Master of Finance program at Di Tella University in Buenos Aires and the Master's program in Agri-business at Austral University in Rosario. Apart from these commitments, I am predominantly involved in seminars and lectures. Furthermore, even in more informal capacities, I coach and mentor individuals within the industry.

Preparing for classes, creating presentations, and keeping them current demands considerable time. It extends beyond the hours spent in front of the class. When presenting a class for the first time, I may invest up to 10 hours in preparation for a one-hour session. Once I've created the slides, updating them for subsequent classes typically requires one to two hours per session. However, developing a new theme from scratch consumes significant time.

Recently, I compiled a presentation on population dynamics and its future implications on food demand. This endeavour entailed extensive preparation, including reading many books and articles, conducting research, and verifying information by contacting the authors of relevant pieces.

Occasionally, I deliver presentations virtually, which offers the advantage of saving time and transportation costs. Nonetheless, I prefer teaching in person; it facilitates a stronger connection with my students.

Navigating diverse skill levels among students poses a challenge. There's a risk of speaking at a level that may be too advanced for some while too basic for others. The key is maintaining a balance, ensuring everyone can understand the material while occasionally introducing concepts that challenge the more adept learners.

Furthermore, adjusting the teaching approach when transitioning from instructing young students one week to addressing executives the next presents its own set of complexities.

What makes a good teacher?

Practical experience holds significant value in the realm of commodities. Students become highly engaged when they perceive their instructor has practical expertise. For many, studying commodities isn't purely academic but a way to advance their careers.

Remaining current with the subject matter, such as incorporating recent real-world examples, is essential.

A dynamic presentation style is crucial to maintain student engagement. Occasionally, introducing surprising or even controversial concepts can stimulate lively discussions.

Drawing connections between commodities and various disciplines such as economics, politics, geopolitics, agronomy, meteorology, and new technologies enhances understanding.

What else? When discussing commodities broadly, it's imperative to transcend specific geographies or products, ensuring a comprehensive approach. It is especially true in Geneva, where students have different perspectives and origins. You need to avoid falling into the trap of being a hyper-specialist.

Reflecting on my transition from trading for Cargill, where my focus was intensely narrow—mainly dedicated to predicting soybean and later sugar market movements—I now embrace a broader perspective. I derive satisfaction from forging connections and appreciating the larger picture.

Do you teach people how to trade?

I'm uncertain whether one can truly teach someone to become a trader. However, it's possible to refine and enhance the skills of those with a natural trading aptitude. Specific innate capabilities, such as risk appetite, are essential for success in trading and cannot be taught. While some individuals possess a high-risk appetite, others may have little or none. Beyond risk appetite, there are other qualities required for trading success. Once you have identified these abilities, you can nurture and develop them through training and education.

The analogy to a sportsman is a good one. Much like you can't create a player like Messi out of thin air, you can improve Messi's skills through proper training, discipline and nutrition.

Economics plays a pivotal role in equipping traders with foundational knowledge. I utilise a triangular framework to elucidate how commodity prices are determined.

Microeconomics constitutes one angle of the triangle, with supply and demand as the primary price determinant. Macroeconomics forms the second angle, explaining how macro variables such as growth, inflation, and interest rates influence price dynamics. Investment funds represent the third angle of the triangle. They are the catalysers of price movements but not the determinants. When futures markets are well designed, prices always converge to fundamental values.

The interplay among these three realms—micro, macro, and funds—accounts for the dynamics of price movements. Microeconomics elucidates the fundamental factors driving price trends, while macroeconomics illustrates how external economic conditions influence this trajectory. And the funds act as the catalysts for price movements.

What educational advice would you give young people looking to enter the agriculture commodity sector?

When I began my career in South America, companies typically required candidates to hold degrees in economics, accounting, business administration, statistics, or agronomy to enter agricultural trading. However, upon relocating to Europe, I was surprised to discover that some of my colleagues held bachelor's degrees in art, languages, psychology, law, and international relations. This diversity enriched our discussions, adding depth and richness to our perspectives.

The landscape has evolved since then. Employers now seek candidates with additional quantitative knowledge and basic programming skills.

While having a master's degree may be advantageous, it's not a prerequisite for entering the trading profession. However, the Master in Commodities program at the University of Geneva offers a unique advantage–a blend of practical work experience and academic learning. With students spending 70 per cent of their time gaining hands-on experience in a company and 30 per cent attending classes at the university, this program offers a potent combination, particularly when the sponsoring company has a well-organised training system.

Once you embark on a trading career, trading a diverse range of commodities, especially those with varying delivery mechanisms, is beneficial. Or if your company is not involved in different markets, it's always interesting to have exposure to different qualities or distinct origins. The delivery mechanism significantly impacts trading dynamics. For instance, in my experience trading soybeans, where delivery primarily occurs along the Mississippi River, you learn how the delivery mechanism affects premiums and spreads in a certain way. In the sugar market, where delivery occurs worldwide on a FOB basis, futures are a source of origination, creating a completely different trading dynamic. Delivering sugar around the globe at a uniform price makes premiums more stable but time spreads much more volatile.

My last piece of advice is to 'Choose your boss wisely.' A supportive and inspiring boss fosters motivation, curiosity, and continuous learning. You may not always have the luxury of selecting your boss, but when given the opportunity, prioritise not just the job but also the individual you'll be working under. It will have a significant impact on your career.

FIVE MORE QUESTIONS FOR THE AUTHOR

Which is the most critical profession in the ag supply chain – and why?

CEOs and company leaders often get bad press, but they play an essential role in setting a company's culture and strategy. Management consultants may talk about 'bottom-up' organisations, but as far as I can see, most of the good stuff comes from the top. Even so, are CEOs essential in the supply chain, or could life go on without them?

In my conversation with Nicolas Tamari, he admitted that although he is involved in the company's day-to-day operations, Sucafina could operate quasi-normally without him. When I asked him if his company still function if he were to sail around the world for a year, he replied, "I would say for a couple of months, but not a year."

The same applies to traders. A company and a supply chain could run for a while without them, but they would soon grind to a halt if no one bought or sold anything – or if people stopped taking risks. A trading company without traders is like a sailing ship without wind.

Could the same be said of risk managers, the people who kerb traders' worst instincts, their excesses and their (occasional) irrational exuberances?

Risk managers did not exist when I started in the business. Each trader was a risk manager, and the head of the trading desk oversaw the overall position. Today, risk managers impose VAR (Value at Risk) limits (they didn't exist when I started) on each trader and desk. Accidents still happen, but (and I have no statistics to back this up) they probably happen less often. Risk managers add considerable value to the supply chain, but it would not seize up without them.

The same applies to brokers. (I am an ex-broker, so I am allowed to say this.) The supply chain would still work without them. It would work less efficiently, but it would still work.

However, the supply chain would stop working almost immediately if operators were not there to ensure that ships get loaded, documents issued, and payments made. Operators play the most important – or at least the most urgent – role in the chain.

I would argue something similar for shipping. Without shipowners and charterers, commodities would stay at the port. Nothing would be shipped.

You could put finance and insurance in the same boat. The sector would grind almost immediately to a halt without those two professions.

I would categorise all the other professions as "without them, the supply chain would gradually seize up."

Lawyers and arbitrators? It would take a while, but counterparties would eventually stop trusting each other to perform, and the system would slowly cease functioning.

Communication and PR professionals? They are critical in maintaining the sector's social licence to operate – as are sustainability professionals.

Educators and talent managers? It might take a generation, but where would we be without teachers and mentors?

All this begs a follow-up question: If other professions in the supply chain are as crucial as traders, why are traders paid so much more?

When I asked Jeremy Reynolds, one of the most experienced operators in the business, this question, he replied,

"Although it pains me to say it, I think it is justified. Physical commodity merchandisers drive a trading company's profitability. They bring the clients

to the table, negotiate the deals, and manage the price risk. They get paid more because they create more value. It's as simple as that. If they create value, they get well rewarded. If they don't, they get fired. It comes with the territory."

I would argue that it is more of a question of supply and demand. Trading is a high-stress, full-on job that does not suit everyone. And, as various people have argued in this book, traders are born, not made. You can mentor a good trader to become an excellent one, but you can't turn a lousy trader into a good one. Good traders must have a risk-taking mentality and a drive to make money. Demand exceeds supply.

Why are there so few women in the sector?

It is a question that I get repeatedly asked and have repeatedly posed to my interviewees.

As Maryana Yarmolenko Stober pointed out in her interview, women make up about 30 per cent of the workforce in the (Swiss) commodity trading and shipping sector, which is not out of line with other unrelated sectors in the Swiss economy.

The percentage is much lower in the on-ship maritime sector, but everyone I spoke with thinks it is normal. They argue that on-ship work is more physical than onshore work and that women don't like to spend months away from their families. I am unsure if I agree and don't understand why there are so few women mariners.

Nor am I sure why most women in the commodity trading business fulfil back-office roles; they are underrepresented on trading desks.

In the old days, merchants would travel the high seas journeying to far-away – and often dangerous – places to originate commodities. Today, they do so from the comfort of their offices or, increasingly, their homes via a video conference call.

Traders are now less hunters and more gatherers. This shift may suit women more than men, and I expect to see women gradually replace men on trading desks. These structural shifts take time, but they do happen.

Even so, finding women to interview for this book was challenging. I wanted 30 per cent of the interviewees to be women, reflecting the gender balance in the workplace. I succeeded, but it was a struggle.

Maryana Yarmolenko Stober suggested it was because I wanted to interview senior people, while women comprise only 20 per cent of senior positions. She may be correct, but even when I found them, they were at least twice as likely as men to refuse an interview or to drop out halfway through the process. Some even dropped out once the interview was over and I had transcribed and edited it.

So, in answer to the question as to why there are so few women traders, the answer must be that it is a function of historical attitudes that are rapidly changing. As to why so few women accepted to be interviewed, I will leave that to someone who is better qualified to answer.

What are the most significant changes you have seen over your career?

The agricultural commodity markets have had two tectonic shifts in the past forty years. The first has been China's growing importance as an importer of foodstuffs. The second has been the growth of biofuels and the diversion of food to fuel. Both are enormous subjects, enough to fill a library of books.

Perhaps the most significant change in the business has been the change in the attitudes of those in it.

A coffee trader recently complained that the business has gone WOKE; he wasn't 'allowed to say anything anymore.' I answered him what I always answer: "My mother told me that if I didn't have anything nice to say, then I shouldn't say anything at all."

He then, with a laugh, accused me of being WOKE. I replied that I didn't understand the term WOKE and substituted the word 'compassionate'. So, if he was asking me if I was compassionate, my answer was, "I hope so."

A different trader once complained that certification and sustainability created a significant extra workload of bureaucracy and was 'driving him mad.' I replied that the sector had no choice but to maintain its social licence to operate it. Consumers demand that their food is produced in an environmentally and socially sustainable way, even if they are reluctant to pay for it.

"Besides," I continued, "aren't you happier working in a sector that protects the environment and its workers?"

There have been many other positive changes.

Agricultural yields have improved, meaning the world's farmers can feed a growing and more affluent population without bringing in too much extra land.

The supply chain has become more efficient through increased scale, for example, with bigger ships and more technology, such as GPS tracking.

Communications have become cheaper. When I started the industry 40 years ago, we had to book a telephone call to Moscow a week in advance. When I started my company, telephone calls were my most significant expense; they are now effectively free. The same applies to a lesser extent with travel.

Communication has also become more accessible. I remember buying my first fax machine; it cost over $1000! I remember sending my first email, a trade confirmation, to Glencore. I remember our first group calls (between offices) on Skype! And I remember with great excitement when we connected our office full-time to the Internet, no longer having to dial in each time through a phone line!

Many traders complain that the Internet and social media have led to a democratisation of information that has reduced trading margins (often to zero) and made it harder to make money. However, margins were already nearly non-existent when I joined the business. We made money by taking advantage of mispricing along the supply chain and correctly predicting future price move movements using detailed fundamental analysis and risk management.

The ease of communication has led to a hard-to-manage deluge of emails and data. As an inter-trade broker, I spent all day on the phone talking with clients. When mobile phones became a thing, we had to hire an extra broker to handle the additional phone traffic. By the time I left the markets in 2016, I could easily spend all day answering the hundreds of emails I received. And I could easily miss an important one!

Technology has taken time to resolve the data overload issue, but more on that below.

Some traders complain that introducing VAR limits means they can no longer trade as they used to.

In the old days, if a trader thought he knew something – for example, that a crop was smaller than anticipated or that an importing country had imported more than expected – they would take a medium- or long-term view and continue to buy scale down until the market caught up with the news and turned around. Today, their risk manager would stop them out of their position before the market finally turned.

As Fausto Felice told me in my book Commodity Crops,

"Trade houses have less appetite for directional trading and flat price positions than in the past.

"In the mid-2000s, financial institutions – hedge funds, banks, and Commodity Trading Advisors (CTAs) – came into the commodity derivatives markets in a big way. They have changed how markets behave. They often accentuate directional moves well beyond what physical commodity trading houses think are justified by the fundamentals. These external money flows were, and continue to be, huge; they overwhelm even the large trading houses.

"It has forced trading houses to change how they manage flat price risk and adopt the same risk management systems as the financial institutions. All trading houses now use VAR (Value at Risk), stress, drawdowns, etc., to measure risk. As a result, they all trade in the same way.

"The grain trading houses still have a competitive advantage in the amount and quality of information. Still, I would argue that they are giving away that competitive advantage by trading and measuring risk in the same way as the pure financial players. The trade houses are now forcing themselves out of positions even when they believe they will be right in time.

"*I fully understand why the tradehouses have had to adopt the same risk management tools as the financial markets, but I find it a little unfortunate. They have diluted their competitive advantage of knowing the fundamentals.*"

However, as Ralph Potter told me in his interview for this book,

"*The worst thing that can happen is when a trader thinks he knows something and disregards his rules. It can be when he has invested so much of his credibility – and so much of his personality – into putting on a trade, it makes it hard to exit. It's hard to change your mind. That's why you must have a risk point.*"

One final and most unwelcome change is that narcotics traffickers are increasingly using agricultural commodity flows to move their products. While interviewing people for this book, I was shocked and saddened by how drug traffickers have infiltrated the agricultural commodity business, threatening supply chain professionals and their families. I sometimes felt the fear in their voices. Violence has increased. It is a significant change.

What do you expect will be the most significant changes in the future?

I once asked an AI expert whether AI would eliminate the trader's role. He replied that it would only do away with traders who don't use AI. It was an excellent answer.

AI will empower everyone in the supply chain, including humble bloggers and authors like me. My son, Oliver, taught me how to use ChatGP and encouraged me to upgrade to the paid version. I refused but am now tempted. It would mean I could finally have a research assistant and only pay $20 monthly for the privilege!

Just as everything is moving – or has moved – from websites to apps, the world of commodity trading is moving from emails to platforms. I interviewed some of the start-ups in this book; competition is ferocious, and there will only be a few winners. But in a few years, trading will move from WhatsApp to platforms just as it moved from telephones, telexes and faxes to Skype (and then WhatsApp.)

On the sustainability front, I expect governments to take responsibility away from traders and certification agencies. For example, the Ivorian government, not traders or chocolate companies, will be responsible for ensuring that their farmers grow cocoa without deforestation and child labour. We are already seeing this move with palm oil in Indonesia.

Over the centuries, the ag supply chain has experienced a significant shift in market power, from farmers to traders, processors to retailers and now to consumers. The democratisation of information has accelerated this trend (think price-comparison sites and online shopping). Consumers now hold the market power in the supply chain, squeezing margins and leaving many farmers unable to make a living.

The result is we do not pay the actual cost of our food. We do not pay the externalities of environmental damage that our food causes, nor the social welfare costs of obesity and poor health, nor the government's farm subsidies. We may pay $6.29 for a McDonald's Happy Meal®, but the cost is much higher.

So, what is the solution? I asked that question back in 2015 to Sunny Verghese, the co-founder and Group CEO of Olam International Limited. He replied,

"My answer is simple: you take all the subsidies – the $387 billion – that the rich world gives to farmers who don't need the money and instead subsidise food for the poor. We need to use those subsidies to ensure that high food prices do not impact people below the poverty line."

The most significant change I expect (and hope to be alive to see) is that consumers begin to pay the actual cost of food and that governments subsidise those who cannot afford it.

What did you learn from writing this book?

I recognised the critical role of each profession in the supply of agricultural commodities. A hospital cannot function without thirty-plus professions, nor can an agricultural-commodity trading company.

The media likes to present the big agricultural trading companies as faceless organisations, but they aren't. They are real people trying to do their best for their company, their families and the global good. Of course, there will always be people in every sector who prioritise their self-interest above the general good. The good news is they tend not to last long.

But I think I knew that already.

www.ingramcontent.com/pod-product-compliance
Lightning Source LLC
Chambersburg PA
CBHW071910210526
45479CB00002B/363